Racing to the Sky

One Woman's Extreme Adventure in the 2015 Red Bull X-Alps

By Dawn Westrum

Edited by Elegant Editing, Los Angeles, CA

Front Cover Photo Credit: Felix Wölk

Back Cover Photo Credit: Vitek Ludvik

Maps: Map tiles by Stamen Design, under CC BY 3.0 Copyright OpenStreetMap contributers

Table of Contents

Foreword

No one truly understands the Red Bull X-Alps until they have competed in it. Despite several books, countless articles and endless media coverage available, the race is, in reality, a very personal one. Sure, the amazing shots of mountains, paragliders soaring on thermals and the grueling hardship as athletes climb precipitous alpine paths by foot make great video. However they capture nothing of what goes on inside the athletes' minds.

Because it is here that the race is truly fought. No matter how good you are at flying paragliders, and how well prepared you are physically the difference between those that become one with this race, embrace it, grow stronger from it and continue to excel against all odds and those that are simply spat out by the system is all about mental attitude.

In this book we get a glimpse into that very personal world, told by Dawn Westrum, one of only two female athletes competing in the Red Bull X-Alps for many years. This is the story of her race, competing in the 2015 Red Bull X-Alps.

Reading this book, it is clear that Dawn did not have the best-prepared team in the race, nor was she the best pilot, nor probably the strongest physically, but Dawn has that special quality so critical for the Red Bull X-Alps. That rare mental ability to become stronger in the face of adversity, to deal with every challenge head on and to simply get on with it.

In this book we hear of Dawn's intent to prove that a woman can compete with the men in this toughest of challenges. Simply getting accepted in the Red Bull X-Alps proves you are an amazing athlete and taking on the race in the way Dawn showed that she was indeed an extremely worthy contestant. But while others were eliminated or retired from the race she continued to battle on. I would suggest that, if Dawn competes once again, she can put aside any comparison with the men in the race. Her competition is with herself to continue to be stronger, better prepared and show that her amazing internal strength can drive her further than she ever dreamed possible.

I hope Dawn competes again in 2017, but in the meantime, enjoy reliving her journey from 2015, full of ups and downs (pun intended). It is a great read!

Jon Chambers,
Red Bull X-Alps competitor in 2011 & 2013
Author of 'Hanging in There', the story of his 2011 race

Preface

I am going to suggest that reading this book might be a little like my preparations for the Red Bull X-Alps; it started out slowly and then got more exciting. Race day seemed to take forever to arrive, but once the journey started, it felt like each flight and each day of racing got better than the last. The danger factor also increased, as I flew from familiar territory into places where I hadn't ever visited.

Training for a race of this proportion was scary, and there were a lot of unknowns. Information about the event was scarce, which is a big reason why I felt the need to write this book. Along with the day-to-day story about the 2015 Red Bull X-Alps, I share knowledge and information which might be helpful for athletes selected in future editions of the Red Bull X-Alps.

The 2015 Red Bull X-Alps was an exciting race to watch on many levels, and caused a loss of work productivity (and sleep) during July for paragliding fans all over the world! With up-to-the-minute live tracking on each athlete, fans were able to watch their favorite athletes all day or night long; as they battled the weather, the mountains, and each other. The race for 3rd place in in the 2015 edition was truly epic. So I've also included stories from the other athletes who were having their great adventures concurrently with my own.

Perhaps these pages will someday inspire you to submit your own application for this amazing race!

-Dawn Westrum

Isaiah 40:31

...those who hope in the Lord
will renew their **strength**.
They will soar on
wings like eagles;
they will run and not grow weary,
they will walk and not be faint.

A Note on Units of Measurement

I struggled with the units of measurements for this book. As an American, I think in pounds and miles, but in Europe everything switches to kilos and kilometers. Some of both are found in this book and here is a chart to help sort out the confusion.

1 Kilometer = .62 Miles
10 Kilometers = 6.2 Miles
1038 Kilometers = 645 Miles   (Straight-line race distance of the 2015 Red Bull X-Alps)

1000 meters = 3281 feet
2000 meters = 6562 feet
3000 meters = 9842 feet
4000 meters = 13,123 feet

1 Kilo = 2.2 Pounds

Acknowledgements

First of all, let me thank my husband Jim Sorensen, who supported me when this race was just a pipe dream. He was there every step of the way, both in training and during the race, selflessly driving along crowded highways while I was far above him as a speck in the sky. I couldn't have done this without you!

Thanks also to my supporters during the race: Chuck, Mike, Boga, Cano, and Eileen. I appreciate the time you were willing to spend to help speed me along the course.

A big shout out to Red Bull for being willing to organize such a great race. Every sport needs a flagship event to draw new faces and encourage innovations and new products. For the sport of paragliding, the Red Bull X-Alps does just that!

Thanks to Tom Payne for providing maps of this year's race.

Thanks to Krischa Berlinger, who put his heart and soul into supporting athlete USA4 Dave Turner, and then wrote about his experience for me in "Spotlight: Day in the Life of a Solo Supporter".

Thanks to Chuck Savall, who wrote a supporter's version of the race in "Spotlight: Red Bull X-Alps from the Ground".

Thanks to Kari Castle, who paved the way for women in this race back in 2005, and was willing to share a little about her experience.

Thanks to Jon Chambers, who by writing the first book about the Red Bull X-Alps, helped me plan my own race, and also inspired me to start writing my own book!

To Cindy W., who knew nothing about the race on the first day, but quickly became addicted to live tracking. She would get up each morning and check where I was in the race, to the point where her husband would wake up and say "Good morning, honey, how is Dawn doing today?"

Thanks to Matt at Ozone Paragliding, who stepped in to save me when I ordered the wrong wing size and needed a last minute change before the race.

Thanks to my fitness trainers Jesse and Sylvia at Lifetime Fitness. They got me strong and fit and helped avoid injuries and overtraining.

A big thanks to Mary R, who along with her daughter organized a prayer chain across prisons in Texas and beyond. I'm sure their thoughts and prayers helped keep myself and everyone in the race safe from harm.

A BIG thank you to my sponsors, in no particular order:

Ozone
Foundation For Freeflight
Eagle Paragliding
FlyNet XC3
Goal Zero
Salewa
Garmin
Icaro2000
US Paragliding Team
Powertraveller
Salt Cycles
Black Diamond

Finally, I thank God for keeping me safe during this adventure!

Section 1: THE RACE

History of the Red Bull X-Alps

The Red Bull X-Alps is the world's toughest adventure race. It's a bold claim – but one it surely deserves. It's difficult to think of another race that demands such a high level of fitness and technical skill – or lasts so long. The rules are simple. Athletes must race across the Alps, by foot or paraglider via set Turnpoints, usually a straight-line distance of over 1,000km. Over the years, the race has attracted and tested to the limit some of the world's top adventurers. It demands not only expert paragliding skill but extreme endurance. Some athletes will hike over 100km in a day and will cover hundreds of kilometers on foot – and 1000's of meters in altitude – by the time the race is over!

Each team consists of an athlete and their supporters. The supporters are there to help with logistics, strategy, food, medical support, and provide psychological assistance. The role of the supporter is hugely important – they are the unsung heroes of the race. However, supporters cannot offer physical assistance; athletes must carry their own paraglider, harness, helmet, electronics and other mandatory gear. Athletes race between the hours of 05:00 to 22:30. Since 2013, athletes have been able to pull a Night Pass, which allows them to push-on through the night on foot, normally a mandatory rest period. New in 2015 was the Powertraveller Prologue, which saw athletes compete in a one-day hike and fly battle in the hills outside Salzburg, three days before the main race start. The top three winners of the prologue were awarded an extra night pass.

http://www.redbullxalps.com/race/about.html

The year 2015 was the seventh running of the Red Bull X-Alps. The event has been held every other summer since 2003. The race always starts in Salzburg, Austria, and always finishes on an inflatable raft in the bay of Monaco. From start to finish, athletes race on foot and in the air between varying turnpoints, through the countries of Austria, Germany, Italy, Switzerland, France, and Monaco.   Athletes are chosen via a highly competitive application process. In 2005 there were two women contestants, but all other years until 2015, only men competed.   This wasn't particularly because the race didn't accept women, I just don't think any applied! According to the race director Christoph Weber, for the 2015 edition, three women applied, and two were selected.

So, for the 2105 race, two women and thirty-one men were chosen from eighteen countries.   Nineteen of these athletes were rookies like me, with fourteen coming back from previous editions, including three-time winner Christian Maurer. I was delighted to see that four athletes from the USA were selected. For 2015 the application process had changed a little, with the race committee selections based on qualifications, rather than country or previous race entries. Just because you got in last time didn't mean you'd make it in again.   This meant that some countries, like Germany, Switzerland and the USA, had four athletes each.

A few notes about the rules: One athlete would be cut every 48 hours from the back of the race. The race continued until the first person reached Monaco, and then everyone still racing had another 48 hours (or 12 days total, whichever was longer) to attempt to finish.   Because the race starts at midday, finish times might be confusing compared to the number of days they have raced. For example, finishing on the morning of the tenth day means a finish time of 9 days, 22 hours.

2015 Red Bull X-Alps Turnpoints

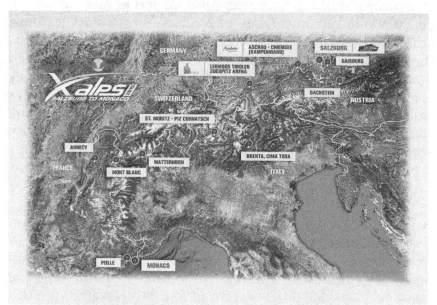

Photo Credit: Red Bull X-Alps Media

Main Race: July 5-17, 2015

Start: Salzburg, Austria
Elevation: 424 meters
Distance Covered: 0
Distance to go: 1038 km

Turnpoint 1: Gaisberg, Austria
Elevation: 1,287 m
Distance Covered: 5 km
Distance to go: 1,033 km
Coordinates: N47.80413° E013.11091°
Athletes must sign the Turnpoint Board at summit

Turnpoint 2: Dachstein, Austria
Elevation: 2,995 m
Distance Covered: 58 km
Distance to go: 980 km
Coordinates: N47.47107° E013.62078°
Athletes must fly through a 400-meter cylinder or sign the Turnpoint Board

Turnpoint 3: Kampenwand, Germany
Elevation: 1,669 m
Distance Covered: 158 km
Distance to go: 880 km
Coordinates: N 47.753644° E012.352900°
Athletes must land and sign the Turnpoint Board

Turnpoint 4: Lermoos Tiroler Zugspitz Arena, Austria
Elevation: 2,962 m
Distance Covered: 276 km
Distance to go: 762 km
Coordinates: N47.4015735712° E010.8792329°
Athletes must pass north of the Zugspitz summit, then land and sign the Turnpoint Board

Turnpoint 5: Brenta, Cima Tosa, Italy
Elevation: 3,173 m
Distance Covered: 412 km
Distance to go: 626 km
Coordinates: N 46.175238° E 010.875920°
Athletes must land and sign the Turnpoint Board

Turnpoint 6: St. Moritz – Piz Corvatsch, Switzerland
Elevation: 3,451 m
Distance Covered: 498 km
Distance to go: 540 km
Coordinates: N46.408246° E009.816083°
Athletes must pass north of the summit of Piz Corvatsch

Turnpoint 7: Matterhorn, Switzerland
Elevation: 4,478 m
Distance Covered: 671 km
Distance to go: 367 km
Coordinates: N45.97651° E007.65832°
Athletes must pass through a 5.5 km cylinder

Turnpoint 8: Mont Blanc, France
Elevation: 4,810 m
Distance Covered: 735 km
Distance to go: 303 km
Coordinates: N45.83249° E006.86427°
Athletes must pass north of the summit of Mont Blanc

Turnpoint 9: Annecy, France
Elevation: 950 m
Distance Covered: 785 km
Distance to go: 253 km
Coordinates: N45.853203° E006.223084°
Athletes must land and sign the Turnpoint Board

Turnpoint 10: Peille, France
Elevation: 600 m
Distance Covered: 1,036 km
Distance to go: 2 km
Coordinates: N43,75594° E007,41082°
Athletes must land and sign the Turnpoint Board. Official clock stops here.

Finish: Landing Float, Monaco
Elevation: 0 m
Distance Covered: 1,038 km
Distance to go: 0 m
Coordinates: N43.74450° E007.43400°
Athletes must swim to or fly down to the float in the Mediterranean Sea.

Race Orientation Week

Jim and I had the distinction of being the first vehicle to arrive in the Red Bull X-Alps athletes' campground by the lake in Fuschl am See, Austria. Soon enough, other athletes started showing up in force. By the end of our preparation week, the area was super crowded with teams, supporters, family and friends, all there to cheer on their athletes. While the Red Bull Headquarters IS in Fuschl am See, the company itself really doesn't have anything to do with the Red Bull X-Alps race (beyond sponsoring it). The race details are organized and directed through a company called Zooom Productions. Luckily, Zooom is also headquartered in Fuschl, so everything we needed was close at hand.

Athletes and supporters were required to arrive almost an entire week early to prepare for the race. The first couple of days were very busy with registration, clothes and electronics issue, and sorting equipment. Each day we had a short mandatory class on important race topics, which included race rules, airspace restrictions, and safety briefings. We also got technical information about the new electronics we would use during the race. The rest of the time, we spent getting our equipment inspected, while figuring out how to operate the phone, variometer, camera, and GPS that the race had supplied. We also spent time with race photographers doing pre-shoots. This meant posing with all of our race gear, including a Leatherman knife, and the obligatory can of Red Bull!

The worst part of it the whole week was putting the official decals on my wing. Imagine trying to lay a sticker on fabric that isn't smooth, has lots of seams, and with random lines sewn on to boot. I'd never done it before and really didn't want to screw it up. The main Red Bull logo in the middle was quite big, came in pieces, and needed to be stuck in just the right place. Luckily an intern from Zooom Productions and the South African supporters of athlete Stephan Kruger were ready to help us.   The key was that all of them had applied these stickers before, so they knew how to do it!   The process of applying nine different logos on my wing still took most of a day.   It was tedious and slow work, with the wing laid out in the school gymnasium and us walking all over it (in socks!) trying to get the fabric smooth enough to eliminate bubbles.

By the last few days all of my supporters had arrived (I'll introduce them later), and we finalized our plans for meals, sleeping, cooking, and finding each other out there in the mountains.   At least we did as much as we could in advance, not knowing which country we would be in each night of the race, much less which town!

We all managed to find time to go flying between the mandatory classes.   That's what we were there for, after all! The weather was really beautiful for the whole week we were in Fuschl, and both athletes and supporters were exploring the area and flying the course whenever possible.   It was only about 30 minutes' drive to Salzburg, and along with many others, I was able to fly between Turnpoints 1 and 2. Now only if I could do it in the race!

Hanging out in the athlete camp
Photo Credit: Chuck Savall

Powertraveller Prologue - July 2, 2015

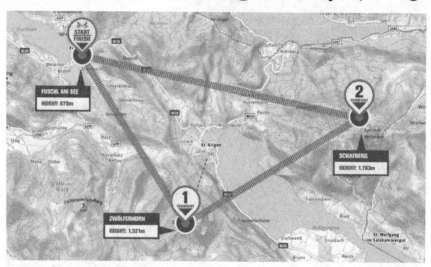

Prologue: July 2, 2015

Start: Fuschl Seebad
Elevation: 670 m
Coordinates: N 47.794166° E 013.298907°

Turnpoint 1: Zwölferhorn
Elevation: 1521 m
Coordinates: N 47.742466° E 013.351535°
Athletes must fly or walk through a 50-meter cylinder centered at the summit of Zwölferhorn

Turnpoint 2: Schafberg
Elevation: 1782 m
Coordinates: N 47.776399° E 013.434060°
Athletes must fly or walk through a 50-meter cylinder centered at the summit of Schafberg

Finish: Fuschl Seebad
Distance Covered: 36 km

The Prologue
Photo Credit: Chuck Savall

Fuschl am See, Austria
Hiking 16 km
Flying 15 km
Total Time: 6 hours 15 min

In the middle of the race preparation week came the prologue, sponsored by Powertraveller. The prologue was a new addition that year, and not one welcomed by everyone. This one-day race fell on July 2, and it both started and finished in Fuschl am See, Austria. With just two nearby mountaintop turnpoints, the course was short, less than 40 km.

Let me be completely clear about the prologue. I hated the idea of it. The prize for winning was a 5-minute advantage during the main race start, plus an extra night pass. Kinda cool, but I would never, ever win it unless the universe as I knew it turned upside down.

I have an extensive background in long-distance racing, running, adventure racing, etc...but the fact that I can go long distances doesn't have anything to do with speed. In fact, I'm quite slow. If I break 4 hours someday in a marathon, it would be an absolute speed record for me. I think I have a pretty small heart and lungs, which means my VO2 max never gets very high, and I don't go very fast. My heart rate DOES get quite high, quite quickly, and fans watching my heart rate monitor during the prologue probably wondered if I was OK! So my cardiovascular capacity almost always limits my speed, not my legs. This might be why I've stayed almost completely injury free over the years. Though that's not always much consolation when sometimes I just want to be able to go really fast!

Anyway, the prologue was too short to show off my endurance skills. Coming just 3 days before the start of the main race, I wanted to take it easy, not work too hard, and get through it injury free. The organizers had made it clear that we had to finish the prologue (I had been secretly hoping they didn't care about finishing it all, but no such luck).

The start of the prologue was the beach on Lake Fuschlsee, very near both Zooom headquarters and our athlete campground. From the beach we would hike up to Turnpoint 1, then hopefully fly across the Wolfgangsee Lake to Turnpoint 2, then finish the triangle back to finish on the lake. In bad weather, Turnpoint 2 would be dropped, but no such luck. The day of the prologue was sunny and clear with rising temperatures.

Prologue Start
Photo Credit: Cano

During our race preparation, the weather had been getting hotter and sunnier every day, and the clear blue skies on race morning said it was going to be more of the same, with stable air. This makes XC (cross country) paragliding both uncertain and difficult.   It also makes walking after sinking out a hot, tiring option.

We were supposed to wear our race jerseys for the start, which were long sleeved and would feel really hot, even just for a few minutes to pose for the cameras. I'm sure there would have been heat stroke and annoyance if we had all raced out of the gate, then all stopped to take them off 100 meters down the road.   Luckily saner heads prevailed, and we left them in our packs for flying, as the jerseys had been mainly designed to keep us warm in the air!   It's always surprising how much temperatures vary in this kind of race...from 100 degrees on the ground to near freezing in the air. Being dressed appropriately can make or break a good flight.

At 10 am the race was on!   I ran dutifully out of the starting gate for the cameras, and then settled into a strong walk with about half the field.   This included 3-time race winner Christian Mauer, who didn't seem concerned about racing during the prologue.   The helicopter followed the speedy guys off into the distance as they vied for the win.   I assumed that conditions on launch wouldn't turn on until later, so I didn't care how long it took me to get up to Turnpoint 1 at all.

The hike up to launch was about 10 kilometers, first flat on the roads, then climbing ever more steeply to the summit. Jim had set off to hike with me, but he was having trouble keeping up, which was very uncharacteristic of him.   Jim usually walks uphill faster than I do, especially when I am carrying a pack and he isn't! He told me later that he drank a highly caffeinated beverage just before the hike, and then felt like he was having a heart attack on the steep sections. Yikes! I think it was his last caffeine of the whole race (besides coffee); we didn't want a repeat of that. Trying not to worry about Jim behind me, I arrived at launch, if not last, then close to it.   Quite a few pilots had already taken off, and not only that, they were climbing up and making the lake crossing quickly too.   It's possible that the winners made it back to Fuschl not too long after I was just launching! But there were still athletes on launch, including a few who had overdone it in the hot conditions and ended up with a bit of heat exhaustion.

After seeing the conditions, I launched quickly in an effort to keep some competitors around me. Unfortunately, I and a few others flew off straight into a down cycle, and we spent the next hour almost sinking out, and then clawing our way back up to launch height, only to sink down again. I came close to swinging through the treetops a few times as I was eking out every bit of light lift I could find.   For a while, my options were pretty bleak; either land at the bottom of the hill, and hike up again for another attempt, or cross the lake very low and hike even further up to the second turn point. I didn't like either option, and grimly hung on, slowly creeping higher until that magical moment when I finally thermalled up above launch elevation and heaved a sigh of relief.

There wasn't much extra height to gain on the stable day, so I crossed the lake low, finding strong, nasty thermals waiting on the other side. It was enough to climb about halfway up to the hill, and then I just couldn't seem to get higher. One by one, the wings around me caught those magical thermals that break through to the higher layers, tagged the turnpoint, and disappeared. Dave Turner (USA4), who had landed out at the bottom and hiked up halfway, launched near me in a good cycle and immediately climbed out and away. I pushed for another location that might get me higher, but only found sink, flying deep into a treed valley with no landing options. Eventually I made it back to where Dave had launched from, and made the hard choice to land there and hike up to the turnpoint. The wind, which had been east in the morning, now switched to north, and I was afraid if I sunk out further I'd have even a bigger hike. By then I was pretty sure I was dead last, and knew I just had to get to the top, relaunch, and hope for a good glide. With a headwind to the finish I was in for a tough day. Luckily my landing area was a grassy knob, and aside from scaring a couple of women hiking on the trail, it was an easy touchdown.

The hike up, which was about 400 meters of climbing, was hot and windy. I (unfortunately!) hadn't thought I would be hiking it, and hadn't brought any snacks with me at all. I rationed my water and of course had money to buy more at the hut (aka monstrous building) at the summit. My Flymaster never beeped to tell me I made the turnpoint, so I went right up to look over the cliff at the top before digging it out of my pack. Luckily along the trail there were nice grassy slopes for launching. Although it was in the lee, I felt nice cycles coming up from the hot afternoon sun.

I hadn't flown in this area before, and wasn't sure if it was possible in the headwind to fly to Lake Fuschlsee and the finish. The winds seemed to be switchy, and with no idea where to look, and after launching I never felt a thermal all the way down to the ground in the valley! So I played it safe, flew over a big pasture, and landed near the main road back to Fuschl. Race headquarters called not a minute later to ask where I was (didn't they see me on live tracking?), to tell me I was doing fine, and said I was only 4 kilometers to the finish. Mentally I was having a tough day, and a few tears might have escaped as I was packing up. Was this how the real race was going to go?

It was moments like these that self-doubt crept in. Did I really deserve a place in this race? Did I have the stamina to keep up with the guys even though they could beat me in a foot race? Was my flying good enough to get me over and through some of the biggest mountain passes in the Alps?

I wiped my tears while I packed up, telling myself that many people had convinced me I could and should do this race. All I had to was give it my best, because as usual I would find a way to rise to the occasion, and outperform expectations.

My supporters Chuck and Boga showed up within minutes of my landing to shower me with fresh water bottles and get me on the road again. I knew I didn't have far to go and I was relieved to not have tired my legs out too much, even if all the other competitors had already reached the finish line ahead of me! There was road construction on the highway, and fresh blacktop. It was HOT. I walked in the gravel to keep out of the sticky stuff, and fantasized about jumping in the lake when I finished.

All of the employees of Zooom came out to the rooftop of their headquarters when I walked by, clapping and whistling. It spurred me to run the last few hundred meters to the finish line, where quite a few people were still around to cheer. Or perhaps they were just sunbathing on the beach and stood up when they saw me! Either way, I gave a short interview, dropped my pack, and dashed headlong into the lake. I'm sure I heard a few people shouting something about my shoes, but they were hot too. After a thorough dunking, I came out to chat with my supporters, before going back in the water for round two. It was heavenly to finally feel cool again.

The inflatable finish line was dismantled almost as soon as I finished, yet I walked back to camp with shoes squelching and a light heart. Sure I had a tough day, but it could have been worse for sure, and I had managed to keep my physical effort low enough that I would be ready for the main race. I knew the chances to show my strengths would be there.

That evening we had the welcome parade and dinner. To put on a little show for the locals, we made a short little parade to the lake, lined up in order of our prologue finish, while carrying the national flags from our countries. It was mildly embarrassing to wag the tail of the procession as the last place finisher, but I was happy to see the Yvonne Dathe (GER2) quite a few places in front of me. At least one of the women had done OK in the prologue!

Turnpoint 1
Photo Credit: Cano

Stanislav Mayer, Paul Guschlbauer, and Gavin McClurg
celebrating their win after the prologue!
Photo Credit: Markus Berger

The Powertraveller Prologue was won by Paul Guschlbauer in
2h 21m. Stanislav Mayer (CZE) was 2nd in 2h 22m and Gavin
McClurg (USA2) came 3rd in 2h 24m.

My Support Crew

Rules for the Red Bull X-Alps have morphed between editions, with limitations about supporters changing every year. In the first race, only one supporter and no outside help was allowed. I'm sure that wasn't easy to enforce, and didn't allow fans to hand an athlete a bottle of water without breaking the rules! I think in subsequent races this was relaxed a little, and in 2013 two supporters were allowed.

Although the athletes are not allowed to be pushed, pulled, or otherwise helped along the course, supporters can do almost everything else to help they can think of.   This includes preparing foot, sorting gear, exchanging clothes, carrying non-essential gear like food and water up to launch, as well as studying the course and suggesting routes.

For 2015 I had planned on using two supporters, but when the rules were announced for this edition, it stated that all athletes would have one official supporter. Uh-oh. Since I already had two lined up, it would be really hard to choose. Before I got too upset, I asked for clarification, and was informed that one official supporter would need to interact with the race officials during the race. However, I could have any other help that I wanted.

So at that point I started accidentally collecting supporters. My official supporter was Jarek, who I thought was knowledgeable about the Alps and would be a resourceful guy to have during the race. I was hoping to find someone who could study the tracklogs of other athletes, give me timely advice on flying routes, and check the upcoming weather forecasts. Perhaps I wasn't clear enough about what I needed, but Jarek turned out to be not very helpful at all, and although he studied the tracklogs incessantly during the race, he didn't seem to want to share the knowledge with me? He turned out to be a disappointing choice, but Jim and my other supporters made up for his ineptness.

We weren't the only team to have supporter / athlete issues, by the way. Asking someone to take a support role for up to two weeks on the go is a big commitment, especially when high levels of stress, physical exertion, and mental tiredness are added in!

My other supporters were great. My husband Jim was there for me every day, both in training and during the race. He kept track of my clothes, food, shoes, and gear, plus got everyone on the team organized while I raced. Jim was there for me to rub my aching feet every day, and to walk the last mile with me to camp in the evening.

My friend Chuck Savall volunteered to help me out of the blue. I guess he wanted an adventure in Europe for the summer! With his own vehicle, Chuck was able to push ahead of me during the race to check out the valley winds, as well as arrive quickly after I landed. He could be counted on to resupply me with water and snacks, and even let me take a nap on the mattress in his van when I couldn't walk another step. He was my secret source of chocolate cake, and would go far and wide to resupply his snack stock. Chuck also stepped up to fill Jarek's role, and with his myriad of electronic gadgets studied tracklogs and weather to keep me as informed as possible.

Mike, Boga, and Cano were also there to help out where they could. Boga loved to cook and whipped up some delicious pasta meals. Cano was just excited to be in Europe, as this was his first time visiting from Chile. At least he got to see a lot of scenery along the race! Mike was visiting from the US, and stopped by for a few days to follow along and cheer me on. He volunteered to stay awake during my night pass on Day 3, and drove Jim out to me, so that they could both help keep me moving and resupplied during the long rainy night.

All the help made quite an entourage. Jim and I had rented a small motorhome for training and the race, which had sleeping space for four, a tiny bathroom/shower, a fridge/freezer, and table big enough to spread maps out on. It was perfect for training but got a little crowded by race day. Mike, Boga, and Chuck all had vehicles too, so at times there were four cars following me around!   Sleeping arrangements were interesting too....we had the motorhome, a van, a tent and a hotel room at times and just hoped no police would bother us in our exhaustion.

So, when the race started I had 6 supporters, which lasted for a while.   Mike and Cano left after a couple of days, and then I had 4 supporters for most of the race.   Even that was really too much.   Feeding 5 people and keeping track of everyone is quite time consuming, and really too much help. The problem with too many people is management.   With only one supporter, that person knows s/he has to do everything.   Each added person COULD do something to help, too, but then it's harder to keep track of whether everything has been done or not.

In my case, I had a couple of supporters that really didn't do anything but ride around in the vehicles.   Which is ok, except it's just more people to keep track of, feed, and find places to sleep.   For the last few days of the race, I had just Jim and Chuck, with two vehicles.   I thought that was really a perfect combination of support.   Two vehicles made it possible to split up if needed, and also have a backup if anything went wrong. Two supporters were nice, because it allowed me to have someone walk with me at times and then get picked up later. Any more than that, and I hoped the supporters were just enjoying themselves, because they weren't really necessary!   If I were going to do it again, I would want at least one person to have lightweight kit and be able to hike and fly with me.   Help in the air was probably the most helpful thing I DIDN'T have, but I sure could have benefited from it.

My unplanned for but totally amazing supporter back at home was my mom Eileen, on the farm in Iowa, USA.   While out on the road during the race, we usually had very poor Internet connection.   This meant my supporters and I couldn't see the live tracking, and had trouble knowing what was happening in the race around us. My mom had a speedy data connection, could study the route, check out the news, and then give me race updates each day by cell phone. With the 7-hour time difference between there and Europe, she didn't get much sleep either! She usually woke up early to watch me fly, and stayed up late at night to give me race updates when I woke up in the morning.

My supporters Cano, Jarek, Boga, Chuck, Dawn and Jim

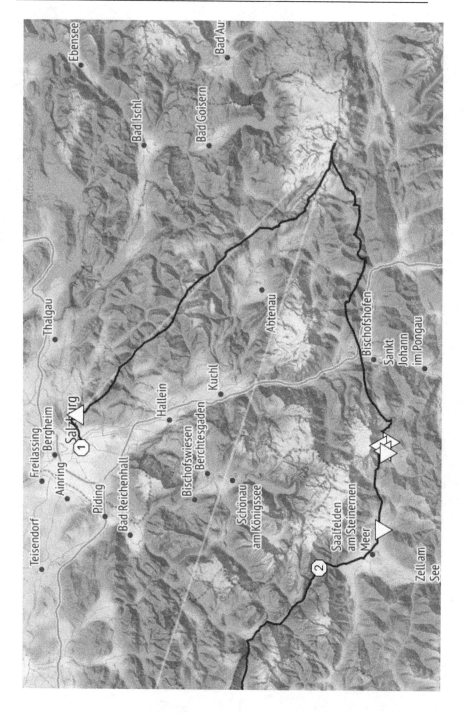

Day 1

Salzburg to Saalfelden, Austria
Turnpoint 1 - Gaisberg
Turnpoint 2 - Dachstein
Hiking 25 km
Flying 110 km

July 5, 2015. At last, the big day had arrived!   In the days since the prologue, I had been waiting impatiently for the race to start.   The weather had been wonderful, and along with many of the competitors, we had been having great training flights and praying for the same on race day.   I had mostly rested the day before the start, finally done with all the details like grocery shopping, placing stickers on my wing, charging my electronics (and learning how to use them), etc.   The waiting game was probably the hardest part of the whole race. Physically and mentally, all the athletes had been preparing for months and even years, so by now, we just wanted to get racing.

The weather on race day was looking hot and stable, but really nice in the higher mountains. As always, it was a question of whether we would be able to fly away from the Gaisberg, our first turnpoint and our first launch site. The Gaisberg Mountain looks down over Salzburg, and is on the very northern edge of the Alps, influenced by the stable weather of Germany's flatlands.   When pilots are having great flights closer to the high spine of the Alps, flights near Salzburg may still fizzle and die.

In any outdoor sport, the weather can be your friend or enemy. The overall temperatures in the Alps for the 2015 edition of the Red Bull X-Alps were unseasonably warm. Record heat was recorded in some places in Europe on July 5, the first day of the race, but the high pressure continued to plague us all the way to the end. Contrast this with the weather from the summer before in the Alps; Jim and I had traveled there to think about signing up for the race and to see Europe. These same two weeks in July, it rained for 12 days and nothing was flyable! On the whole, I think I prefer high temperatures and sunshine.

On race day, from our campground in Fuschl am See, the athletes were transported by bus to the city center in Salzburg by midmorning. In the Mozartplatz square, we hung out and did interviews as the sun beat down and crowds started to gather. My supporters had scattered, with Chuck and Boga heading up to the launch at Gaisberg, while Jim, Mike and Cano met me at the start.

The iconic start in the Mozartplatz was where it began to sink in; I was heading off to race with some of the best pilots in the world. Luckily the cameras seemed interested in the top competitors, and I happily watched from the background. Jim pulled up a spot in the shade and our friend Tony from California showed up out of the blue...we had friends emerging from the woodwork here! I autographed a backpack, gave a couple of short interviews, and tried to stay relaxed. Mostly I tried to stay hydrated; it was already hot with the sun beating down on us.

With a few minutes to go until race start, it was time to switch on all my electronics (more about these later).

Flymaster Live. Check.
SPOT Locater Beacon. Check.
Garmin Oregon GPS. Check.
Two phones. Check.

The Start of the Race
Photo Credit: Jim Sorensen

I also doused my head and shirt with water, but that lasted about 2 minutes before I was totally dry again. It was so hot we were melting in the shade.

At 11:30 the three winners from the Powertraveller prologue were off and running. Then it was our turn at 11:35. I'm sure everyone was taking photos of the athletes, but what I wanted was a photo of all the cameras pointed at us! The runway was lined with people as the clock counted down.

Finally we were off and running on the 7th Edition of the Red Bull X-Alps! My goal was to run fast enough to keep someone ahead of me in sight, so that I didn't go the wrong way in town. While I love navigating with maps, I've always found that getting in and out of towns is the hardest part of adventure racing. There are just so many confusing streets and options. With the cheering crowds running along with us, my energy level was high and it was easy to lope along.

Once across the river, everyone spread out and most disappeared in the distance. The guy whose backpack I had autographed hiked with me for a bit, but I outpaced him, and then I started asking the fans at every intersection which way to go. They seemed to point me in the right direction and soon enough I was climbing up to the trail on the Gaisberg. I wasn't sure if I was the last one on the course but assumed as much. I was hoping it wouldn't matter because the flying conditions would be better later in the afternoon.

Launching at the Gaisberg
Photo Credit: Markus Berger

To my surprise, three teams passed me on the climb, so I hadn't been last, but now I was. The blue sky was still free of wings as I ascended the steep trail, whose saving grace was that it was mostly shady under the trees. A helpful fan had doused me with water from a hose on the road, but I was dry again quickly. Once I was within 10 minutes of the top, I finally started to see white wings take to the air, and I knew I wouldn't be far behind.

My supporter was waiting at the top of the trail with water and my national flag. Yes, I had a US flag with my name on it! It was rather surreal to run across to the summit waving the flag, to sign the turn point board and head to launch. I'm sure there were crowds cheering me on, but my eyes were focused on getting in the air. It was kind of chaotic on launch with people getting kitted up everywhere, but I had practiced my launch sequence a lot, and was confident I could be in the air quickly. Chuck had my extra race gear, and with wings climbing strongly above me it was time to go. It was just a matter of stowing my hiking poles, layering warm clothes over my soaked t-shirt and shorts, and drinking some water. I waffled about putting on my lightweight down jacket, (it was so HOT on launch too) but Chuck gave me a look and pointed at the athletes climbing high above me. It was going to be a good day! I put it on.

The only snag was when I thought I better take the chance to use the bathroom in case of a long flight. The drawback was there were no bathrooms. With full race clothing on, I pushed through the crowds and through some weeds to get out of sight. Unfortunately the weeds turned out to be waist-high stinging nettle! Luckily my wind pants blunted some of the stinging, and I didn't need the towel I was carrying for privacy.

Just that quickly, I was buckling into my harness and launching. Chuck said later he was impressed how quickly I got in the air. Honza Rejmanek (USA1), who had arrived almost 30 minutes earlier than I had, was still conferring with his supporters on the ground. Compared to some of my previous flights from here, climbing out was easy. Too easy, actually. For the first time, I had to think about airspace and staying below it. We all did. The race officials had provided Flymaster flight instruments, which were programmed with the airspace, and would alarm when we were 300 meters below (or next to) the restricted area. That's about 1000 feet and seems like a lot, but in a strong thermal it's good to leave early to avoid getting a penalty.   The airspace around Salzburg is quite complicated, and there were multiple layers to know about and avoid. Secretly I hoped that someone would violate airspace. The 48-hour airspace penalty would put someone very far behind and save me elimination...but all the athletes managed to avoid any violations.

And then I was looking down on the launch, circling with a lot of white wings (race rules specified the color white for the fabric) and making the first move toward the big mountains. Often in my gaggle, all of our Flymasters would alarm simultaneously as we flew along, to warn us of approaching airspace, which would provoke a few kinds of descent techniques to stay below it. Paragliders don't descend very well in rising air, and I used a combination of collapsing the outer edges of my wingtips, (called big ears), and my speed bar to descend and avoid airspace. It was a good problem to have! Some pilots were spiraling down instead, as a few types of paragliders didn't really perform well with big ears. Either way, we had a speedy flight to Turnpoint 2, especially as the airspace limits got higher when we progressed along the course.

Unfortunately none of my supporters had thought to remind me to apply sunscreen, which I thought about (of course) AFTER I launched on what would be a long flight through the middle of the day. I hadn't worn my balaclava, thinking I wouldn't be high enough or cold enough to need it. Oops. I attempted to pull my jersey up over my lower face but that was a temporary solution at best, falling down every time I moved my arms.

Yvonne Dathe and I flew together for a while right from launch. Our flight speeds seemed quite similar, as they should be...she was flying an Ozone Alpina 2 as well, an XSmall whereas I had the Small. The flight to the Dachstein was pretty straightforward; this would be the 3rd time I had flown this same route, and the key was to stick to the high ground and keep moving toward the big mountains and Turnpoint 2. Often other competitors would get low around me, but everyone managed to get up again. At one point I had moved up into the middle of the pack on the live tracking, but in the air I was just happy to be flying and keeping up with everyone. The Dachstein! This turn point had been more in my thoughts than any other section of the race. In fact it was the highest turn point where we had to physically fly or walk over the peak (later turnpoints like the Zugspitz, Matterhorn and Mont Blanc didn't require actually arriving at the top, just flying close or around them). This one was at 2,700 meters and had never been flown in Red Bull X-Alps race history, so I'm sure we were all pretty stoked to be looking down on it! I had been dreading the steep climb up and over the glacier and the difficult snow launch at the top. It had been my biggest prayer that I was able to fly over this section.

It's hard to convey my absolute glee at flying high above the Dachstein on race day. I looked down at the snowfields I wouldn't have to walk over, and felt euphoric. In fact, this moment totally restored my faith in God. Here I had hoped and planned and prayed and trained for 12 months, and it had all come together. After 12 years of doubting my faith, I suddenly knew without a doubt that someone up there was helping me along. At the same time, I needed God more than ever...I was now an insignificant dot moving across the sky, flying under fabric inflated with just air. I felt both vulnerable and safe, while looking at the thin lines connecting my harness to my wing.

So I became quite giddy in the air. I found myself laughing aloud as I made the final climb to be able to fly over the Dachstein turn point. In fact, I confess that I really didn't care how the rest of the race went...I was so happy with the first day of flying that I felt I could relax and enjoy it! By now the airspace limitations were really high, and we were all comfortably flying at about 3,500 meters. I was chilly but not too cold, even though I could feel that my shirt and shorts were still wet with sweat, and sticking to me. The leaders weren't too far ahead, and we crossed paths in the air as they turned west to fly to Turnpoint 3 in Germany.

We had one more section of airspace to duck under as we flew west, and I wasn't sure exactly how high it allowed us to go. I took the safe route and pulled big ears to stay well under it at about 3000 meters. There were wings far above me but with no danger of sinking out it didn't matter much. To be honest I hadn't thought we would fly this far today and I hadn't reviewed this airspace like I had the closer sections to Salzburg! It was quickly behind me and I was soon climbing with a gaggle of competitors below me.

This would prove to be my undoing later though. All alone now, I squinted to see wings ahead of me but nothing was very clear. Below was the big valley crossing over Bischlingshofen, probably the toughest move of the day. I was very high and knew I would make it, but shadows had started to fall across the eastern side of Hochkonig peak on the other side. I was reassured by a wing far below me, and kept an eye on him as I sunk lower across the valley. Competitors were climbing along the cliffs and I headed there, but unfortunately I made a few poor choices. Two wings just behind me found a thermal, and instead of going back to it, I pushed on, getting lower and lower. Even a magic convergence area I had found on a previous flight didn't help out. I hung on in light lift, watching Turner (USA4) sink out below me. I should have (in retrospect) been more patient to get the light lift working to carry me up to the sunny warm cliffs. Instead I attempted to fly over to the nearby pass. With not much air below me to bring warm air up to climb in, I sunk out. And landed in fresh cow poop.

Looking back on the race, this was probably the crux of the whole race for me. Thermalling up here would have meant easily flying another 40 or 50 kilometers, staying up with the middle of the pack, and avoiding a section of the course where it was difficult to find launches and fly. It would also have meant staying ahead of bad weather. Plus with other competitors around me more often, I probably would have gotten a lot further along the course. But that's all conjecture. I might have also crashed, injured myself, etc.

At the time, though, I was quite happy with my flight. I had just flown 100 kilometers over a huge psychological barrier of the Dachstein turnpoint. I had landed near the pass, and I was hoping I could walk around the corner into the sun and relaunch quickly. My supporters reported that there were four or five competitors behind me, so at least I wasn't the only one to land out early---if landing after 100 kilometers could be called early. I packed up after cleaning the cow poop as best as I could, and started hiking. It was a quick walk to get around the corner, but I didn't really like what I saw--a shallow valley and another high hill in front of me. I kept going along the contour of the hill, finally finding a grassy hillside with nice thermal cycles. I hoped. It was getting late, around 5:30 pm or so, and my chances of thermalling weren't that great.

With my paraglider spread out, I suddenly realized that Turner (USA4) was spread out only 200 meters below me, and probably hadn't seen me. Before I had a chance to shout, he was launching and in the air, and would quickly land down in the valley. Oops. Hopefully I was high enough to avoid that fate. In the air, I spent a few precious seconds turning up the volume in my Flymaster, but it was too late. The lift wasn't there, so I top landed again a little below my launch. It was time to pack up and climb even higher onto the shoulder of the peak of Hochkonig. I could see nice launches high above me, but it would take a while to get there.

It was a long climb, and I was happy to drink the pineapple juice I had carried all the way from launch that morning. I wasn't so happy about still carrying my Via Ferrata climbing harness and kit, which was completely unnecessary now that I had flow over the Dachstein massif. In fact I hadn't seen my supporters all day, since my landing at the pass had been on a trail high above the road. Luckily I had brought enough water and food to get me up the first climb, my flight, and even a second hike, so that I could be self-sufficient for quite a while.

I switch-backed up the trail to about 2000 meters, and saw what I believed to be another competitor climbing up below me. (I was trying not to think about the stragglers flying over my head). We were rather identifiable while wearing our race clothing. He eventually caught up and I realized it was just random chance that this guy was wearing a blue Salewa shirt and orange Salewa shorts and carrying a big pack, the exact clothing that the men were wearing in the race. This day hiker, though, definitely wasn't in the competition.

By the time I had climbed almost up to the top of the ridge, shadows were lengthening and I knew I had probably missed my chance at another big flight. But the cliff rocks were still hot, and my new goal was to get across these winding valleys and into the flats near the town of Saalfelden. Indeed, to my supporters watching below, I had a magical evening glide, flying at a 15:1 glide ratio at times along the cliffs. (Normal glide is more like 8:1 or 10:1). The long glide allowed me to clear a couple of small passes (by only 20 feet in one case!) and bypass a lot of winding roads. It was the next best thing to not sinking out. Turner (USA4) was only 5km in front of me at that point, but he had done a lot more walking to get there, after sinking out below me earlier.

A parade of supporters arrived when I landed near the road near the town of Maria Alm am Steinernen Meer. Jim and Jarek were in the motorhome, Chuck in the van, Boga and Cano in the car, and Mike in his rental. I know, it was too many people, but they wanted to help so why not? They were happy for my great flight, and gave further reports on the athletes behind me. I unloaded all my flying clothing and via ferrata kit, and got more water. Eventually they all went ahead to Saalfelden to order pizza, and we agreed to meet up in the center near a spot I knew. Jim and I had passed through this area a few times in training, and we knew it quite well. In reality, one supporter found me with a box of pizza, and walked with me for a while out of town while I ate, bypassing everyone else and leaving them uncertain where I was going. This was a hint of how confusing it would get with too many supporters, and I would leave it up to Jim to organize everyone to avoid this in the future. I guess they eventually got more organized (more or less), but I was only seeing snippets of their day when I would meet up to eat, change shoes, reload on water, and continue on.

From Saalfelden I had a route choice of two valleys, and I had trained in both of them. In the end it was an easy decision to go with the shorter option, which had no airspace issues, even though it meant a longer walk to a good launch. Even better, it was pretty flat all the way from here to the next turn point, so it would be the fast option, even if the weather was bad.

I set my sights on flying off Lofer peak in the morning, and sent the cars ahead about 6 km, which I figured I could make before the evening time cutoff at 10:30 pm. I was even familiar with where we would stop for the night, having walked this narrow valley before. With a headlamp on and full dark settling in, it was a race to make the vans as 10:30 approached. In fact I made it with about 5 minutes to spare by running a bit along the trail! I had only walked about 25 km this first day, so I was still fresh enough to run easily with a pack on my back.

Then we crossed our fingers that our vehicles wouldn't be noticed for the night. Chuck was sleeping in his passenger van with the seats rearranged out of the way. Jim and I were in the motorhome, Mike had gone to a hotel for the night, and everyone else was in a rather large tent. Tent camping being rather illegal in Austria outside of designated spots, we were taking a chance of getting kicked out if noticed by anyone.

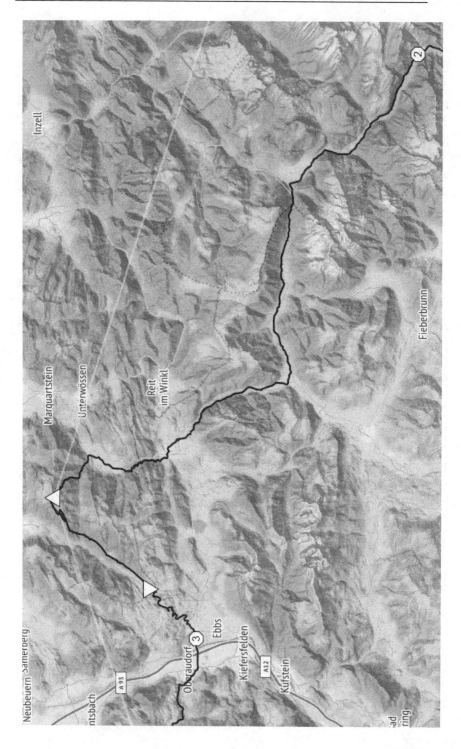

Day 2

Lofer to Niederndorf, Austria
Turnpoint 3 - Kampenwand
Hiking 75 km
Flying 11 km

Despite a quiet night with no tent evictions, unfortunately I was only able to get about one hour of sleep, being too excited and definitely not physically tired enough to fall asleep. I think this is a peculiarity of women athletes during endurance events. At an expedition race in Scotland back in 2012, my three male teammates were able to nod off for a couple of hours sleep each night (and in fact needed the sleep to keep going), while I was unable to get more than one hour of sleep (total) over the first three nights! I have since read other reports of women who are unable to sleep for a night or two after starting a difficult endurance event. In any case, after years of working the night shift as a soldier in the US Army, I knew that missing a night of sleep wasn't that big of a deal, and I would be able to stay alert the next day with no problems.

The weather wasn't going to cooperate with me though. At my 5 am start, it was warm and muggy as I walked down the trail, with most of the crew still asleep. First there was some fog, and then it unexpectedly poured. Out came the poncho. My planned launch that morning obviously wasn't going to happen.

So instead, I kept a steady walking pace, and caught up on the news of the day. Although I didn't have much time at night to study what was happening, I could walk along during the day and follow the other athletes by reading the Red Bull X-Alps news snippets posted to Twitter. These showed up as text messages on my phone and gave me a snapshot of the race. I also checked weather websites, posted Facebook updates about my day, read the encouraging replies from everyone, and checked the PilotFinder list repeatedly. Pilotfinder was a spreadsheet of all the Red Bull X-Alps athletes, and told me where they were in relationship to me along the course. While I couldn't get live race tracking to work on my slow data connection, I could get Pilotfinder to update quickly. So I knew that when I started out that morning, Turner (USA4) was 5 km ahead of me, while Dathe (GER2) was about 10 km behind me.

Little wonder my phone needed charging twice a day during the race!

I was motivated to catch up with Turner (although I never did, it seemed he had LONG legs), and stay ahead of Yvonne (we managed the same pace almost all day). But flying was out. It poured on me as I turned the corner to Lofer, so I continued walking the valley heading to the town of Kossen. In the middle of the rainstorm, the motorhome of helpers caught up to me with a smoothie, which I took to go, and drank as I walked. I wanted to crawl in the motorhome for a break, but It didn't seem like a good idea to go inside and drip water all over the inside. While drinking my smoothie in the rain, I came across a public bathroom. Score. Still nursing my smoothie, I then found a very nice wading stream with a built-in dock and a bench. Double score. While still wearing my bright red poncho in the pouring rain, I doffed my shoes and socks and stood in the knee-deep stream for a while. Any chance to soak my feet and legs was worth doing. They weren't too painful yet but it was just a matter of time.

After walking past the town of Lofer and over a small (very small) pass, the rain stopped and the sky started to look better. Unfortunately I was in no-man's land for flying. Ahead of me was Kossen, with a big wide valley and narrow funnel leading to the Kampenwand, Turnpoint 2. I had been here before several times, and had never managed to fly across the valley, not even close. My personal thoughts on the area went like this "All good flights end in Kossen." So although there was a shortcut to climb up the ridge to my north and launch from the

Fellhorn mountain, this was a marginal day, and I figured I would end up landing in Kossen. Plus, at a walking pace I should make the next turn point while it was still early enough in the evening to fly off it, but rolling the dice on a steep climb and earlier flight might make me miss the 9 pm cutoff. So it really wasn't worth the hike up for such a flight. I passed it by and kept on walking around the bend, finally heading north and straight to the checkpoint.

Author's Note: Both Samuel Vurpillot (SUI2) and Dathe (GER2), about 10 km behind me, WOULD hike up and fly from the Fellhorn. Both of their flights ended in Kossen and they missed the chance to fly from Kampenwand that night. Whether they could have made it there faster on foot instead of flying isn't clear.

What was clear was that it was getting really hot. Jim walked with me for a while along a river, and I was desperate to soak my feet again somewhere. It wasn't the nicest river for doing so, really fast moving and rather mucky, but I wasn't going to be picky. Then it was time to hike solo again, really put my head down and get myself to Kossen.

As I walked past the gondola and met up with my supporters, I needed water and an umbrella. Not for the rain anymore, but the sunshine...I was broiling in the heat. I stopped to say hi to Pier in the Parashop Kossen on the way by. Pier was worried when I came in that I needed a repair, but then gave me a big smile and a hug and sent me on my way again. He had repaired my wing from an earlier eagle attack, and helped adjust my new race harness when it arrived, so it was fun to stop in the race for a second, and get out of the sun. I found my supporters again downtown. It was too hot to stop, so on to the river and to dunk myself in the cold water before taking the trail through the forest. My mom, following me via live tracking, texted me to ask "Are you taking a swim in the river?" I found it hard to convey how hot I was.

The cold water wore off very fast even in the shade. In the next village, I was met by my train of supporters and their cars, including my main supporter, Jim, Chuck, Boga, Cano and Mike. I'm sure my face was very red from the heat, which was almost unbearable. Although I was drinking loads of liquid, I couldn't stay ahead of dehydration. It was Boga who found the brand new cattle trough filled with cold water near the motorhome. I wandered over, took off my shoes, and gratefully submerged my whole body under the water. I could even drink from the fountain at the same time! My supporters thought it was hilarious and took lots of photos.

Cooling off in a horse trough!
Photo Credit: Boguslawa Majorek

Eventually they made me get out of the trough and continue walking. I quickly dried in the sun, as afternoon shadows got longer. The climb up the backside of the Kampenwand actually didn't seem as hard as the first time I did it in training. My supporters had left me with a little water and some snacks, and were now driving around to the west side. There they could take the gondola up to the Turnpoint, and hoped to make it there before me. As I approached the Steinberg-Alm hut, a car drove past me, and a bottle of water dangled out the window. Although I had enough fluid to make the summit, I couldn't say no to cold water! It was the owners of the Alm, who had been tracking me on the website, and wanted to hike up with me to the checkpoint. We conversed in broken English and German, and the distraction helped me push quickly up the steepest part of the climb at the end. This mountain is a very popular paragliding launch, and I could see lots of (non-race) wings flying merrily above me. Everyone was reporting that conditions were still good if I could hurry to the top. Hah. Given that I had already walked 60 km that day, I thought I was holding a great pace, although my shins started to hurt on the ascent.

There were many people at the summit, and I managed a run across the pasture to the Turnpoint sign. A voice over the loudspeaker kept shouting, "WAIT" and soon enough a man came running up to interview me for a couple of minutes about the race. I have no idea what I said but could tell that Jim was impatient to get me flying as it was past 7 pm and there wasn't much left in the day. Still, I got launched with a bit of lift yet, and was able to climb a little and work my way back south...this was the furthest north our race would take us. A couple of my crew launched with me and we got together in the air for a nice final glide. When I landed, a guy in a convertible stopped for a minute to tell me that I could get another glide down to the Inn River if I hiked up a few hundred meters to the west.

That seemed like a good idea, so I packed up quickly and set off back up another hill. After 60 or so km of walking for the day and a semi-hard landing, my shins were barking a little but I figured it wouldn't be far.   It wasn't, only a couple of kilometers, but on the other side, the hill was very shallow. Plenty of pastures to launch from, but none of them seemed steep enough. I walked to one that would work, behind an active dairy farm, and asked the farmer if I could launch. He told me no, the grass was too high and it would damage his crop.   Bummer. The wind at that moment seemed to start blowing down hard anyway, so I continued walking down the road, winding my way down to the river. Actually, I started limping my way down to Niederndorf, and texted down a request for some Advil and my Black Diamond trekking poles. I hadn't thought I would need them anymore at the checkpoint, and had sent them down the gondola with Jim.

Chuck showed up quickly and followed me back down the hill. It really was only a small hill, maybe 500 meters of descent, my first downhill of the race.   And a shortcut on the route as well...I would have come this way whether I could fly or not. Still, not flying down on a perfectly beautiful evening felt sad, not to mention painful. My left shin was really hurting, and I used my poles as a crutch to take a little weight off of each step. I found I could move quite quickly, sort of leaping over my poles onto my good leg and covering some ground.   This final descent would take me up to 75 km for the day, though, and I told Jim I couldn't make it across the river tonight. He managed to find a spot behind a grocery store, where the lady next door was following our race! I limped in sometime after 9 pm to a big plate of Boga's yummy pasta and an early bedtime. An Advil PM assured I would sleep well.

The quirky aside to the day was the bizarre penalty meted out by the race officials to most of the athletes, for short cutting the obligatory route up to the Gaisberg (through Salzburg) on the 1st day of the race. For some reason, they had made the route deviate from the shortest way up the mountain by one city block, which added maybe 100 meters to the route distance. The officials told us the route wouldn't be marked in town, but that a guy on a bicycle would show us the way. That's all well and good for the leader, but for the athletes strung out along the route, we all just hoped to follow the guy in front of us.   I had even asked the spectators at times which way everyone else went.   So 28 out of 32 athletes got this penalty for not following the official route, me included. Chrigel Maurer, the 3-time winner and race favorite, was also penalized, and we were told it would be a 6-hour penalty starting the next morning after the mandatory rest period. That seemed like an insanely high penalty for what was an accidental mistake, which maybe only saved us a minute or two on the course.

My mom back in the States, who had been following the live tracking closely, filled me in on all the details when I called her on the hike down the hill.   I put in an official complaint about the penalty, as did many other competitors I'm sure.   Word came back pretty quickly that the penalty had been reduced to 2 hours and would be enforced the next morning.   It still seemed a high penalty for what was a completely innocent mistake, especially since 90 percent of the athletes were getting the penalty.   This should have shown the race officials it was a problem with THEIR course marking, not the athletes. However, in the end, I'm fairly sure that the penalty had no effect on the overall standings, and from what I heard afterward, most athletes were more than grateful for the extra sleep!

Turnpoint 2
Photo Credit: Boguslawa Majorek

Daily Race Rituals

It seems odd to need to be reminded to brush my teeth, but when mind and body are really tired, thinking becomes difficult. With that in mind, I knew I needed to establish a daily race ritual ahead of time for the morning and evening. I knew this would mitigate some of the worry that comes with being tired and not being able to think linearly. It also helped me sleep better!

Therefore, I taped the lists (below) onto a wall of our motorhome, where I could glance at them before bed and before heading out in the morning. This way, I never walked off without turning on my live tracking, or forgot any essential race equipment. It went unsaid that I always had my wing, harness, reserve and helmet with me, even if they weren't on the list!

Foot care was high on my priorities. Even a small blister can turn into a big problem. With the mileage I would be putting in during the race, I didn't have time for foot problems. To take care of my feet, I employed a few tactics, and I'm sure they all helped. To start with, in the mornings and after shoe changes, I applied waterproof lube to my feet. Essentially, the lube coated the skin with a high-tech type of Vaseline, preventing the wrinkles you might see on feet and hands after spending too much time soaking in a bathtub. Blisters are caused by three variables: heat, moisture and friction. By eliminating moisture with waterproof lube, even in hot temperatures blisters were much less likely to form. In fact I only had 2 blisters over the whole race, pretty minor considering I walked 468 kilometers in 11 days!

Muscle soreness would also be an increasing problem during the race, and my husband Jim gallantly offered to give me a foot rub each night before I went to sleep. It's amazing how much a foot rub helped with recovery. My feet usually went from aching to relaxed within a few minutes, and it helped a lot with circulation too. Spending so much time walking made my legs swell a little, and manipulating my feet each night got everything moving again. To help with my foot rub, Jim used fractionated coconut oil, mixed with a few drops of essential oils. There is no danger of essential oils interacting negatively with each other, so I added all the oils which might help me with recovery, including peppermint, clove, frankincense, lemon, helichrysum, lavender, eucalyptus, ginger, and basil. If nothing else, the oil helped my skin heal from a day stuffed in sweaty shoes, and smelled really nice!   I also rubbed an essential oil mix (similar to Icy-Hot) on my calves. It smelled like it was helping whether it did or not! Over the top went my compression calf sleeves, which I wore each night to sleep.

Whenever I could during the day, I stopped for a few minutes to soak my feet in cold streams or rivers along the route. Cold therapy does an amazing job of mitigating swelling and muscle damage.   Even 5 or 10 minutes can mean a measurable difference in muscle soreness. I also took cold showers each evening in the motorhome. It may sound really wimpy, but I slept a LOT better when I was clean and my sweaty skin wasn't sticking to the sheets!

Morning Race List:

Brush Teeth
Lube Feet
Mix Perpetuem Drink
Gear:
> Poles
> Clothes
> Food
> Water

Check Weather
Electronics:
> Turn on Flymaster
> Turn on GPS
> Phones (2)
> Back-Up Battery
> SPOT Tracker
> Garmin Fenix GPS Watch

Evening race list:

Clear Trash from Pack
Lay Out Clothes for Next Day
Soak feet
Foot Rub with Essential Oils
Eat
Drink
Download track logs from GPS if needed
Charge:
> Phones (2)
> Flymaster
> Watch
> GPS
> Back-Up Battery
> SPOT

Check Maps
Check Airspace
Calf Sleeves

Day 3

Niederndorf, Austria to Kreuth, Germany
Hiking 35 km
Flying 15 km
Night Pass Hiking 41 km

The two-hour penalty from the Gaisberg shortcut on Day 1 enforced that morning meant that I could sleep in an extra couple of hours. Together with an early stop, this meant I got a full 8 hours of sleep! This was nice, as the next night I would be using my night pass, meaning that I probably wouldn't get much sleep at all. In the early morning sunshine, I crossed the River Inn and was back in Germany again. Actually, yesterday I had hiked from Austria into Germany, flown down from the Kampenwand to literally land straddling the border, and slept in Austria. Now I would be back in Germany until almost Turnpoint 4. As an American in Europe, I actually enjoyed all the border crossings. Of course these days no passport is required, but since I hadn't left the USA at all until I was 16 years old, such casual country hopping still seemed fascinating.

The motorhome had hit a snag that morning. Our Goal Zero Yeti power supply, which was charging the myriad of electronics I carried each night, had gone dead. Evidently the cable we were using to power it (via the cigarette lighter) wasn't working properly. So Jim went off to a campground to plug into a power outlet and get everything charging again. After some research, he realized that it would take 18 hours to fully recharge the batteries, so he ended up purchasing a power inverter for the motorhome to keep everything charging as he drove.

I had hiked the road up to the launch at Bayrischzell in training, and knew it would be a pleasant, easy walk. It was about 20 km, which would take about 4 hours, but the day was hot even when I started out at 7 am. Everyone had been planning to come up to Bayrischzell to fly with me. After all, it was a drive-up launch on what could be a key flight if I could get some distance in the air. Plans changed with the discovery of the dead charger, and it looked like I would be on my own. Chuck and I worked our way slowly up the hill. He drove up to scout the road ahead, then back down into town to look for breakfast and ice. Breakfast turned out to be chocolate cake (my favorite!), but there was no ice to be had. Sheesh, in the USA every gas station would have loads of the stuff for coolers, etc. Here in Europe, it was really hard to find. A real bummer as it was a scorcher of a day. Temperatures were again heading into the 90s F (35 C). Chuck managed to grab some of our dwindling supply of ice in the motorhome and I put a Ziploc of melting ice under my floppy hat. It was great while it lasted, for sure!

The last part of the climb up to launch was in full sunshine. Since this launch was really an afternoon site, when I arrived at 11 am Chuck and I went straight into a restaurant/hut there for a big glass of Apfelsaftschorle (half apple juice, half carbonated water) and some chocolate ice cream. Then we waited on launch for conditions to get better. A few pilots showed up, and greeted me like they already knew I would be there. Guess they were following live tracking! I took a few photos with them and they were happy to be my test wind dummies, so that made up for the motorhome being stuck back down in the valley.

The first guy launched, flying straight out and up and making conditions look really good. Then he just kept flying straight and landed out down in the valley. He would eventually come back up and fly with me, but landed out again!?! Then it started blowing down, which it did for almost half hour, a long time. Another pilot who was ready to launch just packed up his wing and went home. So much for my wind dummies.

By 1 pm I was ready to go whether it was good or not. I could see Alex Villa (COL) flying a few peaks ahead of me, but he wasn't able to make much distance that day either. When I did launch, I scratched for a long time before climbing out, still not getting very high. The problem was that I wasn't really thermalling as much as just climbing up on ridge lift in the northern Bavarian winds. The day was actually pretty stable, and I had several big crossings ahead of me. Unfortunately the first one proved to be my undoing. I crossed the valley and approached the small hill to the west, debating to myself...sunny side or windy side? I ultimately chose the windy side, which kept me closer to the main valley and the trails I would need if I sunk out. And sink out I did...feeling almost no lift at all on my way to the ground.

I was quite unhappy with myself, and sorely wished my supporters would have been flying with me. Of course, once I had packed up alone in the scorching hot valley, and set off to hike up the next hill, that's when my whole parade of supporters showed up. Where were they when I needed help flying on the hill? I knew I was being unreasonable, but I had been really hoping for a good flight. Looming ahead of me was my night pass, and I knew from training in this area that I needed to get across two more big hills before I could get to a straight, flat road for the night hike.

At noon I had declared to the race officials that I was using my night pass, which I could use once during the race. Tomorrow morning at 6 am the first athlete would be cut from the race (and again each 48 hours during the race). There were 3 athletes behind me, but anyone could still catch me by walking all night, so my only choice was to do the same.

So that became my new mission for the day, to get over the hills in daylight so I didn't have to walk the mountains at night. I had flown this area before, and I knew where the launches where and what to expect. That was the good news. The bad news was that it was so hot I could barely stand it. I exchanged empty bottles for a lot more water and pineapple juice. It was too hot to eat, so the calories in the juice were keeping me going.   In an angry haze, I walked right past my trail junction, and had to backtrack to the right intersection.

Shortly past this, I came to a big signs stretched across the trail saying "STOP" and a picture of a hiker with a big X across it. I took it to mean the trail was closed, and in my weakened mental state, almost came unglued. I sat down and called Jim, barely coherent. After reviewing the maps a little, I determined that there were two trails beyond this point so it was unlikely they would both be closed. Ducking under the sign I continued on, hoping the bulldozer there meant it was just a short section of trail closed.

A little further on at the junction was another sign with even more dire warnings in German of how the trail was closed. My only option was to take a longer trail, going almost around the mountain rather than over it. This would bring me to a launch I hadn't seen before, facing SW rather than NW. Plus it was almost 2 km longer, which seems like agony when I was racing the clock for a late launch that evening.

I must confess that while walking up this hill, I cried several times. Perhaps bawled might be a better word. I would have to walk all night now just to stay ahead of elimination, and it suddenly all seemed like too much. I'm sure my pace dropped to that of a snail, my phones and live tracking weren't working at all in the trees, and I was drinking water only to have it leak out of my eyes. All things considered, it was the hardest/worst hike of the whole race. I was embarrassed at landing out, sure that everyone else was having great flights, and stuck on the ground detouring a long way around a trail that should have be open, darn it!

Eventually I climbed high enough to get the phones working and called Jim, who gave me a pep talk. Talking to him helped me feel a lot better. Other athletes were having similar short flights in the area and I should be safe from elimination, as Dathe (GER) was behind me and hadn't pulled her night pass. In a better mood now, I continued on, with the scenery getting nicer too. As I hiked by a high mountain lake, I called my mom for good measure, just to pass the time, and get the low down on where everyone else was along the course.

My supporters were giving me updates on the weather too, and looking for launches on the southern end of the mountain. The main wind was coming from the north, but I would arrive on the SW side of the hill. As I got up to the Rotwand Hut, I could feel nice cycles coming up along a nice sunny bowl, and would have easily launched here without having a second thought. My supporters insisted that I continue around the ridge and feel the northern wind, which was quite strong. I'm convinced now they saved my life when I complied, because the wind was really howling from the NW once I turned the corner. If I had flown from the south and thermaled up, at some point I would have encountered the strong rotor, plus I would have landed somewhere not nice, and definitely not in the right direction.

Anyway, in the wind I could feel strong cycles and a few lulls. I picked a nice grassy steep face just below the summit to lay out my wing and waited. I drank my last sip of water, and waited some more. Finally I felt a big lull and pulled up my wing. It immediately got away from me though, and I quickly started flying sideways and heading for a fast landing while still facing the hill. Somehow my muscle memory helped me pull the correct brake. I spun around in the air and I was flying up and away. Even then it wasn't easy, as there was really no thermal lift, just ridge lift. Where I needed to fly was against the wind and down to the small lake on the way to the next summit. With the strong winds it would be another sled ride, and I just hoped that there would be no rotor in the narrow valley. Altogether it wasn't a very nice flight, and I was back on the ground across the lake at 6:45 pm. A frantic call ensued to Jim for more water, as I needed to hike up yet another ridge and fly down before the cutoff at 9 pm. Luckily Chuck was nearby and showed up in minutes. I dumped four empty bottles of water and juice, and got 4 more. I think he was amazed at how much I was drinking. I could have died for a cold bottle of anything, but in this heat and lacking ice for a cooler, I had to be content with just lukewarm instead of hot.

Luckily I had hiked this exact route in training, and it was only about 5 km to a wonderful grassy launch that I knew would have the afternoon sun and would be flyable. As I passed a hut, I eyed the cold drinks inside, but I had enough with me to keep me going. A mountain biker saw me pass, shook my hand and wished me luck. Then he came running after me so he could get a photo together! I still needed to hurry but I was pretty sure I would make the 9 pm cutoff for flying easily, and chatted for a minute with the biker. In fact I made it up to launch before 8 pm, after climbing another 500 meters of vertical. It was too late for any thermals, though, and all I could manage was a sled ride to the official landing zone in the town of Rottach-Egern.

YAY...I had made it to the main road! From here I could head south and then west on pavement, which would lead me all the way to Turnpoint 4. The difficult part of the day was over, and I could take a minute to relax before heading out on my night pass. At least now I didn't have to race to get anywhere, just keep plodding along. The caretakers of the little hut at the LZ came out to meet us, and talked to all of my supporters while I hopped in the shower to cool off after what had been a really tough day. They were excitedly following the race because they had helped to train Sebastian Huber (GER3), who would go on to finish 2nd in the race. They were incredibly nice, and arranged for the motorhome to stay there for the night with a power outlet, to continue charging our still half-charged battery. (All of my electronics plugged in overnight really drained it). I eventually walked out of town with the promise that Boga would make some delectable pasta and Jim and Mike would come find me later with dinner. My supporters then hung out at the hut and shared a beer with their new friends. Turns out one of the caretakers had participated in the Red Bull X-Alps a few years back. Evidently his race had derailed the first time he had to walk down a hill, as he hadn't trained for the downhills!

I spent the next hour or so walking along a river trail with darkness falling, enjoying the dusky views and finishing up in almost pitch black before emerging on the road to turn west. At just that point, Jim texted dinner was on the way, and I stumbled upon a large picnic table. It was too much to resist, and when they arrived I was sprawled out with my feet up, starving. Boga's pasta was perfect, along with a few other snacks and inevitably more bottles of water and some Coke to get me through the night. I stuffed some chocolate in my pack for the midnight blues, hoping that the air was cooling off enough to not melt it.

In fact it was about to rain, and drops started falling as I chased the last bit of pasta off my plate. The poncho went on and the guys took off, promising to come back in a few hours so Jim could walk with me through the wee hours of the night. What ensued was one of the most fantastic lightning storms I've ever seen. I was walking on a road now, and would follow it the whole night, so I didn't have to worry about route finding, and traffic was sparse. With raindrops pelting me, my shoes and socks were soon soaked, and the thunder and lightning was intense. One driver even stopped to see if I was ok. I guess a hunchback figure in a bright red poncho walking in the pouring rain at 11 pm WAS a little weird.

Evidently the race officials even called our supporter race phone to make sure that I was ok. On the road, I was well away from dangerous objects like falling trees, and it was windy but not terrible. Kruger (RSA) wasn't so lucky. He and his supporters were making dinner somewhere southwest of me during the rainstorm. A microburst hit them, and two or three rather large tree branches fell on their vehicle, narrowly missing supporter Konstantin's head. They would spend some time the next morning clearing the branches away before they could move the vehicle, and were really lucky that the damage was minor.

The storm passed and I was left with squelching shoes on what became a rather nice starry night. I begged Jim to bring me dry shoes as soon as he was ready. My feet were already tender from the 145 km I had walked in the race so far, and I didn't want to get blisters.

Supporters with new friends in Rottach-Egern
Photo Credit: Boguslawa Majorek

Equipment and Electronics

Here's the mandatory equipment I used during the 2015 Red Bull X-Alps:

Wing: Ozone Alpina 2, size S   Weight: 4000 g
Harness: Ozone Ozium, size M/M   Weight: 2000 g
Reserve: Supair X-Tralite   Weight: 999 g
Helmet: Icaro 2000   Weight: 390 g
Pack: Ozone   Weight: 500 g

Altogether my base kit weighed about 8 kg. I'm not including extras like trekking poles and clothing in the total, because I switched out gear depending on weather and conditions.

Let me say that I was really happy with my kit provided by Ozone Paragliders. I had been flying an Ozone Delta 2, and switching to the lightweight version in the Alpina 2 was great. It launched and flew wonderfully in conditions that were trying at times to say the least. I owe some of my safety to the fact that my wing was solid above me and didn't take unnecessary collapses.

Matt Gerdes from Ozone was really nice to work with, even when I had trouble getting the sizing right on my gear. I had been wondering which size of wing to use, which included factoring in my body weight, my equipment weight, the feel of the wing under different loads, etc. Being heavy on the wing makes it fly and sink faster, whereas lighter means less sink but also less speed. Ozone wing sizes are based on body weight + gear. Unfortunately, I fell right between two sizes. This meant I needed to either lose weight (about 4 kg) to fit into the XS, or carry extra ballast to fly on the S.

Originally I went with losing the body weight, and ordered an XS, then realized that doing so would be really difficult while training, and changed my mind. Plus a larger size meant I could eat an extra slice of black forest cake occasionally and not feel guilty! So for a while I had two training wings before selling the XS wing. It's not that I couldn't have flown the XS over the weight range (people do all the time) but for the Red Bull X-Alps I would be weighed and measured, and everything had to be within the official weight limits.

The problem came when I went to order my wing for the race. I thought I had checked the order but evidently not, as I ended up with an XS race wing! Doh. This I found out only three weeks before the race, and made a frantic call to Matt at Ozone to order the correct size. It had to be white, or I could have flown my training wing, but in the end Ozone delivered a new S wing quickly and I was saved.

Race electronics:
When athletes arrived at race headquarters about a week before the race, they were handed a large goody bag. Or should I say a heavy goody bag. The array of electronics we were required to carry was staggering.   These included:

Flymaster Live Variometer (Live tracking, airspace notifications, and everything I would need in the air to gauge my flights)
Garmin Oregon GPS (Backup logger, and a heavy brick of a GPS)
Red Bull Mobile Phone (Voice and text but no data) The best thing I can say about this heavy phone was it seemed to hold a charge for days, probably because I wasn't using it. It also had an emergency crash feature, if the phone hit the ground too hard, it would beep and send an emergency message to the race officials as a safety backup. Athletes could be seen "testing" this feature over and over during prep week!
Backup Battery and Cables (Needed to recharge batteries as we raced that didn't last the full 18 hour day)
SPOT tracker (A last minute addition when athletes realized that we didn't have failsafe backup method of beacon tracking when out of phone signal range)

Personal iPhone 5 (Needed because the race phone didn't provide data, and I had already downloaded electronic maps and other navigation aids)
Garmin Virb HD Camera (Optional to carry)
Garmin Fenix 3 Watch (Watch/GPS combined into my favorite gear of the whole race)
Flare Gun (In an emergency we had a tiny flare gun with some extra flares)

You guessed it. All that gear was heavy. I didn't actually weigh it, but I had a huge pile of electronics every night to recharge and I think it was close to 2 kg. That seemed a little over the top, as some of it was obviously redundant. The athletes all spent some time complaining about it to the race officials, and each other; after all, we had carefully removed each gram we could from our equipment, including the harness padding that would save us in an accident! Now we were saddled with all this! But in the end, since we all had to carry it, it was fair, just not very fun.

In addition to the required kit, I usually carried some small snacks, chapstick, foot lube, and a little bit of extra brake line in case I snagged my wing and needed to do a repair on the hill. Water was the biggest weight, adding up to a kilo or two before each hike. That might sound like a lot of water, but in the heat I was drinking several bottles during each climb up to launch.

My clothing stayed pretty consistent. Lightweight shorts and t-shirt, a floppy hat, wool socks, and lightweight running shoes. I usually had a light pair of arm warmers stuffed in a pocket, and if I got chilly those would do the trick. When heading up to a launch, I would bring gloves, sunglasses, wind pants, fleece jacket, down jacket, raincoat or windbreaker, and my race jersey. Four layers might seem like overkill but up at 4000 meters it was essential.

So I'm guessing that my 8kg pack became 10kg with electronics, and then went up to 12 or 13 kg with clothing, food and water.   Of course, if I was walking down the road, I could dump a lot of extra weight and be back closer to 10kg.

I didn't have the lightest pack out there by far.   Some athletes had really cut back and were using pod harnesses near 1 kg and wings closer to 3 kg, with a base weight of 6-7 kg. A few athletes were carrying even more than I was, because of a bigger wing or a harness with more padding.

The trail is closed. Where to go now?

Photo Credit: Vitek Ludvik

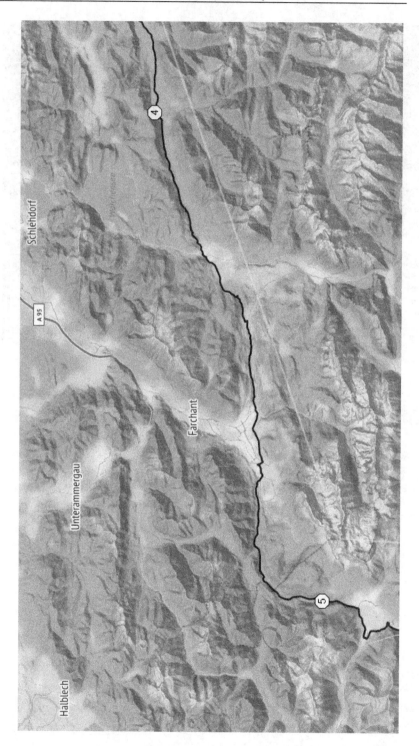

Day 4

Kreuth to Lermoos, Germany
Hiking 48 km
Flying NONE

Midnight came and went as I walked down the deserted road using my night pass. A trucker slowed up when he saw me in his headlights, and I'm convinced this saved him from hitting a rather large deer that ran across the road right in front his vehicle. Otherwise the road was really silent. I was overjoyed to have Jim and Mike show up with dry shoes and socks, as my soaking wet feet were starting to get unhappy. I pulled on my Seal Skinz waterproof socks just in case it rained again (as forecast), and more skin lube. Seal Skinz keep my feet snug and dry even in the pouring rain.

Jim got lucky to avoid all the rain that night, and walked with me for a couple of hours when the weather was perfect. No wind, not hot, not cold, drying conditions, a few stars, and a deserted road. My feet were feeling quite painful though; even the quick rub after my shower earlier hadn't helped much. This is a common problem for long-distance hikers, I believe...after being on my feet for so long, they just felt really sore and ached a lot. There was nothing to help them except rest and put my feet up, which wasn't an option. As the pavement dried, I took short rest breaks right in the middle of the highway, lying down, leaning on my pack, and putting my feet in the air. After all, I had covered 35 km of hilly walking that day, and would do another 41 km on my night pass. I didn't even want to think about tomorrow.

We passed Kruger (RSA) and Villa (COL) somewhere that night according to the Pilotfinder list, although I never saw their vehicles. Behind me, Neynans (NZL) was also pushing hard, but Vurpillot (SUI2) had walked only far enough to get ahead of Dathe (GER2) for the morning elimination. According to the website, they were only 1 km apart, but only showed their location along the course line. In reality, which I didn't know until later, they had taken wildly different paths and were a long ways from each other on the ground. I had envisioned them in a footrace to avoid elimination, but of course that wasn't quite the case. In front of me, Ha (KOR), Turner (USA4) and Colas (ESP) were all within reach if I could push the pace and keep moving through the night. I didn't really see much alternative, as the motorhome was 30 km behind me parked for the night. I had nowhere to sleep even if I did want to stop!

At 3 am or so, Jim and Mike left to catch a few hours of sleep back in the motorhome. I passed over the bridge of a large lake, chatting with my brother and my mom via text messages to pass the time. I had landed near here in training, and knew it was quite picturesque, but in the dark everything looked the same, but eerie. Especially weird was hearing what sounded like a family of groundhogs alongside the road, screaming. Their cries seemed to follow me for a while, and be quite near me. I walked faster and left them behind.

Chuck, who had slept a few hours, woke up and caught up to me just before the next rainstorm hit. I gratefully crawled in his van for a break, putting up my feet and resting for the first time in hours. I delayed getting back on the road as long as possible, but eventually and painfully continued walking. My feet were quite sore, and under the triangle of my little toes, I could feel little blisters forming. My pace at that point was pretty slow, hobbling along at only 4 or 5 kph, even on the flat while using hiking poles.

By 6 am I had reached a beautiful stretch of toll road along a river. I had also reached the end of my abilities. My pace was so slow that it wasn't really worth moving anymore. What I needed was a little sleep, and some Advil. First I had a quick foot soak in the clear blue river water. That helped my legs too. Chuck had a mattress in the back of his van, and as the pain medication kicked in, I knocked off for an hour's sleep.

While I slept, Yvonne Dathe (GER2) was the first athlete (and first woman) eliminated in this year's competition. That had to be heartbreaking, after so much preparation, to only race for three days. It left me doubly inspired to keep racing, and to stay ahead of at least one guy for as long as possible. I vowed I was NOT going to be the next one eliminated!

Before falling asleep, I told Chuck to wake me up when the motorhome arrived, with the intention of crawling into my own bed for even more sleep. After all, I had only walked the whole night of my night pass just to prove that I could do it. With more rain expected, I really didn't need to get anywhere that day. My supporters had other ideas though! As I slept for that hour, Villa (COL) had passed me by, and they were worried that if I rested too long, my efforts during the night would be wasted.

I wasn't going to argue (too much), and walked off again at a quicker pace. The short nap had helped, along with the arrival of daylight. There is something about walking at night that makes it really hard to keep up a quick pace. I've done several multi-day adventure races; and I know that hiking in the dark, when it's hard to see what's coming, when my body wants to rest, makes it a challenge to keep moving with a purpose. Seeing the first glint of light in the east was a relief. It also helped when an official race photographer arrived, along with Kruger's (RSA) supporters, and I could focus on something besides my aching body.

Even the motorhome eventually showed up. Jim had gotten some sleep, and now everyone was back trying to stuff more food into me. Actually leftover pesto pasta tasted pretty good but they all had this curious idea that I hadn't been eating enough, and tried to feed me at every stop. I was rarely hungry and usually just wanted water and juice and chocolate. (It wasn't until a few more days into the race that they realized I had a pretty good idea of what I needed to keep me going. After all, I had walked some pretty amazing distances in the heat, and hadn't bonked.) But I tried to eat to appease them!

Also waiting for me was my daily water bottle mixed with Hammer Perpetuem, a concentrated powder with long-chain carbohydrates. It was specially formulated to keep endurance athletes fueled and performing at their best. I had used this orange-flavored drink mix during many triathlons, Ironmans, and expedition adventure races, sometimes for days at a time. The taste was pleasant and I had always enjoyed drinking it. In fact I was counting on this being a staple of my race calories. I had lugged two large canisters from the USA and planned on drinking it throughout each day. Unfortunately for me, somehow from the very start of the race, I now hated the taste of this Perpetuem and had to choke it down each morning with Jim insisting that I drink it. Chuck had a canister of it in his van as well, but he could never convince me to drink more during the day. I couldn't understand why I didn't like the taste as I had used it many times before.

The joke is on me, though! It wasn't until after the race that I realized my big mistake...the two canisters I had brought over weren't the same. Chuck had gotten the Perpetuem container, and the one in the motorhome was Hammer Recoverite! Same canister, same flavor and same label markings. I had just overlooked the name difference when I purchased them. Big oops...if I had ever mixed up something from Chuck's container I would have realized the difference, but since I hated the taste of the Recoverite, I never did. Oh well. I ended up drinking a LOT of pineapple juice to make up for it, which always tasted cool and refreshing.

Anyway, I was resigned to walking the rest of the day, as launches were limited in this valley, and rain showers came and went. It was a dreary day with low hanging clouds, and one rather nasty rainstorm. By then I had walked away from the river, through a town, and was taking a shortcut away from the main road. Luckily my poncho showed up just before the rain! I had been discarding clothing in the vehicles to keep my pack light, but getting the poncho back was a day-saver. It rained so hard I was soon walking through puddles. In the midst of the downpour, suddenly a car pulled up ahead of me and a lady popped out. She called me by name, and offered me apple juice and coffee. I don't drink coffee but gratefully accepted the juice, thanking her for the kind gesture, especially in the pouring rain!

I hoped this would be the last rain shower of the day, and was as bedraggled as a soaked kitten by the time I reached a small lake. Here I was dismayed to find that my shortcut included hiking up and over a small hill to get back to the main road. It was probably only 100 meters high, but in my state that seemed like 99 meters too much. Not helping was the map on my phone, which didn't seem accurate here so I spent some time walking back and forth along the lake trying to latch onto the correct trail.

Waiting for me on the other side of the hill was an unexpected sight: official race vehicles and a team car. It was Colas (ESP) getting looked at by the race doctor. He had injured his calf, and although he hoped it would get better as the race went on, he was walking pretty slowly and painfully on this grey day. My own supporters were waiting for me another 5k ahead, but this suddenly seemed like 5k too far. I called them back for an earlier stop, and gratefully took the opportunity to rest a minute. Colas caught up to me there, and we had a brief conversation about the race. It was looking doubtful that he could continue on much further, and I somewhat tactfully brought up the topic of elimination vs. quitting. He assured me that he would continue on as long as he could. I could only hope that he had understood my broken Spanish, as my ability to continue on in the race in the coming days would depend on me having competitors still behind me.

Also at this rest stop was a race official, here to check that I was carrying all of my official gear, and to exchange SD cards from my Garmin Virb camera. I didn't have much footage, as the camera battery seemed to be dead every time I wanted to use it. Oh well. Also suffering from technical problems was the blogging application on my race phone. It was supposed to be pretty seamless, as we could text updates and add photos and videos with a quick link to upload everything to the Red Bull X-Alps websites. In reality, while practicing before the race, I couldn't get photos or videos to upload at all. So I ended up with short blogs, which made no sense without the attached photos and videos. Doh. During the race, the blogging app never worked at all. My attempts generated messages saying "Unable to upload blog at this time, it will be stored and published later." Later never seemed to arrive with this phone, and when I reached an absurd number of failed attempts, I quit trying and did updates on Facebook instead. At least there I could see if it was working or not right away.

These electronic problems seemed insurmountable and yet unimportant as I trudged down the road. The main highway was pretty busy but most of the time there was a bike trail alongside it. I put my tired feet on autopilot and hoped I could make the turnpoint in Lermoos that night, before I crashed into some much needed sleep. I could tell Colas (ESP) wasn't too far behind me, as his supporter kept driving ahead, parking the van, and running back past me to find him again. Also behind me but closing fast was Nick Neynens (NZL). His supporter Luis walked with me for a few kilometers, but since Nick passed me while I was eating dinner in the motorhome, I never saw him. Neynens had charged his way from last place in the race, and would soon reach Monaco in 10th place...mostly while wearing flip-flops!

Suddenly catching up to me at a run was Kruger (RSA). I think he wanted to have someone to walk with for a while, as we were both in tough shape. We stayed together for a couple of hours, and it helped us both to maintain a quicker pace. We also met up with his supporters, and they showed me the tree dents in their van from the rainstorm the previous night. They also offered pasta, which I couldn't pass up! In a light rain shower, we darted into a little woodshed while they changed the dressing on a rather nasty blister Kruger was sporting on the side of his foot. I guess the owner of the shed wasn't too happy, because he came out and gave us a long sermon in German which none of us could understand. Since we were on a public bike path I wasn't too worried, but we kept saying 5 minutes and got ready to walk again. He just kept standing there speaking in German but eventually gave up and walked away.

Turnpoint 4 in Lermoos wasn't too far away (as the crow flies) but there was quite a big shoulder of the Zugspitze in the way. The majestic summit of Germany's highest peak was shrouded in cloud, and we didn't get the great views possible in the Garmisch valley. Unfortunately there also were no launch spots anywhere on the hill except near the summit of the Zugspitze itself. That would be quite silly though, as the Turnpoint in Lermoos required me to land down in the valley and sign the official race board. So we stayed on the main road and walked a big loop around the hill. A bike path paralleled the road, so walking was safe enough to be pleasant, if my feet hadn't hurt so much. I passed by my supporters again near the campsite where we had stayed a few days in training. I was sorely tempted to stop and take a shower, or maybe even stop and sleep for the night! Instead, Jim promised me a plate of pasta if I kept walking, and I was still buoyed up enough from the company with Kruger that I agreed. I had walked the day away, and by now it was late afternoon, with the turnpoint still 20 km away. Kruger was determined to make it that night, maybe even catch up to Ha (KOR) just a couple kilometers ahead, but suddenly I just couldn't maintain the fast pace. I let him go ahead, and sunk down to rest on the bike path. The distances I had covered the last 48 hours were catching up to me, and my feet hurt with a fire that I couldn't quench. After all, I was approaching 115 kilometers of walking since starting yesterday morning and continuing through the night and all of today!

The motorhome and the promised pasta seemed to take forever to appear. I was walking quite slowly by then, and on the verge of tears. It was maybe 7 pm when I got to the vehicles, and I collapsed onto the bench to eat with the energy of a slug. Rotisserie chicken and pasta tasted good, but I really wanted to do was stop for the night. I fought tears at the news that I really needed to make it another 5k down the road, so I would be in position to find a launch the next morning, if weather conditions improved.

Even spending an hour in the motorhome didn't help much. Jim and Boga both worked on my feet as I ate and rested. My shins had been hurting again, although they really hadn't bothered me at all since getting a good night of sleep on Day 2. I suppose spending 2 days and a night walking without stopping is enough to aggravate any minor injury into something bigger?

Anyway, neither tears nor begging convinced everyone to stop here for the night. Jim and Chuck went ahead to scout out a place to sleep, as I refused to walk another step without knowing there would be a destination. The valley was quite narrow here, and I was afraid that there might be nowhere to park. I was completely unable to run to make up ground right now, and that 10:30 deadline would sneak up on me.

They did find a spot 6 km down the road, and Jim walked with me, along with Colas (ESP) and his supporter. It was a very painful walk, I was terrible company, and none of us enjoyed it at all. Along a busy road as night was falling, with me whimpering at every step and trying not to cry from the pain. Limping along at 4 kph, it did seem to take forever, and it was fully dark by the time we arrived at camp. Here I found out that the race photographers wanted to video my preparations in the morning. I could only think of a three-letter word: BED. Advil PM would be my friend tonight, after 125 km of walking (with one hour of sleep) in the last 38 hours.

The South African team and I would spend a lot of the race together

Day 5

Lermoos, Germany through Austria to Merano, Italy
Turnpoint 4 - Lermoos
Hiking 28 km
Flying 76 km

The photographers, true to their word, were outside my door in the morning before it was even light enough to film. With Colas (ESP) and me in the same parking lot, it must have been too good to pass up. I got dressed pretty quickly, gave a short interview, and was still on the road and walking by 5:01. Somewhere around this moment, my pack became a part of me. I no longer noticed the weight of it on my back, and the sleep had done wonders for my morale. I was ready to get walking again, and hoped to get in the air too.

First on my agenda was a phone call to my mom. She had become my reliable source of information about my competitors, because I didn't have strong enough data connection to see live tracking. It became our habit to talk when I started walking in the morning, to help me to get a feel for where everyone was in the race. Then she would go to bed (7 hours behind me in the central USA), and wake up again near midday in Europe when I might be flying.

My immediate goal was Turnpoint 4 in Lermoos. It was only about 5 km ahead, which seemed much more doable this morning after some sleep. I was back to my normal pace, although my shins still hurt and the blister under my little toe was a bit painful. The turn point itself was right in town, but at six in the morning almost deserted. Kruger (RSA) had just come through, having slept in an extra hour in a hotel in town. Knowing that he was just ahead of me had me hurrying to catch up so we could hopefully fly together. Waiting at the checkpoint was an American couple who had seen me on the live tracking, and was willing to get up early on a grey day to wait by the signboard! I appreciated their enthusiasm and

regretted I couldn't fly off or anything...the turnpoint was on
the valley floor. Kruger's supporters were still there as well,
and took a few photos of me signing the board. It was nice to
see them so lively.   My own supporters were noticeably
absent. I ventured a text to Jim about breakfast, and got a
sincere apology. They had fallen back asleep! No doubt that
EVERYONE was a little tired today, after pushing hard
through the day-night-day to support me during my night
pass.

Kruger soon appeared ahead in the distance, and together we
met up with our vehicles to formulate a plan for the day. The
weather looked windy but flyable. Again, our first move would
be the hardest, as we would have to fly across the wide Inn
valley right off the bat. We had several launch choices, and we
could see what wasn't working. Ahead of us, Villa (COL), Ha
(KOR), and Colas (ESP) had chosen to hike up to the closest
launch, a saddle overlooking the Inn valley. But it didn't have
a great launch, and the most they were able to do was a sledder
to the next hill in the middle of the valley. We decided on a
west-facing launch to take advantage of the winds, which
Rejmanek (USA1) had used for a good flight the day before. I
called up Rejmanek, who was happy to describe the launch as
"super steep" but worked very well.   We decided to go for it,
and brought our warmest flying clothes hoping we would need
them.

The first part of the climb overlooking the Fernpass wasn't too
steep. The gravel road switch-backed up to the Muthenaualm
Hut, situated in a bowl on the hill with tall trees all around.
Our launch was supposed to be up here somewhere, it didn't
really look promising. Since it was only about 11 am and still
pretty cool and cloudy, we retired into the hut for lunch. The
goulash soup was wonderful, and so was sitting in the hut next
to a warm fire with my shoes and socks off. The chill in the air
outside was actually kind of nice, but sitting by the fire was
even better. The soup revived us, but it was hard to get
moving again, knowing that we still had to find the launch.
The owner of the hut told us in broken German that we should

head south to a launch, rather than north where Honza had gone. It was only a 5 minute detour to check her suggestion, but it turned out to be a very shallow opening with no way to clear the trees below. Doh. So finally we headed to the original launch, somewhere to the north at 2000 meters. Considering we were only at 1700 meters, there was still some climbing in our future.

The grassy area behind the hut was pretty flat, and all we could see around us were trees, except for the steep grass high above us, on what was essentially a scree slope. Honza hadn't been kidding when he said it was steep. I had been secretly hoping he had overlooked somewhere easier to launch, but no. The climb up was trail-less. It started steep and got steeper, until I was scrambling on hands and knees to get to the top. When we stopped to rest, I had to carefully make sure that my pack didn't go rolling down, or it would have been a several hundred meters of vertical to retrieve it!

The weather didn't seem to be cooperating. At this elevation, the winds should have been fairly strong, but we barely felt a puff of wind in our face. The only thing to do was wait. "The clouds are supposed to clear and we will get a good flight." I repeated this like a mantra to Kruger, who probably got tired of my hopefulness. But we did need a great flight, as we were now next to last on the course, and might face elimination soon. Only Vurpillot (SUI2) was behind us. Ahead a short distance, three or four competitors were waiting on the next ridge to the south, so we weren't too far behind the middle of the pack. Way ahead, race leader Maurer had just rounded Turnpoint 6 in Switzerland, and we hadn't even made it to Italy yet :(

The puffs of wind on launch got stronger, and it was time to start laying out our gear. The problem was that the grade was so steep my wing kept sliding down the hill after me! I had brought a couple of clothespins with me to try and clip the wing to some grass to keep it from moving. These proved to be useless and the best I could do was spread it out and hope all of the lines were free of rocks. All of a sudden the sun came out and the wind picked up. It was time to go and soon seemed like it might be too strong.

We had one chance of either launching or sliding down the steep grass and ending up in a tangled heap of lines far below. Kruger launched just before me with a cravat on one wing tip, but at least he was in the air. He would spend more than a few minutes getting it out, all the while climbing steadily in strong lift. I was right behind him, unable to do anything but get below my wing and hope for a smooth launch. I started backing/falling down the hill, the lines all came free and the wing came up. Whew. I was flying! Thank God, that was a scary steep slope, and I was ecstatic to make it in the air safely.

The wind gradient was forecast to get a lot stronger above us, which meant we couldn't climb too high, or we might find ourselves in exceptionally dangerous conditions. A small airspace restriction nearby kept us from ascending too much anyway, so there was no temptation. After a short time hanging in ridge lift, I was ready to make the first valley crossing. The air was very buoyant and windy, so essentially I was a Frisbee blown along in the current. At the next ridge, a large bump across the Inn valley, Kruger and I weren't able to gain much height but worked the lift patiently in very windy conditions. Finally we let ourselves get blown over the back. We had no way of communicating except for hand signals. Kruger wasn't sure which way to go from there, so I led the way into the Oetztal valley, having flown near here in training.

Once in the Oetztal, the route was pretty clear for a while, down a narrow, windy valley. The strong conditions meant that I didn't want to come too close to terrain, and I patiently worked the edges to gain lift without approaching the jagged rock faces. Kruger managed to climb higher than I did at the valley entrance, and he floated above the peaks for a while, while I found myself sliding downward into the valley on the lee side of the hills. The valley flow was strongly north; much stronger than when I had flown here before, but my experience flying in training would come in really handy! Finding myself almost sinking out in the same spot as I had before, I went to a small hill that faced the valley winds, and ridge surfed my way back up. The first time, I had spent almost an hour parked over this hill, but today I climbed out fairly quickly. I won't say it wasn't terrifying, though. I was parked over a steep waterfall with nothing but trees below me, and I couldn't let the thought of landing in them enter my mind.

I gained some minimum altitude to go over the back of the hill and connect with the steeper mountains along the valley. I found the valley winds to be so strong that my flight consisted mostly of fast downwind runs, and then slow climbs along the windy northern faces. My supporters driving below me found it hard to watch, they too knew the winds were high. Talking with Kruger about the flight later, he said he kept flying only because it was scarier to think of landing in the narrow valley with such a strong valley flow. But I had lost track of him in the air and was flying on my own.

At least I was alone for a few minutes, until white race wings suddenly seemed to be around me everywhere. I had caught up to the athletes in front of me! It's always nice to fly with others, and as we got closer to the Timmelsjoch pass, I finally climbed above the peaks and could thermal up to 3200 meters. Up here, it was COLD. My hands wrapped around the brake lines were almost totally numb, and my teeth might have been chattering.

I had a great debate going on in my head concerning my willingness to fly over the pass. Conditions that day were strong North Foehn. Foehn is a term used in the Alps to denote the pressure difference between the North Side of the Alps, and the South Side. When the pressure difference is large, like this day, the wind can rush up the north side, which was where we were flying, and down the south side, just like a strong waterfall. This causes dangerous lee side rotor and can be the source of bad accidents. Today the Foehn report was for the highest potential of Foehn, an 8. I had decided before launching that I wouldn't fly into this waterfall of rotor, but when I found myself sky high above the pass, it seemed like a shame to waste it...and landing in the wind at the pass might be equally dumb. What would I do then?

I called my supporter in the air to get his opinion, and he reported that conditions were getting lighter and that I was probably ok, as others were flying over it and continuing on down the course. He advised me to follow the highest line of mountains to the south, which I could see that Gold (AUS2) was doing right in front of me. It was a very scary line, in very rough conditions. I had almost been forced down to top land on jagged peaks a couple of times that day, once in sinking air so strong I was free falling towards the rocks! I only pulled out a few meters above the ground, which was NOT cool. Waiting to the south was jagged rock, with deep glaciers and nothing but sharp peaks.

My final decision was that everyone else was doing it, and to stay in the race I needed to follow the leader. So finally, with some trepidation, I crossed into Italy and flew across the main ridge of the high Alps! Timmelsjoch Pass at 2500 meters was far below me. I had flown this Italian valley in training, albeit much, much lower. With freezing hands, I decided to play it safe with the Foehn winds, and pointed my wing away from where the invisible waterfall could be, across the crooked valley and down to Merano. Kruger reported later (after I landed) that he had gone over the highest peak, and then found 9 m/s sink on the other side. That's really scary. Witschi (SUI3), already in Switzerland, had encountered some really nasty rotor, been forced to throw his reserve parachute, and landed in a lake. Luckily he only had a short, cold swim to escape the water. Gold (AUS2) had a rough top landing above Lana (near Merano) and would end up hiking down rather than flying.

I wouldn't know any of this until later, so I was concentrating on the Merano valley. If winds were strong, which of course they would be, I knew landings were very limited in this valley filled with vineyards and apple orchards. These weren't nice orchards like I was used to, as the small trees were staked out with sharp sticks, just like the vineyards. Of course, I could possibly fly over the valley, but the race route from there got narrower and more difficult. In the end, I just didn't want to continue flying in the Southern Alps on a day with strong North Foehn. It would be really dangerous. So I made the difficult but safer decision to land before Merano, setting myself up for a longer walk that evening and the next day.

Even here, landing wasn't easy. I could see the trees below me whipping around in the wind, and picked a long grassy field. I turned upwind at the windward side of the field, just in case I would be flying backwards, and basically sunk straight down.

Of course nothing is as smooth as that makes it sound, and in reality I was jerked higher, then suddenly freefalling, then climbing again. A few prayers went heavenward, and eventually I found myself landing between trees, the river, a chicken shed, power lines, and a couple of fences. I may have kissed the ground.

It took me a while to both warm up and calm down. I was really pleased with my flight; after all I had flown across a huge pass and bumped myself up a few places in the standings! I knew I could have gone further, but it didn't seem worth the danger factor. When the wind gusted up even stronger after I landed, I knew I had made the right decision. My main supporter wasn't terribly pleased when I called him, though. He thought I should have kept flying, and immediately started talking about finding a place to hike up and relaunch. I had to make it clear that the conditions down here weren't safe and I would spend the rest of the day walking. Everyone was still driving down from the pass, and would catch up to me right after I had packed up.

It was already past 4:30 pm, so I didn't feel too bad about not flying anymore. Instead my supporters went ahead to find a "real" campground in Merano, which was mostly on the way to the next launch. I only needed to walk about 11 km and I would have an early night stop. It felt almost decadent not to be walking into the night! A trail along the river led from my landing zone right into town, so I had a peaceful walk to the campground, no longer in a hurry. Behind me, both Colas (ESP) and Villa (COL) had landed still in Austria, on the other side of the pass. Villa (COL) was in a particularly tough place, having followed Ha (KOR) up a side valley rather than the main pass. Ha (KOR) would fly over it and was now ahead of me. Villa (COL) would end up walking over a 3000 meter pass, a difficult undertaking even on fresh legs. Vurpillot (SUI2) had walked up to my steep launch, albeit much later in the day than Kruger (RSA) and I had been there. For some reason Vurpillot never launched at all; it might have gotten too strong perhaps. So I knew I had an advantage on a few pilots, which gave me some breathing room for elimination.

My first stop was by the river for a while to soak my tired legs. My blisters still hurt, and now one of my little toes was going a bit numb, probably from some nerve aggravation because of so much walking. This toe didn't hurt exactly, it just felt weird, and would make me hobble each morning for a few steps until I got used to the numb feeling and could ignore it. My ring finger of my right hand was also a little numb, caused by the brake line wrapping around my fingers with frozen hands up at altitude.   Both of these numb appendages would be annoying but not debilitating.   If that was the worst the race could throw at me, I wouldn't be unhappy.

By early evening I arrived at the campsite to find that everyone had barely finished checking in. What? Evidently the guy at the check-in counter was quite drunk, but still insisted on seeing everyone's passport and filling out lots of paperwork. No one had eaten much that day either. It was time for me to lecture my supporters on how they needed to take care of themselves as well as taking care of me! We retired to a Chinese restaurant very near the campground, where I ordered two entrees and ate every morsel. It was great to put my feet up, with ice packs on each shin, and even nicer to sit and relax for a bit. The winds stayed strong even late into the night, almost blowing our tablecloth away a couple times. Jim was happy to see me eating so much, as I had been picking at my food and living on juice and snacks in the heat. I left everyone to order dessert, and instead took my first hot shower of the race. It was heavenly, and I stayed in the shower for a long time. Luckily there was no limit on hot water, as in some campgrounds where one Euro only gets you 3 minutes!

We spent some time discussing my planned launch for tomorrow (which ultimately was the wrong decision for the conditions). But I'll address that during the next day. Suffice it to say I successfully negotiated a 5:30 start from my taskmasters, earning an extra half hour of rest!

The Zugspitz looks on as I walk in the early morning
Photo Credit: Jen Hohmann

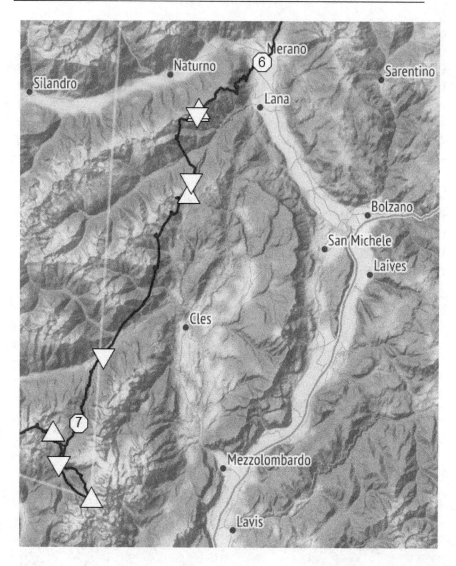

Day 6

Lana to Madonna di Campiglio, Italy
Hiking 35 km
Flying 36 km

I could really get used to getting a full night's sleep in this race. But first I'd get back to my route choices for the day, and our decision-making process about the flying conditions. I had three choices of launches near Merano. Lana had an official paragliding launch with a cable car overlooking the Merano valley, at around 1400 meters high. This was about 10km away and would have been a nice choice if conditions looked strong. Higher above that, which meant hiking up to about 2100 meters, was a grassy ridge. It was about 20km away. The problem with both of them was that my first flying move of the day would be to cross a wide valley, and fly over a 2000 meter pass at Passo Castrin.   In training I had attempted this pass and not made it, forcing me to land on a road between trees near a tunnel, scraping up my hands and cutting a line on my glider.   The problem with the area is that south breezes normally push up and over this pass, making it hard to fly over at a low altitude, with limited landing places. My third option was to forgo trying to fly over the pass and just walk to it, hiking 37 km but at least I would be over it and could launch from there to continue on the route.

In our discussions about my options, my supporter thought the lift wouldn't be enough to get me away from the low launch above Lana. Sinking out from there would mean walking up to the pass and wasting my flight. But the air would be better if I could launch from above 2000 meters, so I could walk 20 km or 37 km. Choosing to walk to the pass probably should have meant walking longer last night, but again we wanted to have power for the motorhome overnight to continue charging our battery, which still wasn't getting full for some reason.

So I opted for the 20 km launch to be able to make it by midday. It turns out that might have not been the best decision, but of course hindsight is 20/20. It was a couple of kilometers across the valley first, and my shins were quite painful. My legs were noticeably swollen and I had limited mobility in one ankle; it literally hurt too much to move. Luckily walking up hill was the easiest, least painful movement I could do, so I looked forward to the climb for once. The trail I took started climbing steeply right after leaving the valley floor, and continued steeply all the way past the official paragliding launch above Lana. As I climbed I could look down on the Merano valley, full of vineyards and orchards. Across the huge expanse, I had a lot of trouble picking out even ONE nice place to land. I was doubly happy I hadn't tried flying into this valley in the high winds the day before!

It took me about 4 hours to make it up to the top of main cable car, and it was really nice to see Jim and Boga waiting with a smoothie, snacks, mashed potatoes, and other goodies. I ate as much as I could, to make them happy, but their picnic could have fed ten people! As long as those ten people only wanted to eat potato chips, mashed potatoes and apples with peanut butter....

Back on the trail, the hardest part of the climb was done. Now I just needed to curve around the ridge and keep gently climbing up to tree line. The graded gravel road took me under a single person chair lift to the eastern summit of the ridge, then further along to the west. By the time I arrived at a good launch, it was about noon, and conditions were looking pretty good. I figured waiting a little bit might improve my chances of crossing the pass to the south, so I hung out longer. My mom was giving me race updates via text (she had woken up early again in the USA to watch me fly), and could see that several athletes who had hiked up to the pass were already flying and getting up to about 2600 meters. This wasn't high enough for me but it might be as much as I could get.

Not too much later, my mom told me that Kruger was very near me on the hill. He had actually landed just north of this launch, but for some reason had hiked almost around to the Lana launch before coming back up here again. He wasn't very happy about going far out of his way for no reason, but we were pleased that we could fly together and hopefully make the crossing.

By then it was time to get going. The launch was grass with scattered boulders, and a few bushes waiting to snag lines. I got off smoothly but found the lift very weak, and landed again on the hillside before I could sink down below the tree line. Nearly out of sight, I could see Stephan pulling up his wing multiple times. I guess his lines were getting snagged on the bushes or something. This gave me time to hike back up the hill a little with my wing bunched up over my shoulder. The second time, we launched almost simultaneously and both climbed out above the peaks.

Still we weren't able to get much above 2600 meters, and found some remnants of the North Foehn in the rotor as we attempted to make it across the valley to the pass. So we came in low and had to scrape above the trees below the pass, on the wrong side of it. I thought for a minute that I was destined to land in the same crappy place on the road I had last time. We found a scrap of lift, then a little more. It was enough to get us above a nice pasture to land in, and we both concluded independently that further attempts to fly in the rotor on the lee of the pass wouldn't be smart. Stephan was out of water and had been for a while, so he headed to a farmhouse to fill his bottles. Then it was a relatively short level hike for a couple of kilometers to the pass.

It was nice to finally crest Passo Castrin, which had been such a source of angst both last night and today. Of course, with better flying conditions it wouldn't have even been a blip on the radar, but we were there today and had to deal with the low base. The other athletes who had flown from here earlier were all making it to Turnpoint 5 in the Brenta, but it was past

3 pm now, and our flying time was limited. In front of us there was not a nice valley to fly down, but a series of short fingers to cross. The route for the 2015 Red Bull X-Alps was some of the most difficult terrain to fly across in the history of the race. This day in particular was a great example of that difficult terrain for us.

Even harder than flying this section would have been walking it. I had driven this way before, and had deemed it "The section I most wanted to fly". The roads were narrow, twisty, and hot. The path to the turnpoint was anything but a straight line. I would have had to walk miles out of my way to avoid going up and over these ridges jutting out from the mountain range to our west.

So luckily for us, we were now poised to fly this section. Others had done it today so we knew it was possible. The downside was that neither of us had flown it before. I had heard nothing from Jarek about the best route but by this time I had realized he really didn't care to help me, and figured I could fly this just fine without his advice.

We did do just fine. With a hot south wind, it was more ridge soaring than thermalling until we were able to climb above the peak and back up to 2600 meters, which today was hard to break. From there we slowly made our way across six ridges, climbing at each one before continuing on. By the last crossing conditions seemed to be lightening, as it was past 5 pm. I think we were lucky to just sneak over the last ridge into the main valley, the Val Di Sole.

Once in there, the north side of the ridge was in shade and the winds became really confusing to me. The south winds seem to have disappeared and now there was a quite strong valley wind from the east. Unfortunately I took too long to figure this out, and found myself speeding along the valley looking for a landing spot. At least the winds were blowing me in the right direction!

I didn't exactly land going backward, but I didn't really have much headway either. Fortunately my landing zone was a HUGE field with very few obstructions, one of the largest I would find in the race. Stephan came down close to me too, and all of our supporters arrived quickly. Jarek was quick to question why I hadn't taken a deeper line in the mountains like the previous athletes, and why I hadn't crossed to the sunny side to get back up and fly to the turnpoint. Since I hadn't heard from him all afternoon, I wasn't sure how I could have possibly known to do either of those things as I didn't have access to live tracking. I just shrugged. Kruger said he had also thought of crossing to the sunny side. I wish he had, because I would have followed him, but we had no way of communicating in the air. It would have been nice to make that flight instead of struggling our way another 20k on foot to the checkpoint. Too late for that, though, and there was no point in beating up on myself for what I could have done. I was a rookie, having never flown this section before, and I'm not a mind reader, so I wasn't about to feel bad. In fact, I felt pretty good at what I had flown that day, as it had saved me walking some really horrible terrain and going far out of the way on the roads.

Still, in retrospect, today was one of my biggest wasted opportunities of the race. Athletes who had been just kilometers ahead of me at Passo Castrin would go on to finish the race and arrive on the float in Monaco. Their ability to fly to the Brenta Turnpoint and beyond now put them a full day ahead of me rather than just a few hours. With changing weather conditions ahead on the course, this would be very key.

But that's Monday morning quarterbacking, and back in the moment, it was about 6 pm with four hours of walking to the checkpoint. I suppose it would have been possible to walk there that evening, sleep at the hut, and fly down in the morning. But with good flying conditions forecast to continue, I felt that I could stop early, get up to the hut in the morning, and make a good midday flight from there. The tricky part was that the Brenta Turnpoint was deep into a west facing bowl, and it would be later in the afternoon by the time we could fly out of there.

Also arriving at our impromptu gathering of teams was a Garmin technician. It always felt strange when race crews would show up out of the blue to my location. It's one thing to know that I am being tracked live all over the world, another one to see people who actually know where I am and show up right there! The Garmin tech replaced my Garmin Virb HD camera. I had been having trouble with the battery life, just as other athletes in the race had experienced.

As we considered our flying options, Stephan and I started hiking our way up to Madonna di Campiglio, the small town below the checkpoint. Once again it was hot in the valley, and even the evening shadows weren't helping much. Our tired footsteps found a faint rhythm on the trail, and then faltered again on the blacktop. This side valley actually climbed quite steeply up to the skiing town of Madonna, and more ascent would be needed to get up to the Turnpoint. We decided to go another couple of kilometers and call it a day. My legs had already summited more elevation in one day than I had wanted. The bottoms of my feet were starting to hurt again, and my shins were still pretty painful.

My supporter was convinced that our best move would be to fly from Turnpoint 5 early, and then climb back up to a SE facing launch for an earlier start. With the west wind forecast to pick up later in the afternoon, we knew that flying to our next pass would be key. Even better, supporters from both teams would be able to fly with us by using the chairlift to launch. This meant an early start, and part of me really wanted to relax a bit and make a flight from the Turnpoint, but I could see the sense in what was suggested. We had a dinner of pizza and turned in relatively quickly.

Photo Credit: Boguslawa Majorek

SPOTLIGHT: Following in a Legend's Footsteps, Kari Castle: 2005 Red Bull X-Alps

Author's Note: Kari Castle was one of two women who were the first to compete in the Red Bull X-Alps during the second edition of the race in 2005. She was also the first American to take part in the race. Unlike my preparations, Kari was asked compete just three months before the race and didn't have much time to prepare. She still accepted the challenge and did her best to race across the Alps. Kari is a legend in the paragliding and hang gliding world, and is a three-time world champion as well as a fourteen time U.S. National Champion. After Kari competed in the Red Bull X-Alps, it would be ten years before another woman would take part in the race.

Dawn Westrum: How did you come to be in the Red Bull X-Alps?

Kari Castle: I was lying on my couch with my knee iced and elevated the day after I had knee surgery. I received a call from Hannes Arch, my friend and the event organizer for the Red Bull X-Alps, asking if I would be interested in competing in the event. He said they really wanted to see a woman enter the race and he was confident that I would not get hurt or kill myself doing so. I told him about just having knee surgery yesterday and he assured me 3 months would be plenty of time to prepare for the Red Bull X-Alps!! Ha ha ha...

DW: Had you heard about the race before?

KC: Of course I had heard about it, and loved the concept of hiking and flying, two of my favorite things to do. But I really didn't get to follow the first race much, because of travel and my paragliding competition schedule in the summer. I do recall asking Will Gadd who had entered the race in 2003,

about what is was like for him. He called it a "suffer fest"! I loved the term but it also scared me. Knowing Will and if he's calling it that, then I have no business entering the race, is what I thought. I asked him if Will would do it again this year and his response was a very clear "hell no".
So I agreed to enter the race anyway. WTH....

DW: How long did you have to prepare for the race?
KC: Almost three months. In that time I needed to rehab my knee, learn about the Red Bull X-Alps race, try to figure out the course, get maps, figure out gear needed, find a supporter, organize myself and my crew in Europe. At that time there was not a lot of information out there for us and the "internet" was not what it is today, let's just say!

DW: What was the race like?
KC: It was pretty exciting to be part of such a cool race. Once we got to Austria and started preparing the few days before, it started to sink in just how far out of my league I was. But I tried not to let it bother me, I figured I would do the best I could and go from there.

DW: How far did you go?
KC: For me it felt FAR but in terms of the distance of the course it was not far. I made it to the first turn point, the Zugspitze in Germany and a bit further. My goal at the end was to at least make that turn point and the 200k mark. I reached both of my goals.
The problem was every day I wanted to quit because of the pain. After day one I had blisters covering the bottom of both feet on the pads of my forefoot. So every step was excruciating pain and no matter what I did to try to relieve it, blisters continued to fester and multiply. Other competitors were starting to drop out because of pain or injuries. So my goal was to "not quit", so I was happy to reach that goal as well.

DW: Who supported you?
KC: I asked my cute new Australian boyfriend to crew for me.

He was a new pilot himself and thought it sounded like fun. I was use to organizing myself in the flying world so it didn't occur to me how important this position was in order to be successful or not. We were both wonderfully clueless!!

DW: How many days did you race?
KC: My best guess is 13 or 14 days I believe. I'd have to dig around through my records for the exact number of days. I completed the two days they allowed racers to keep going as far as they could after the first person crossed the finish line.

DW: Were there eliminations?
KC: No. Luckily for me there were no eliminations that year. I was able to go as far as I could which I was grateful for. Even though I had only put in three months of preparation it would be a huge let down to be eliminated after a few days. I do understand why they have to do this (eliminations), I was just happy I was given the chance to finish my own race.

DW: How did you know where to go?
KC: That's funny, I didn't! The maps I had found sucked. Asking other pilots about their plan was useless for the most part since everything about this race was so foreign to me including the route and potential flying sites. Once on course I pretty much walked on pavement the whole time because it was raining or the cloud deck was so low it wasn't inspiring to hike up and try and find a launch somewhere. I could not even see the mountains for the most part. I remember one day after walking in the crap weather for so long I decided to hike up this mountain and fly off even though it was off course and would most likely not get me any further on course. While hiking up cloud base lowered, the rain started to fall so I sat on top and waited. Luckily for me there was a beautiful restaurant serving hot food!! To my surprise the clouds lifted, the sun came out for a brief moment so I decided to fly off while I could. The only sled ride that felt better was my very first one ever!!!

DW: What electronics did you have?
KC: They gave us instruments to use as a vario and that would track us.
They also gave us cell phones that we used to send our mandatory daily text messages to HQ with updates. Internet was not possible unless you were in some big city sitting in McDonalds believe it or not!!! So we had no weather updates, no idea what and where other pilots were etc. I would get text messages occasionally from friends and family, which would help lift my spirits.

DW: I know you suffered with blisters; how did you get through that?
KC: I kept repeating my mantra "I love this sufferfest"...."don't quit."

DW: Did your recent knee surgery hold you back or not?
KC: My very first landing on day one I landed funny and it hurt for the next couple of days but the blisters won over in the pain department after day 1.

DW: Did you ever think of doing it again?
KC: Of course, I love to dream about being one of "those pilots" that could do well in a race like that. The level of skill it takes to win or complete this race is truly inspirational to say the least!!! But honestly I don't have the drive it takes to do this race...YOU HAVE TO REALLY WANT IT. And then you have to have the fitness and skill.

DW: What were the rules? Could you race all night or was there time to sleep each night?
KC: We / they could race all night. I had no problem stopping each night when it got dark in order to rest my feet and my soul.

DW: What was your favorite day?
KC: Day one when we were on launch at the start of the race, we were all still in first place!!! I absolutely loved that launch

even though it scared the shit out of me because we could not see the ground!! Below us sat a layer of clouds, which they assured us would clear enough to fly down through. I had to trust what they said and no one else seemed to be worried about it so I followed along. The flight was magical, we all glided for about 20km in the most buoyant air you could imagine and landed all over the place.

DW: A funny moment?
KC: On day one I landed in a field with this famous British Pilot, I remember talking with him as you would after a magical flight. He was in such a hurry to pack up and get out of there. I couldn't figure out what the rush was and why he wouldn't wait for me so that we could walk together. He packed up and left. I was hoping he could help give me some pointers ....ha ha ha. That was the last time I saw any other pilot.

DW: Any scary moments?
KC: Yes I almost killed myself. I'm pretty sure the story would have said I committed suicide, which made me laugh. There I was, hiking up over this little mountain in the middle of a valley. Nice walking path up and over. I had my ear phones on listening to music when I came up to this funny red and white striped barrier that I had to walk thru switching directions every 5 or 6 steps, then I remember looking ahead at the red and white strips and wood path crossing the railroad tracks, thinking how pretty and neat and tidy everything was. As soon as I took my first step onto the tracks I heard this very loud foreign sound (the train blowing their horn)...I looked left and to my horror I see this very large train coming at me full speed ahead. It was too late to stop and go backwards with the weight of my glider on my back and my momentum so I remember thinking MOVE NOW DON'T STOP GO FAST. I made it to the other side just in time to have the train wiz by me a mach speed. It was so quiet and fast is what I recall, my heart was racing as I realized how stupid that would have been to die walking across the railroad tracks without looking after

all I've been through.   After all flying is supposed to be dangerous right?!

Signing the board at Turnpoint 4
Photo Credit: Jen Hohmann

Day 7

Madonna di Campiglio to Vezza d'Oglio, Italy
Turnpoint 5 –Brenta Dolomites
Hiking 35km
Flying 50 km

It was a bit odd to wake up in the morning and feel a little chill. It had rained during the race, but even then I just threw on my poncho over a t-shirt and shorts, and was still hot. For the most part it seemed like there had been nonstop heat.

The chill didn't last long and Kruger caught up to my earlier start after a mile or two with his longer stride. The town of Madonna di Campiglio was quiet so early in the morning, and then we had a slight downhill to the trailhead of the Brenta Turnpoint. Kruger's supporters and Jim were there to meet us at a parking lot about halfway through the hike, and I mooched a little bit of pasta from Sunshine (one of his supporters) for breakfast. He sure made some mean pasta!

The climb up to the Turnpoint was beautiful, and I was feeling really good. I was even running on the short downhills to keep my speed up. My goal was to get there, and get in the air as quickly as possible, but it was hard not to appreciate the amazing scenery as I walked by it. The Dolomites are some of the most beautiful mountains in the world, in my opinion. The rock spires are just works of art.

The Brenta Dolomites at Turnpoint 5
Photo Credit Boguslawa Majorek

Turnpoint 5 was hidden in the midst of such geographical riches. My supporter was there already, having hiked up quickly without a pack. Quite a few people were up there, but few were interested in us as we signed the Turnpoint board and headed to launch. I did take a photo with a fan or two, but probably not the fanfare that race leader Maurer (SUI1) had when arriving a few days before!

It was 9 am and the sun was fully on the rocks to the south of us. We laid out our wings and launched, sneaking over to the sunny side in the hopes that there might be a smidgen of lift. Town looked a long ways away and it would be nice to land beyond it. I think I made one circle in light lift, but it was just too early to be working yet. Same thing as we flew into the east facing sunny hillside that is the town. Lift wasn't strong enough to turn in, and landing zones were looking pretty sparse. Stephan put down in a grassy spot so small that I lost sight of him even as I flew right over him. I was hoping for some lift, found nothing, and found my LZs were disappearing too. Nothing looked good all of a sudden, except for the straight main road through town! The trees were back far enough from the pavement, no power lines crossed it for a while, and for some absurd reason, there were no cars from either way at the exact moment when I needed to land. Divine intervention, perhaps? I got a nice long tailwind glide, suddenly hoping I would get on the ground before the trees and signs encroached on the good bit of road. Smack down on the road I went, barely ran it out, and my wing slid over to land beside a parked car. Vehicles immediately started driving by me, some of them taking photos out the window! An Italian came out of the restaurant parking lot I was folding up in, shaking his head and pointing to how close the sign and trees were. Oops, got away with one there! Chuck pulled up soon after, asking where I had landed, and got a look in his eye when I said it was right where he was parked.

Anyway, this makeshift LZ had saved me a little bit of extra walking, and it actually wasn't that far through town to the base of the gondola. With all my supporters collected from various locations, it was time for a third breakfast. The chill from earlier was completely gone, and it was hot. Two of our supporters were planning on flying with Kruger and I, so they took the gondola up while we walked in the heat. Luckily halfway up there was an alpine lake. Plenty of people were there hanging out and dipping their feet, but no one was swimming. We couldn't help ourselves; we were so hot from our climb we had to jump in. We found out quickly why no one was swimming...it was COLD. But well worth the shock of the freezing water to feel cool for a few minutes.
I'm sure we looked a bit crazy, throwing down our packs, stripping off our shoes and jumping in fully clothed. We were back out quickly, and on our way before most people realized we had arrived.

The final climb up to launch wasn't too bad. This trail at least seemed a bit more gradual. We had ascended 700 meters to

the Turnpoint, and did another 600 meters up to our second
launch. And all before noon!

Getting to the takeoff at the right time was a big weight off my
mind. I had been afraid that by sledding down from the
Turnpoint, we might not make it to the this launch in time to
make use of the day. But in fact it was just getting good when
we arrived. Our supporters had planned to launch first and
lead us out, but when I saw it was good enough to stay up, I
went ahead and got in the air. It was a slow struggle to climb
above the peaks, but Kruger (RSA) and I managed it together,
and went on to have an amazing flight.

The four of us had radios to communicate with, but our
supporters were a bit behind us and we couldn't afford to wait.
So Kruger and I had this beautiful flight over blue alpine lakes,
glaciers, and some really scary looking terrain. Little tendrils
of fog/cloud were drifting up from the sunny sides of each
spire, and we were able to cruise around the edges of these
ephemeral creations and get enough lift to make it to the next
one.   Conditions were strong but not dangerous, and seemed
to be pushing us toward the pass. I was flying closer to the
rocks than I really liked for a while, and always tried to stay on
the valley side in case I needed to get away from the jagged
edges. Landing up here would be a real no-no.

At Tonale Pass, we were quite high, and needed to make a
move toward the northwest.   The obvious route, which had
worked for me in training, was to fly from the north side of the
pass across the valley to the west. Unfortunately, with the
west wind, we got so low just crossing the pass that we almost
landed up there.   The nice part of our flight was definitely
over.   Kruger's supporter Konstantin was now higher than us
at the pass, but none of us could seem to get much altitude. So
he made himself a guinea pig and attempted to cross the
valley. In other words, he sacrificed himself, soon landing
down in the valley.   Bummer.   Kruger and I would hang out
for a while longer in the air, but we were destined to end up
down there ourselves. I looked at the maps on my phone and

tried to see if there was anywhere else we could fly to get away from the wind. I even called Chuck in the air to see if he had looked at routes of the other athletes. In the end, after looking at everything, we needed to head west and nowhere but west. Stephan went for the shady side of the hill and landed out. I top landed at Tonale Pass to let a dark cloud pass, and then attempted to go back to the ridge we had been happily flying along before crossing the pass in the first place! Unfortunately the west wind was too strong and nothing was working. My only option was to land and find another launch in the morning.

Landing in the valley was another windy descent. Man, it was hot down there too. But once again I had flown over a very difficult pass and that felt really good. It was only late afternoon, so there was time left to walk down the valley. My next move was to climb up and over a saddle for a big shortcut in the race route, but the vehicles would have to drive far around, or go on a very twisty road up and over.

I was feeling pretty good physically, and decided to make the climb that evening rather than the next morning. My next valley crossing would be the biggest flight across anything in the whole race, and if the weather conditions weren't going to be great I could do it as a morning sledder. So all I had to do that evening was to hike up another 1200 meters of altitude! I had already climbed that much this morning, but there were a few hours left of daylight and I figured I could make it.

The heat was crushing as usual, and at one point I soaked my floppy hat with water so that it could cool my head and provide shade as I walked. My face and nose were really starting to suffer from the perpetual sunshine, both when I was walking and when I was flying. Even with regular doses of sunblock, being outside all day every day is tough on exposed skin. As I dumped water from my bottle into my hat, it turned out to be carbonated water! Oops. My head bubbled for a while, but it worked fine.

My real idea for the evening was to see if I could make it up to the mountaintop before 9 pm, in order to fly down a short ways across a plateau. I set that as my goal, and walked about 8 kilometers down the road to pass my support crew, who happened to be wining and dining in a nice restaurant. They reluctantly left their glasses of wine to throw me a bottle of water as I walked by, and said they would meet me at the top of the mountain in a few hours! Actually, I was really happy to be able to give them some down time. They had been working hard to keep me going strong, and I knew it was taking a toll on their energy levels as well. They seemed to forget to eat while they were chasing me along the course.

Photo Credit: Jen Hohmann

So in the town of Vezza d'Oglio, I started the big climb up to my morning launch. Or even an evening launch if I could speed up a little. Yet however I did the math, the numbers weren't telling me I could make a flight by 9 pm, with 1000 vertical meters yet to climb.   It may have only been about 5 km to the top, but it was some of the steepest trail I had been on yet in the race. The first half was paved, and then there was a trail through the woods that would be a significant shortcut (if I didn't get lost). The sun was behind the hill by now, and the woods were steep, dark, and deep. My breath was more like gasping, and even at a slow pace I needed frequent rest breaks after a long day of such ascents.

Daylight was passing quickly, and no way was I going to get to that launch. My supporters were on top of the mountain now, waiting at the place where I could fly off in the morning. That seemed too far to get tonight, as my legs absorbed 2400 meters of vertical and began to get very tired.   The woods were getting darker by the minute, so I convinced everyone to drive closer to me.   I still had to get up to the plateau, but in the meantime they would end up finding the most beautiful sleeping area of the whole race, overlooking the valley where I had just been.

I was still a little lost in the woods, the trail getting fainter until I wasn't sure I was on anything more than a deer trail. I had to backtrack a little, then a little more, then gave up and abandoned the trail completely. Daylight was no more than a faint thought by now. The GPS lock on my phone map app said the paved road wasn't too far above me, so I bushwhacked up a dry creek bed. I was using my headlamp now, and I have to admit it was a little freaky in the deep woods. And still soooo steep!   I was very happy to pop out on the road, and know that I only had a short ways to the motorhome. Jim appeared soon after that to walk with me for the last mile or so. I guess he had learned that the last few minutes were the hardest time of the day for me, mentally and physically.   It was nice to have him there as I took a final limp into camp. Why is it that the last kilometer hurts the worst?

Dinner was a flask full of hot goulash soup that Boga had convinced a restaurant to fill up for me. Yum. Even better news for the day was that flying conditions looked good for tomorrow, so my midday launch was very close, and I could sleep in a little bit.

The Dolomites are so beautiful!
Photo Credit: Dawn Westrum

Flying with Stephan Kruger in the Dolomites

SPOTLIGHT:

A Day In The Life of a Solo Supporter
By Krischa Berliner

Krischa Berliner from Switzerland worked tirelessly as the only supporter on behalf of athlete Dave Turner (USA4) in the 2015 Red Bull X-Alps. We all know supporters have the tough job, but he went above and beyond. Talk about sleep deprivation! Here's how his days in the race went.

3:00 am – Get up to turn off the battery charger so the car will start in the morning!

4.30 am - Start my day. I'll make a light breakfast with some scrambled eggs, just something to get Dave going. While the coffee is brewing, I awake the monster that is sleeping out in his tent. This gives him those couple more minutes of sleep while I get the kitchen going.

4:45 am - Check and turn on the instruments (Flymaster, Garmin GPS, backup battery, SPOT, Phone)

4:50 am - Fill up water and snacks

5:00 am - Send my athlete on his way. It's going to take a good hour until he's actually awake, so until then I can plot tactics for the day,

5:05 am - Check the weather forecast.

5:10 am – Check live tracking, see if other athletes are nearby, and guess what launch they are using. As a sole supporter I have to be quite good at multitasking, so I'll probably be washing socks at the same time!

5:45 am – Drive up to athlete on the road.

6:00 am - After an hour of walking, my athlete's stomach can probably already take my power fruit salad, which could fuel up a Formula One racing car.

6:05 am - While he's trying to force this meal down, I'm giving him all the information he needs for the morning; a quick summary of the weather, route and launch options, and a breakdown of what his competition is up to.

7:00 am - Drive to the bottom of the proposed launch, and look for a good spot to park the van, preferably with an open area big enough to land a glider.

7:05 am -Pack my personal flying gear and all the non-mandatory gear that the athlete needs during his flight. This includes warm clothes, gloves, camera, extra food and extra water. It helps that I am reasonably fit, since all this can easily weigh up to 17 kg. I have to be as fast as the athlete on the trail, even though he only is carrying 8 kg!

8:10 am - Intersect the athlete at the agreed meeting point with maybe a third breakfast, for example a large guacamole. Anytime he's eating, I'll be presenting him with the newest available information of the day, and any changes in the leaderboard.

8:30-10:30 am - We charge up the hill to the launch of the day.

10:30 am - Upon arrival at launch, I'll be readying my gear as fast as possible, and then help with the athlete's too. It's better to double check! After a couple of days into the competition, the human brain just doesn't function that great anymore. Sleep deprivation definitely takes a toll.

11:00 am - If the conditions are not obviously working and great, I'll be launching up front to be the wind dummy and show him if it is good. If he sees that I make it work, he'll be right behind me. Usually I'll be making the first transition as well, to mark the second thermal, so that he gets in the flying groove and climbs as high as possible.

11:45 am – While he continues on, I fly down to the car as fast as possible. Hopefully the valley winds aren't blowing too hard yet...

12:00 pm - After packing up, I'll channel some Michael Schumacher! To be able to be catch up with the pilot, keep radio contact with him, and be there when he lands, I have to break every possible traffic law and gun the engine of my poor little van.

12:30 pm - When I get back into radio distance with the athlete, I'll be constantly updating him with weather conditions and especially on the tactics of the field. Maybe I can give him specific information, which could have an impact on his route or flying decisions. This is very stressful, as I'm trying to figure out what's happening to my pilot with the live tracking,.

1:45 pm - When he gets low while flying, I'll try to be there in case he lands and needs food, or to pass off his non-mandatory gear like clothes and food.

2:15 pm - When he gets high, I can relax a little!

4:00 pm - He landed, and no matter what the result was, I will be positive and keep his psyche going. This is crucial; I'll have to stay positive, no matter the sleep deprivation, the physical exhaustion, and the stressful situation. Also, if there are issues within the team, I have to keep my ego down and keep his spirits high.

4:30 pm – He always lands hungry and I'll get another meal ready for him, maybe some juice and high calorie snacks.

6:00 pm - When the big part of the day is over, I start to relax a lot more. I know most of the cards have been played and the day is coming to an end. Most of the field is on the ground and walking, more or less at the same pace. The magic evening light does the rest, and shows the phenomenal scenery of the Alps in this beautiful mood that we all love. I start to remember again why I am doing do this!

7:00 pm - For a last evening flight I usually go with the athlete, just to keep him going a little better. It's always easier to walk together than alone. It's also easier to keep the athlete hydrated when I'm with him, as he sometimes forgets to drink.

8:30 pm – I land and pack up from evening flight, hopefully near the vehicle.

9:00 pm - The rest of the day I will use to find a good spot to sleep, prepare dinner of pasta and set up his tent. Everything should be perfectly timed, so there is as much time left for a good night's sleep as possible. I have to plan this stop location carefully, so he can just get here before the mandatory rest period starts at 10:30 pm.

10:30 pm – The athlete eats and gets to sleep as quickly as possible. I get the van in order, and then do all the media stuff for Red Bull; including blogging, uploading pictures and posting videos.

11:15 pm - Get all the electronics plugged in and charging.

11:30 pm – Finally get to sleep!

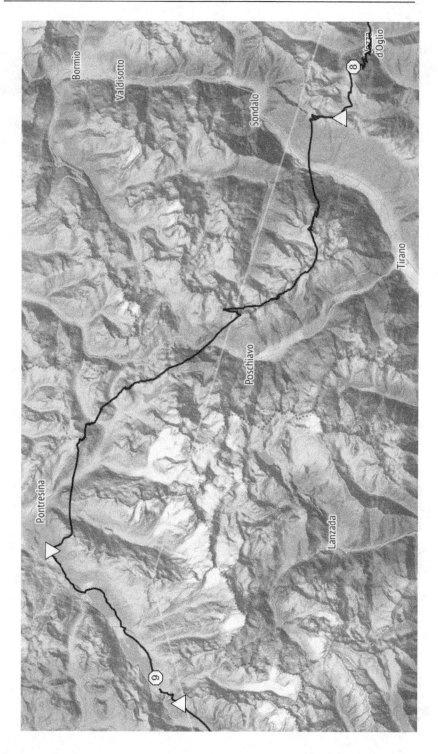

Day 8

Pianaccio, Italy to Maloja, Switzerland
Turnpoint 6
Hiking 24 km
Flying 50 km

I woke up to an alpine wonderland. The plateau looked like the Andean high country, with bogs and grasses and green hillsides. Even better, I was able to sleep in until 7 am (daylight!) which really helped me recover some energy. We woke up to a strange car in the parking area, which turned out to be the Red Bull photographer who had done my race Pre-shoot. Evidently he had knocked on the window about midnight, to ask what time I was getting up in the morning. Someone told him that it would be 7 o'clock, but I didn't hear a thing.

My reward for a really tough climb last night was a gentle morning walk across the plateau as it descended slightly to the west. In the early light it was absolutely beautiful, and I was glad I hadn't tried to hurry through it in the dark. My launch was a slight ridge on the western edge of the area, and I met the motorhome again for breakfast at the trailhead. It wasn't going to be a very hard climb, only a couple hundred meters of vertical, yay! Once again I was putting all my chips into a midday launch, hoping that I would have a good flight. Vitek Ludvig, the Red Bull photographer, was ready to hike up to launch with me to get some action photos, and we set off together for Monte Resverde. My supporter came up behind us. He had thought of flying too, but in the end didn't want to carry his heavier wing up the steep trail. The trail was barely there, unlike most marked trails in this area, just a faint steep goat track marked sparsely with orange spray paint. We climbed in the morning sun, and again it was easy to see that it would be another warm day.

Once on the ridge, there were plenty of launches and I needed to think about my options carefully. The sun was beating on the east face, and if I launched from there and sunk out, I would have a short walk back up from the motorhome. Not that I wanted to hike it again! To the west was the longest valley crossing I would need to make in the entire race so far. It was about 10 kilometers from peak to peak, and on the other side I would be in Switzerland. To even attempt this crossing, I would need to be at least 3000 meters of altitude. There was a forecast slight west wind, which would get stronger as the day progressed. So I'd need to make the crossing against a headwind too. I had successfully done this in training, but conditions had been better then, and I still lost almost 1500 meters of altitude crossing it.

First on the agenda was a nap. It was really early, and launching now would only be altitude suicide. I put on all my flying clothing to protect my skin from the sun, pillowed my head on my thick puffy jacket and rested for a while. It got a little hot even with puffs of breeze, so I finally found a little shade behind a boulder where I could be cooler. Unfortunately it meant I had to be precariously perched on a cliff and folded in half like a pretzel. You can imagine by this time I really didn't care what it took to be comfortable, and any rest was better than none. In fact this felt quite decadent, being able to sit for a couple of hours in the middle of the day during day eight of the Red Bull X-Alps! Vitek the photographer waited patiently for the conditions to improve also. Perhaps he had been running around like crazy too, and with such a beautiful day it was hard not to be content while sitting on a sunny warm mountaintop.

Kruger (RSA) had chosen to stay on the road and hike around the plateau rather than over it, so our paths had diverged yesterday afternoon, after landing quite near each other. He had slept a lot lower, making a bigger hike this morning to get up to launch. He was now at about the same altitude as I was but one peak to the south. Kruger would end up not clearing the valley crossing, and unfortunately I didn't see him again in the race.

Just past noon, the puffs were getting stronger and it felt like time to go. I still chose to launch facing east, as I had a nice bowl funneling the winds up to me. Vitek got a lot of nice shots on the ground, but lost his chance once I got in the air, because I was rocketing up to the moon like I had been launched out of Cape Canaveral. I had a monster thermal and it was taking me as high as I needed to go. I just hung with it and got up to 3000 meters, then eked out a bit more to arrive at 3250. The thermal circles of my flight track were showing me there was a bit of south in the wind, but not too much, and I was pretty sure I was high enough.

As I climbed up in the thermal, I realized that I hadn't put the next Turnpoint into my Flymaster. I guess I had thought I would never need this one as I wasn't likely to get this far! That's a nice problem to have, and soon enough I had it programmed to point me into Switzerland.

The crossing was LONG. Even flying at 40 km an hour it still took at least 10 minutes to fly over the valley. I let go of the brakes, tucked my arms in along my pod, and tried to be aerodynamic while pushing on the speed bar. I had high hopes, vindicated as I came into the hillside at 2000 meters. I was just at tree line, and with the sun hitting the hillside full on, I knew I just needed to be patient and work my way up the slope. Indeed it did work, and it didn't take me too long to get above the peaks. I was at the southern end of a long ridge, and the cluster of peaks were picked up thermals from 3 sides, all funneling up to me. My phone chirped a border crossing just as I hit the strongest thermal of the day.

I thought I was home free at that point, and switched to the western side of the ridge as it was now becoming afternoon and the sun was swinging overhead. It wasn't going to be that easy, however. Suddenly there were no thermals; perhaps I had gotten in the lee of the southern breezes coming over the peak? Oh well. I just kept flying north along the ridge, figuring that there would be lift somewhere. I eventually found it again, and although it was really ratty air I was getting up. I hadn't really gotten low but it's funny how perspective changes in the air. Some days I would be ecstatic to be cruising just below the peaks, but today I was used to flying far above them. In fact the only thing keeping me down today were the clouds. As I came close the rough edges of the cumulous bottoms, I knew it was time to keep pushing along the course line.

Ahead of me was the Bernina Pass. A large lake sits at the pass itself, and it looked possible to fly to either side of it. I had flown up to it but not over it in training, and I pondered aloud to myself about which way to go. I wanted to be sure, though, and asked Chuck via text to check the race tracking to see which way other athletes had flown. A few minutes later he reported either side should work. Eventually I would need to be west of it to start working my way between Turnpoint 6 and the airspace over St. Moritz.

With a tailwind the decision was really a moot point, and I was able to stay high and scream over Bernina Pass, turning only occasionally in strong lift. I imagined my supporters at the pass waving at me, but in reality they were way back at the border crossing. They had needed to drive around quite a long way from launch around the valley to get up to the pass. From Bernina Pass, it was all downhill to St. Moritz, but I was still going UP. In a strong thermal over a mountain peak, I saw 7 m/s of lift. That's the equivalent of going up about 2 floors a second in an elevator! It WAS an elevator of sorts, one that I had to hang on to with every atom in my body. Definitely the strongest thermal I'd ever been in.

This thermal took me all the way up to cloud base at 4000 meters, and it seemed like it would be easy to cut the corner of St. Moritz and start heading west. Turnpoint Six above Piz Corvatch only required that I fly to the north of the peak, and then continue on my way to the Matterhorn and Turnpoint

Seven. So I wouldn't need to land or do anything special, and I was hoping to just continue my nice flight.

Sometimes the ground has other plans. All that lift turned into sinking air, but I was still able to fly over the ridge to St. Moritz fairly easily. Usually in the air, as you get close to a peak or a ridge, there is a nudge of lifting air to let you know that you are over the ground and should expect a thermal or ridge lift. This time, there was nothing. I continued to descend and started sliding even faster over the ground. I had a moment of time to think, "Uh-oh, this isn't right". It's about the same feeling of being suspended at the top of a rollercoaster, when you know the bottom is going to drop out at any second.

Then the bottom did drop out. I was only 50 meters away from the hillside when I hit the biggest waterfall I hope I ever feel. The rotor on this lee side was the trashiest air I could imagine, and my wing was doing everything but flying. To make it tougher, over the town of St. Moritz was airspace that I was desperately trying to avoid. So there I was, trapped between a steep hillside covered in tall pine trees, and airspace that would assess me a 48-hour race penalty.

Far below me on the valley floor, but only about a kilometer to the north, was a thin strip of grass amid a sea of trees. Crisscrossing everywhere were power lines. It was mentally hard to adjust to this new scenario, as my mind was saying "But you were just up at 4000 meters, this can't be happening!" With my wing collapsing and jerking every which way, I struggled to keep it under control and make any progress away from the hill. Although with the power lines below me, at times landing in a very tall tree didn't seem like such a bad option!

I was really happy with my wing at that moment. My Ozone Alpina 2 should by all rights have been balled up and not flying, but somehow it always popped out of each problem and parked itself back above my head. I saw 6.6 m/s down several times, which felt pretty close to free fall (which at 9.8 m/s2 was only a little bit faster!) I fully expected to have to reach for my reserve parachute, but never even came close to needing it. Thank God!

The ground kept coming closer, and still there were only trees below me. I alternated between trying to push some speed bar to get away from the hill, and letting off when the rotor tried to rip the fabric off my wing. Slowly the green patch slid below me, bordered by super tall trees and large power lines. Bicycle riders blithely tooted their horns along the path, unaware that above their heads I was fighting for my very life.

My descent into the pasture was pretty much straight down, alternating with times of being yanked straight back up again. With no padding in my harness at all, I hung my legs down so I would land upright rather than on my back, and let them take the brunt of my fall. The wind shadow from trees in front of me erased any consistency in the wind, and with 10 feet to go dropped out completely. I almost landed on my feet, but bounced off my butt instead, just behind a small tree. A tiny stream padded my landing, with my harness getting wet but my feet staying dry on either side! It took me a moment to realize that I was still all in one piece, and scrambled out of the stream before everything could get soaked. Although the word stream was rather too grand for this tiny flow of water that was maybe 3 inches deep.

I thought I had broken my nose for a second, but in the end it was just a little whiplash, as my helmet had bounced forward to hit my sunglasses on the bridge of my nose. I did need a while to calm down, and flipped my harness over to dry in the sun while I eased the shaking out of my arms. My supporters were still far behind me so I had a while before anyone would show up.

The pasture I had landed in was really more of a bog. My feet sank with every step, as if the ground itself were floating on a lake. I was absurdly grateful to have landed in such a forgiving place. Winds on the ground were quite strong, and as I looked back up at the mountains I was really glad I had made it all the way down here safely.

It wasn't until I had landed that I understood the dynamics of the air I had flown into. This valley was flowing east to west, with a super strong west wind. The Bernina Pass had a strong south wind pouring down over the pass. So at the ridge above St. Moritz where I had flown, both of these winds were meeting and flowing down together. I can't imagine a worse scenario and I don't think any change in my flight path would have helped me escape it. In fact it might have been worse if I had been deeper in the mountains as I could have landed high in no man's land. With winds forecast to be strong over the next 30 hours, re-launching up there wouldn't have been an option.

So all in all, I was really content to be standing in a squishy boggy meadow with damp gear. Eventually I got myself together, packed up my wing without getting it too wet, and got over to the bike path. By then Chuck was close to me, and we met up for a late lunch. Actually I had missed lunch, while napping on launch this morning, and hadn't eaten anything but a few gummy bears during the flight. Chuck hooked me up with some Pringles and a Snickers bar, and reloaded my water supply.

Photo Credit: Vitek Ludvik

My fortuitous landing in the main valley gave me an easy walk for the rest of the day. I needed to head west for a while along the valley, all the way down to Chiavenna, and my path to get there was straight and flat. The only exception to the flat was a sudden drop of about 500 meters, and it would be nice if I could fly this descent rather than walk.

Ahead of me about 15 km and above this small descent, competitor Pascal Purin (AUT4) was also looking for a place to launch on the north side of the valley. He had walked in a big circle up on the hill, but descended without flying back down to the valley floor.   By that time I had almost caught up with him. Jim met up with Purin and his crew at the mouth of the pass while waiting for me to arrive. Purin reported switching and gusty strong winds that just didn't seem flyable. He told Jim that he had promised his mother he would stay safe in the race so he could someday give her grandchildren.   That evening Purin made the decision to drop out of the Red Bull X-Alps completely.

My supporter had been pushing me to get to the pass that evening and fly down if possible, but as I walked by Lake Silvaplauna, the kite boarders were out en force on the east end. The winds were obviously too strong to even think of flying, and I felt no pressure to do so. Plus tomorrow, winds were also forecast to be strong, so I had another whole day to get into position to fly when the weather did improve.

A nice pasta dinner was waiting for me when I finally met up with the motorhome, and I was really glad to see everyone. By this time my team was a pretty well-oiled machine, and Jim had a camp chair and spare shoes laid out for me to change while I ate. Most of my socks were dirty, so we started choosing the "least dirty" pair when I swapped out shoes. The paved hiking trail continued along the lakes, me walking while my supporters drove ahead to the pass, finding a campground for the night right along my route.

I had refused to think about flying in these winds, and calculated that I would arrive too late to make the 9 pm flight cut off anyway, so it was a good night to finish really early and have a lazy evening. Everyone went out to eat, while I had my second hot shower of the race. Wow, it felt like a million bucks. Even putting on the same dirty race shorts afterwards didn't matter. I turned down dinner at the restaurant for a chance to be lazy, lay in bed and look at live tracking. As I zoomed in on race leader Chrigel Maurer (SUI1), he was just top landing after an amazing day of flying...but he wasn't done yet. With only minutes to go before the 9 pm cutoff, he raced back up to a ridge, launched again, and landed down in the valley. It was fun to be a spectator in the Red Bull X-Alps for a second, as most of the time I really didn't know what was happening to everyone else out there racing. I also looked at the race stats for all the athletes so far. Turns out I had walked 387 km in seven days, more than anyone except Turner (USA4)!

Walking further than most of the competitors at this point in the race was both good and bad. As a positive, it told me (and the world) that physically I could do as much (or more) than the men. Gender obviously wasn't a factor, then, which was a point I was trying to make by taking part in this race in the first place.   On the other hand, walking this much meant I wasn't being very efficient and hadn't spent enough time in the air. While I had flown as much as I was willing and able to so far, many if not most other competitors had more paragliding experience than I did. This was evident in the distances they had flown during the race, which were far greater than mine for the most part.

A slice of chocolate cake was my reward when everyone returned from dinner. It was so big that it morphed into breakfast too.   By then I had done my research into the weather, and decided to try for an early flight down from the pass. The rest of the day would be incredibly windy and there was no chance of a midday flight.

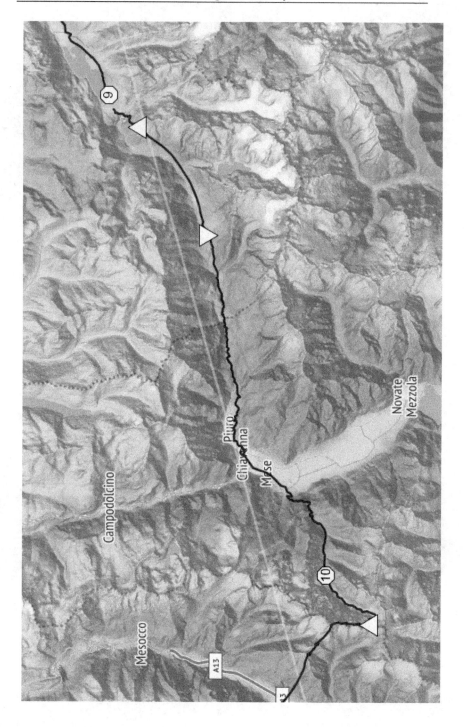

Day 9

Maloja, Switzerland to Gordona, Italy
Hiking 37 km
Flying 9 km

In the morning it was extraordinarily hard to wake up. I had been using Advil PM occasionally to help me sleep and to alleviate the pain in my legs. Without any pain medicine, I would toss and turn at night as the muscles in my legs would cramp, and sometimes jerk uncontrollably.   While I was walking, my legs actually didn't feel sore, but the cumulative miles were definitely making themselves known. My lower legs had been a little swollen for the last couple of days. In such heat, it was hard to keep the circulation going, and a little dehydration didn't help either. Altogether, I was happy being injury free, but that doesn't necessarily mean pain free. Jim had faithfully been giving me foot rubs each night, and I wore my calf sleeves to sleep in, but the Ibuprofen helped with the inflammation too. I tried to keep my use of it very minimal (as it thinned my blood), and I was very cautious of anything that would increase bleeding in case of a bad accident.

It was important to get in the air as early as possible if I was going to get a safe flight down from the pass, so at 5 am I was off and walking.   After inhaling some chocolate cake, of course! The pass descended very near where we had camped, so it was just a matter of climbing up a few hundred meters around the corner, so I could look down into the next valley. I was on the south side, taking a cue from Jon Chamber's book about the 2011 Red Bull X-Alps. Chambers had launched successfully from here and I figured that meant I could too.

At the pass I left the road and started up the trail, first crossing a dam, but the lake itself was completely empty with walking trails at the bottom. It looked weird. My trail did eventually pass a tiny lake (this one filled with water), but at that point I was busy swatting at flies, which seemed to be thick in the area. I also crossed a rather flimsy swinging rope bridge, which amused me even though I could have gone around it faster than going over it! I was hiking in still, steamy woods, but the winds aloft were already very strong from the north. In fact, I could see them, in the form of a fog bank, rolling down over the peaks to the north of me. It was a little eerie, and I knew that I needed to get launched and land quickly before the day started heating up. If the winds were too strong, I could always walk down the trail to the valley. It wasn't too much of a descent and no one was going to overtake me today anyway. By this point, seven athletes had quit the race or been eliminated, leaving just two quite far behind me in Italy.

I curled around the corner, and could finally see the valley below me, and was relieved to see plenty of pastures to land in. There wasn't an obvious launch, because the ground was covered in high scrubby bushes and trees. It actually felt very much like a rainforest, and I could feel that I was on the southern, steamy side of the Alps.   Luckily, as the trail contoured, a nice possible launch came into view.   My launching run would take me down the hiking trail, as long as I jerked to the side at the end to avoid tangling my wing in a tree! I needed to get in the air, and didn't want to waste time looking for a better spot.

With my wing laid out, the air was still, with the occasional puff from behind me. I waited a while to avoid launching in a light tailwind, but finally got airborne. Luckily I remembered to jinkly to expect any thermals, and with the strong winds, Foehn could be a problem. I decided flying straight down the middle of the valley was the safest place to be.

I'm not sure where the wind came from, but my instruments soon began showing me speeds of 70 and 80 kph! Jeez, I really wasn't expecting that. A complete switch of direction from the headwinds of yesterday, and I was now screaming down the valley and flying further than I had planned, which was all to the good. What wasn't good was that I had never flown this valley before, and had no maps of the area, so I didn't really know what was coming. In sinking strong winds, this probably wasn't the best scenario. Ahead of me, the valley narrowed as it descended, and although I was still high, I couldn't see past this gap to know what the ground looked like. Flying sometimes requires some split second decision making, and good judgement about conditions ahead, and the last thing I wanted to do was fly over somewhere with no landing zones while screaming along at 80 kph. So I took the safe choice and turned into wind to land. I had picked a wide section of valley with the biggest pasture around. It was broken up with power lines and some stone barns, but at least I had room to maneuver.

Even landing required some intense concentration this time. Paragliders only fly at about 32 kph. Since my flying speeds (with the wind) were about 75 kph, which put the winds at about 43 kph. (Paraglider speed + wind = flight speed) When I turned into wind, this meant that I was flying about 10 kph...backward. (Paraglider speed - wind speed = flight speed). Luckily, winds near the ground tend to be slower, as the wind hits objects like trees, houses, hills, etc. But to make sure I had a place to land in the field, I turned around WAY before the field, then flew backwards to get there!

I won't say I had a nice landing, as this time I truly was going backwards when the ground rushed to meet me. I narrowly missed a stone barn (yikes), and found it was quite difficult to try to keep my body pointing forward to fly the wing, while looking back over my shoulder to see where my landing might be. Smooth grass awaited me (yay!) when I did touch down somewhat ungracefully, and I immediately fell backwards and slid a few feet as my wing touched the earth. Luckily the ground winds weren't enough for me to actually become a cloth-powered sled for more than a second or two. But I did have to pick grass out of my reserve handle for a few days!

Once again, I stood with shaking legs to pack up my equipment and wait for Chuck. I calculated that this was the

5th day in a row that I had landed going backwards in strong valley winds.   I was beginning to wonder why everyone thought it was so great to fly in the Alps.   A local passed by; shaking his head a bit and pointing at how close I was to the power lines.   Of course I had actively avoided them like the plague, but if he had seen my descent and landing, it didn't look very pretty.

Chuck arrived promptly, and since I would be walking for the rest of the day, I really emptied my pack of all extras and just grabbed a bottle of water and some snacks.   It was going to be a scorcher (again) and I didn't have to worry about flying clothes or rain gear.   Temperatures continued to be abnormally high, and it would get to about 100 F (38C) today. Sweltering was the term that came to mind.

Ahead of me on the road was a short tunnel, and while the rules allow for walking through some tunnels, I thought it would be best to get permission for this one. What we weren't allowed to do is cross under a major pass between two valley systems.   This one was just heading down the same valley descending into the town of Chiavenna.   I fired off a text to race director Christoph Weber, and sure enough a few minutes later got an ok.   The tunnel was really loud, and I'm sure the traffic going by probably thought I was a strange homeless person, carrying a large pack and covering my ears.

Hiking down the valley would only be my third descent of the whole race.   This time I had another 800 meters downhill into Chiavenna, which sits at a low, humid, and hot mere 300 meters above sea level.   Chuck met me again a few miles down the road, I'm not even sure why.   I was happy to see him nonetheless, and looked forward to dropping my pack for a few minutes. Somehow that turned into a few minutes of lying down on the mattress in his van.   I was soon asleep, with my feet sticking out the door and my arms crossed over my chest, like the Lady of Shalott in her boat waiting to float out into the lake.   Jim showed up with the motorhome and I didn't even notice.

A short nap must have been just what I needed though. Fortified with more chocolate and the inevitable box of pineapple juice, I continued down the valley. The road was narrow and cars were whizzing by. My digital maps of the area were less than accurate, but somehow I ended up on a bike trail along the river, and followed it for miles. A plethora of small towns were strung along the valley, but none of them seemed to have a store or a bakery. I would have loved a cold drink and some black forest cake (my two secret cravings the entire race) but alas, nothing.

I was grateful for the occasional shade, but otherwise carried on in hot sunshine. Temperatures were in the 90s Fahrenheit and approaching 100 F (38 F) by the time I arrived in Chiavenna. The river would have been a great place to cool off but it was very hard to get down to the water and I didn't try very hard. I guess I figured that there would be a better place further downriver, but that never came. It was along this stretch that I got the worst news of the race. Colas (ESP) had quit, 18 hours ahead of the next elimination. Since he was the last one in the race, behind Kruger (RSA) and I, we were both dependent on his elimination to keep us in the race longer. The rules stated that if an athlete quits, it doesn't count toward the next elimination. So Kruger was now last, and would get cut in the morning, and I would have to worry about the next one in 48 hours. I did text the race director about it (ok, I was complaining). Christoph Weber responded back that he had tried to talk Colas into not quitting, but wasn't successful. I saw it as really poor sportsmanship on the part of Colas, and I wondered if he realized that he had cut two days of racing from both Kruger and I. If he was trying to save face to avoid elimination, then he failed...there was quite a backlash about his choice from race fans.

I had been blithely thinking that I was safe from elimination and could take the next five days to get as far as possible along the course. I had even started hoping my final stop could be Zermatt, Switzerland, under the Matterhorn at Turnpoint 7. It just seemed so iconic. But suddenly just three days seemed like a very short amount of time to accomplish that. Zermatt was still 250 kilometers away as the crow flies along my route. I really couldn't see any way of doing it...but I was determined to try.

Ahead of me, but on a very different route, was Gold (AUT2). He had tried a committing flight to the north but had sunk out. So while we were a long ways from each other, we weren't too far apart in the standings, and if I could catch him that would earn me another few days in the race.

My supporters had claimed a table at a restaurant right along my route through Chiavenna, and we could commiserate together. We had pizza and pasta, which was only mediocre at best. I had now walked back into Italy, but I've found that Italian food in Italy is either really good or really bad. This fell into the latter category but I was too hungry to really care. I also made a phone call to Kruger, and broke the news that he was going to be eliminated in the morning. He took it fairly well, and assured me that he wasn't going to quit like Colas had!

After the disappointing lunch, I detoured back to the motorhome to rest in the heat of the day. The forecast for tomorrow was looking promising, and my launch wasn't too far away, so I could take some time to rest and recuperate. If that's what you call sweltering in the motorhome, anyway! After an hour, I couldn't take the heat anymore and figured I would just keep walking. I was hoping to finally locate a place to cool off in the river.

While I had sweltered in the motorhome, race leader Chrigel Maurer was flying the last few kilometers to land at the last Turnpoint 10 at Peille. He would win the race in 8 Days and 4 Hours. Race rules stated that everyone else had either another 48 hours after the winner, or 12 total days to finish the race, whichever is longer. So that meant another 3 ½ days for me...if I could avoid elimination.

You might think that with my race looking like it would be a lot shorter, I would rush out and keep going to get as far as I could for the day.   The problem was, my route to the Matterhorn needed to take me back into Switzerland, and straightest way there was up and over a 2200 meter pass.

At the pass, there were a few route choices, depending on the weather.   Since Turnpoint 7 at the Matterhorn was a 5.5 km circle, it was possible to tag this point from any side.   In really good conditions, it could be approached even from the southern, Italian side of the Alps. This would mean flying over several mountains 3000 meters or higher.   Sinking out anywhere in there would mean days of backtracking to get back to the northern side of the Alps, as Turnpoint 8 specified passing north of Mont Blanc.   On the other hand, it was possible to fly to the Matterhorn from the east, although I had been warned there was tricky airspace and some high passes there, as well as a lot of narrow dangerous valleys.

My choice, along with the majority of the athletes given the weather conditions during this section, was to approach the Matterhorn from the north. This meant I needed to cross the main spine of the Alps (again), and work my way around a big half-moon route to the Goms valley. But no matter which way I chose, my first move was to get over this next pass. And since it was too windy to fly today, it ultimately meant I was forced to take my time getting up to the pass. I really didn't want to walk down the other side!!!

A good launch if I can avoid that tree on the right!

Back on the main road out of town, I sweated my way down the sidewalk munching on an apple. The river never materialized and I was grateful to finally start climbing up to the pass. At least the temperature would get cooler as I climbed. A little. I hoped.

To cross this main ridge of the Alps, I had two options, Forcola Pass and a saddle called Forcellino del Notaro. I ended up choosing the latter because it was closer to the valley I needed to fly into. Neither one of them was helpful for a sled ride though. On the western side of these passes, the convoluted valleys pointed almost due north, whereas I needed to fly west. If I wasn't able to climb out in the morning and sunk out, I might be faced with a long valley hike. Actually, I didn't really know what I would be faced with, as I hadn't trained in this area at all. While I walked, my supporters had bought a couple of maps and were looking at my route. I had basic maps on my phone but nothing as detailed as before and really no time to download anything either. I was flying blind.

But all that was a question for the morning, and my job now was to climb as high as I could into the mountains, to save all of us a hot night of sleeping. The pass was almost 1900 meters above me (6000 feet!) and if I could do even half of that I would be really happy. The paved road continued about halfway as well, and soon the vehicles were disappeared in front of me looking for a place to park up in the hills. The sign as we entered the toll road, said that we needed to get a vehicle pass at the bar in town. Only in Italy would they send you to a bar to get a free pass to drive up a toll road! Jim headed up anyway but Chuck went back to see if he could make us all legal.

I turned off the road onto a trail, and followed the steepest set of stairs I've ever seen. They were wide and well maintained and well groomed, and I soon hated every step I took on them. The stairs switch backed up and up and up, and all I wanted to do was get off this hellish climb and get back on the road. At least the grades on a road are usually somewhat restrained!

Finally I did get back on the road, but with no sign of my supporters. The canyon I overlooked was quite popular with the canyoneering folks, as there were signs all over with maps and entry locations. Canyoneering sounded pretty good to me at the moment in the heat...and the water far below me looked green, clear and inviting. Alas, the road was perched high on the hillside, so a quick dip in the water still was out of the question. Bummer.

The locater app on my phone put Chuck below me somewhere, but that must have been a mistake, as the next time I saw him he was coming back down with Jim to see how I was doing. They reported it was only a mile or so to camp. Obviously phone signals in here were nonexistent, so they took my iPhone, which was dying for the second time that day, and drove back up to the cars. I suddenly felt very alone, and very tired. My steps brought me through a little village, and the road denigrated from pavement to rough gravel. A mile passed and I started to wonder if I had missed a turn somewhere. Why is the last mile always the hardest and the longest? Anyway, my lower lip might have started to quiver by the time I saw Jim, who was walking down to meet me.

It was still pretty early, and Boga had warmed up yesterday's leftover pasta, which tasted even better now. I ate it sitting on a boulder in the creek, while soaking my feet in the coldest water I had been in yet. Yes, after all day of wishing for a river to soak in, I had finally found one. And it was blessedly cool up in the mountains so we could sleep a little better than sweltering down in the valley.

My supporter had found a place for me to launch in the morning, and planned to hike up with me. He had talked to a local who was following the race, who reported a competitor ahead of me had landed near here and hiked up to the border to get re-launched. It was a relief just knowing that someone had flown out of here, as I really didn't know anything about the terrain above me.

It's not always easy to maneuver this motorhome through
traffic and towns
Photo Credit: Chuck Savall

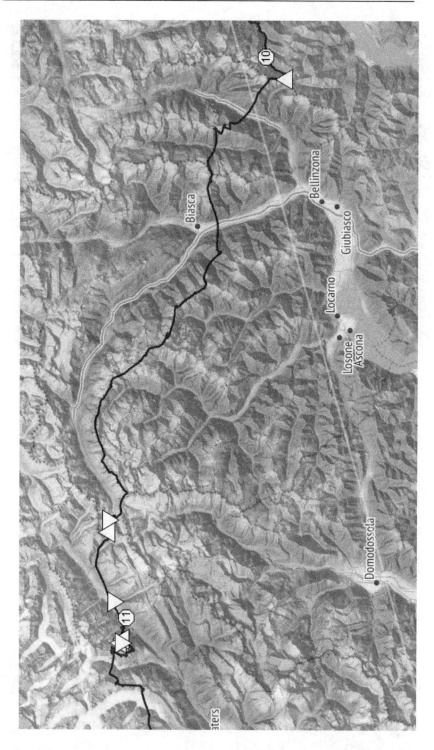

Day 10

Bodengi, Italy to Gluringen, Switzerland
Hiking 12 km
Flying 93 km

Another day to sleep in for me on Day 10, as I only had about 1000 meters of vertical to hike up to launch. You might be wondering why I wasn't racing every minute of the day from 0530 to 2230 as the race allowed. For me it was just some simple math. In a few hours of walking, I might cover 5 to 15 kilometers, but the same time in the air I could cover 50 kilometers or more. So if there was a good chance of flying, I thought it was better to get the extra sleep to be able to focus on a better flight, rather than tire myself out walking. So I was going to make this pass my midday "go for broke" launch again, rather than waste it too early and sink out. I was at the point where my legs were terminally tired of hiking up hills. There had been talk of strategically hiking up early and gliding down to a better launch around the corner, but there was no chance I was going to waste 1800 meters of vertical on a sled ride!

I left at 7 am to make my way up the hill. My supporter had planned on hiking up with me and then down the other side to meet the vehicles. He had done the research the day before on where to launch. The vehicles would have to drive way around to Lake Como, as I truly was going up and over the main spine of the Alps, and it was hard to get from this location to the other side. At the last minute, with no warning, my main supporter decided not to hike up with me. I was extremely unhappy with him by then, and had no information on the location of the launch, but left anyway to hike up, without giving him the satisfaction of asking for help. I had started to think that perhaps he actually wanted me to fail. Choose your supporter wisely is all I can say...I should have vetted him more carefully.

So without any phone contact in this dead zone, race headquarters had lost my live tracking since yesterday afternoon. Eventually I would have to send them my backup track logs to prove where I had been! The vehicles all left to drive hundreds of miles around to arrive on the other side of this ridge, and we had no way of tracking each other for hours. I was truly on my own.

Waiting for me on the quiet trail was another 1100 meters of climbing. I passed a beautiful village seemingly lost in the middle ages, with stone roofs and a quaint look about it. Two dogs vied for my attention at the bridge leading to the village, but I wasn't going that way and they weren't willing to come out any further. One of them looked a bit silly wearing a surgery cone e-collar, but I'm sure the dog thought it looked ferocious!

The trail went gently up the middle of a long valley, which would eventually end in a bowl where I hoped to find a launch. I only saw one person all day, an older Italian gentleman who was headed up to watch for animals on the hillsides. He could only speak in Italian and I could only pretend to understand. He did know about the race, saying that another athlete had come through here and found a launch above me. His directions to such a place were a little confusing and involved a hut. I thought later that I should have had him show me the location on a map while I had someone around. Oops.

The race was finally starting to tire me out, and what I really wanted to do was lay down and take a nap. That wouldn't have been a great idea, so I compromised and began taking a short break after each 100 meters of vertical that I hiked up. I watched my Garmin Fenix 3 closely to keep an eye on my elevation. Sometimes the last few meters seemed to take forever but I slowly got higher. The trail went ever steeper, and the scenery was pretty amazing to distract me. On three sides were big cliffs and rocks spines, interspersed with a few cows on rocky pastures. I had a few choices to try for a launch, and with my exhausted state, I went for the lowest option, still up at 2100 meters of elevation.   The ridge along the spine (which was also the Italy/Switzerland border) looked like the backbone of a dinosaur. Obviously I wasn't going to have an easy time finding a nice pasture to launch from here. The trail meandered up through the steep pasture and through a gap in the spine. On the other side, it was just as steep, and even worse...shady.   The dark cool valley leading into Switzerland would have been a sure and quick way to land at the bottom.

So I paused in the gap to eat some chocolate before it melted. The stretch of relentless hot days in the Alps was a source of amazement for me, as I had packed for and planned on cooler weather. The morning sun was beating down on the east side of the spine, so my choice was to launch here, and hope to thermal up and over somehow. I found a spot of grass to lay my wing out, but it was riddled with boulders. When I had everything laid out, I realized that I would need to hop from one rock down to another as I reversed down the hill to launch. Luckily my Ozone Alpina 2 launched like a dream because I didn't want to mess this up. In other words, I didn't really look at the wing when I pulled it up, just focused on quickly hopping boulders down the slope, and then I was flying.

I had left myself an out; if the air wasn't working I would be able to land somewhere up here to wait for better conditions. I thought for a few minutes I would need them, as I hovered in zero lift and even lost a little height. Then I found a quiet thermal and began to climb.

Looming above me was a corner of Locarno Airport airspace at 2895 meters So as I circled I knew I would need to work my way north up the ridge before I got too high. The area was quite imposing even viewed from the air. It's not like I had missed a really nice launch just around the corner...there really weren't any.   The dinosaur spine continued in both directions for miles, and the valleys were convoluted and steep, difficult to traverse on foot. In other words, a great spot to have a border!

I was very happy to climb above all this and get away from the area. I had really never been here before so I was flying blind. Luckily I could open the map on my phone and see where I was and where I needed to go. My route looked kind of like a fishhook, first I had to make a move into the adjoining valley, and then follow it a long ways north up to Neufenen Pass.

Traditionally I would have followed my valley around to the junction and then continued on in the next one. I was quite high and I knew there were launches down at that corner of the route. However, I was already in the air and didn't want to sink out. I was too tired to hike up again! So instead of curving around the valley, I went straight across the middle hoping that I could use the ridgelines of mountains to get some lift. This was a big breakthrough for me in my flying in the Red Bull X-Alps. I had been playing it safe and sticking with my route on the ground in case I did sink out. But since I had thermalled out on an east face, I figure that if I hopped to another east face across the valley, I could do it again.

I was amazed but not particularly surprised when it worked. Flying this way helped me cross a few spines and each time I chased the sunny side of the cliffs. There seemed to be a little north wind, but not enough to cause any lee side problems, with the sun to overpower the wind and provide thermals.

It was really fun to be successful at my moves and I arrived in my main valley, which would lead all the way to Neufenen Pass. In fact I could see it ahead of me in the distance. It was such a clear day I thought I could see the Matterhorn and Mont Blanc as well. They weren't actually too far to the west of me, but I was playing it safe and working my way around to the north in order to avoid any really high passes. Although as I climbed up to almost 4000 meters it was hard not to think of flying straight to them!

My deep lines continued on the west side of the valley and I made my way to the pass. It was slow going at times and quite punchy in the air. At 4000 meters the wind was quite strong and my progress went almost to nothing, so sinking down a little allowed me to fly faster.

I was in quite a bit of pain now while flying, and had been for a couple of days. My harness, which had felt comfortable in training for up to six hours at a stretch, wasn't feeling so great with my exhausted legs. The lightweight pod didn't have a seat board, so the whole harness cocooned around me and wrapped my hips and legs quite snugly. My feet really hurt on the bottoms as I pushed on the speed bar and tried to keep my legs out straight for aerodynamics, and my hips just ached from sitting in my little cocoon. It's pretty bad when flying hurts as much as walking!

My direction of flight wasn't terribly obvious a few hours later, so I texted Chuck while in the air to see if he could give me an idea where other competitors had gone. Again I was really tempted to head straight to the Matterhorn but my ability to keep flying in the later afternoon hadn't been that great here, so I wanted to get into the Rhone valley.

Near Neufenen Pass, I began to sink lower and not find climbs back out again. I wasn't sure what the wind was doing, and my supporters were far behind me and not able to find wind reports. Fearing the rotor if the wind was blowing down, I landed above and behind the pass in a nice high pasture. Indeed I could feel the wind in my face from the pass to the north. Unfortunately a little bit of pineapple juice had spilled in my pack while I was flying. My backpack had already started to stink from hiking while sweating, and now it was sticky too. I tried to wash it off with a little water but my efforts were rather futile.

While everyone caught up to me on the roads, I leisurely hiked down to the top of the pass, via a few waterfalls and some snowfields. One stream was a little deep, so my shoes got soaked. Luckily I was close now and the vehicles came into sight. At the pass, my main supporter departed; he and Boga had decided to head back to Poland. Now just Chuck and Jim, who had been doing most everything anyway, were left, so our team was finally streamlined. A lot simpler too!

My late afternoon snack consisted of a berry tart they had found in a bakery. Yum. Then I had time to change my shoes and wait for the wind to die down a little bit. It was still quite strong, so Chuck drove down to the next valley to see what was happening there. In the main Rhone valley, the wind was blowing strongly from the NE, and then wrapping around into this little pass blowing NW. If I could fly across the valley, perhaps I could get in the lifting side of this and use it to work my way further down the valley. It was a bit late to think of thermalling, but one could hope.

So I had a very easy launch from the pass on a lovely grassy slope. Jim was there to watch me on launch for the first time in the race since back in Germany. I was able to ridge soar in front of him for a few minutes before heading down to the main valley. Unfortunately, the winds didn't seem to be doing anything useful, so the best I could manage was to fly as far as I could with a cracking tailwind. I was also distracted with my flight deck, it hadn't attached properly and the zipper had undone itself from the wrong end. So it was hanging by one end, and I couldn't see the screen of my vario, which showed my sink rate and flying speed. I managed to rip the deck off the zipper completely, breaking the zipper, which I saw later. It didn't really help though, because without anything to rest on, the angle of the deck was the wrong direction and I still couldn't read the screen. At least it was looking like a short flight so it wouldn't matter. I had a spare deck in my other harness so I could swap it out for the next day.

Now in the Rhone valley, I passed a disused runway with big Xs across the pavement, then another one with gliders parked alongside. By this time I was getting low along the edge of the trees and without any lift I just flew close to the hill. Alarm bells went off in my mind, but only mildly, as I had checked the race airspace maps just that morning and this was not on it. Just past the glider port across the river, I turned into wind and landed.

Perhaps just that quickly, a van showed up with an irate woman shouting about how I needed to come with her to see the boss of the airport. Of course she was shouting in German, so that either made it more scary, or less, depending on what I thought I was hearing! I think I asked if I got to make a phone call first. Ok, I was a little nervous, and fussed around trying to get my wing packed up. There's really nothing worse than having gear spread out everywhere and angry people around. I felt really vulnerable, and psychologically I was much better once everything was back in my pack.

About that time Chuck drove up in the van, and I gladly handed him my race phone and had him call the race director Christoph Weber. Christoph calmed everyone down, spoke to the woman, and worked everything out. I guess. In the end, with Christoph's permission, I rode with Chuck in his van over to the glider port, where we apologized excessively for violating airspace that I didn't know existed until I came around the corner of the valley. Then I rode in the van back to where I landed, and continued the race. A better ending than I had hoped because an airspace violation would have meant an end to my race.

For my live tracking watchers back in Iowa, I found out later, this landing looked very unsettling. I had landed and then went quickly, not walking, in a different direction in a straight line that looked like a vehicle. They wondered if I had been injured in the landing and prayed that I was OK. I quickly made a Facebook entry once I was walking again, to explain the weird tracklog!

In fact my flight today was the day I had hoped for (but not dared to dream about) when I heard the news about Colas (ESP) quitting the race. Today I had hiked and flown about

110 kilometers, and had left myself only 70 kilometers to get to Zermatt, the next checkpoint. I finally felt that it was doable. Even better, I had pulled ahead of Gold (AUT2), who was now 25 km behind me in the same valley!

Looking up at the hills, I could see that every hilltop was grassy and would make a great launch. I wasn't going to win or lose the race on my feet, so we found a nearby campground for a very early stop. I think I only had to walk 5km down the valley, which was heaven. On the way, Jim found a do it yourself pizza shop. He and Chuck crafted three pizzas, had them weighed and then cooked in a brick fired oven. Because it was Switzerland, they cost an arm and a leg, but at least they were delicious! The shower also felt really nice, but rather short. It cost 1 Swiss Franc for three minutes. Jim must have been feeling rather generous that night; he said, "Here, have TWO Francs!"

Supporter Chuck Savall takes out a knot in my lines   Photo Credit: Cano

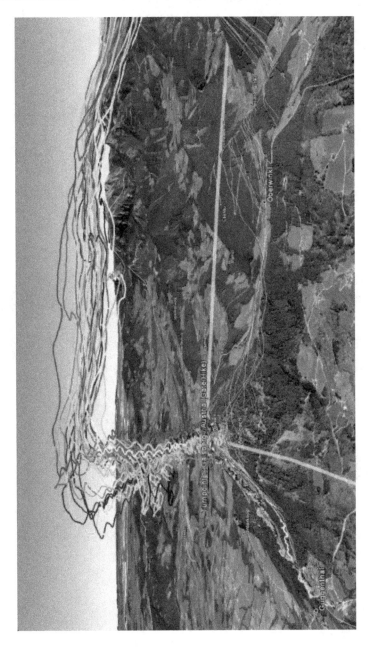

3D Tracklogs from the launch on Day 1 look like a volcano
erupting!
Photo Credit: www.redbullxalps.com

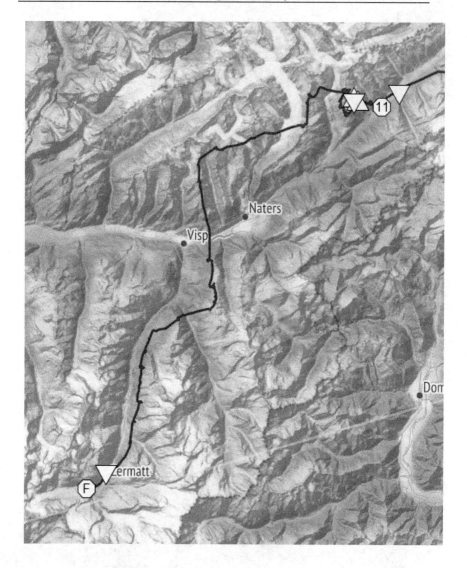

Day 11

Grafschaft to Zermatt, Switzerland
Turnpoint 7 - Matterhorn
Hiking 15 km
Flying 73 km

The Rhone valley of Switzerland is what paraglider pilots wish all alpine valleys would be like. Every hilltop was a green grassy slope, with easy launches and top landings. In the valley there were plenty of places to land, and the higher mountains behind had amazing glaciers and snowcapped peaks. In short, it's a glorious place to fly. Not to mention the valley has quite a few chairlifts heading up right to a great launch.

I was wishing for a chairlift as I headed out of the campground. With all of the perfect slopes above me, it was just a matter of picking the closest one and hiking up. I still had 1000 meters of altitude to gain, so not for the faint of heart. What I didn't have were maps of the trail. I hadn't been able to download digital maps of this section, as I had just plain forgotten to do it before the race, and forgotten again yesterday evening. Oops. My Internet connection on the phone was practically dial-up, so I wasn't able to load them while hiking either. I frantically texted Jim and he came running after me, and I was able to take photos of the maps on his phone, and continue on.

The trail was not gentle, that's for sure. After a nice section along a stream, it turned straight up the hill through the pine trees. It was the steepest dirt trail I've ever walked up, I think. I was feeling quite tired, both physically and mentally. While I had been mentally in the game for 10 days straight, knowing this was probably my last day made me think a little more carefully about my goals. Most of all, I didn't want to hurt myself at the end of the race, when I was tired and not thinking clearly. My pack, which had felt like an extension of my back for quite a few days, was feeling very heavy again. The little toe on my right foot was really numb, which didn't hurt but just felt weird. Plus the ring finger on my right hand was numb too. Argh. So my steps were dragging up the hill, and I was drinking my first Coke in quite a few days. The caffeine didn't really help, and I sent Jim a text as I climbed, stating emphatically: "This. Is. My. Last. Hike. Up. A. Hill!"

Today would perhaps be my last day of the race. Gold (AUS2) was only 19 km behind me, having pushed across the Furka Pass yesterday evening. He hadn't as yet used his night pass, so I would need an extraordinary flight to get far enough ahead of him to avoid this last elimination. Due to injuries, athletes dropping out, and eliminations, I had moved from 30th place all the way up to 23rd place in the race. I had certainly accomplished all of my goals and then some. (Have I mentioned that my original goal of the race was not to be the first elimination?)

I had talked to my friend Chris Bamford the night before about strategy. Chris is a tandem pilot in Zermatt, so I figured he could give me some insight on how to fly into his home territory. I knew the crossing into the Zermatt valley would be tough, and Chris gave me some locations where I definitely didn't want to land out! Otherwise, staying high would be the key as usual, even for the first crossing over to Fiesch, which was a very popular paragliding launch.

The trail broke out of the woods, and finally I was up to a huge expanse of grassy meadow. It looked amazing. It was only about 9 am, potentially my flight could start really early today and I didn't want to let Gold get the jump on me. So I hiked quite a bit higher, getting above 2000 meters, which would get my flight off to a good start.

Gold was at about my elevation but further down the valley. We both (without ever communicating about it) sat down to wait for better conditions. I got ready to fly, covered myself with clothing and closed my eyes for a second. I think that second turned into about 30 minutes of napping, but I didn't miss too much. Or so I hoped. My iPhone had been sitting on my chest, and overheated. For a moment I was afraid that I had slept through Gold flying right by me. But no, it was still early.

Pilots, not in this competition, were launching from Fiesch already, and floating along at about my height without sinking out. Every so often one would come by me, but they were heading east with a tailwind and I needed to go west. Conditions had completely changed from yesterday's evening wind direction, and the top of lift needed to improve a lot to be able to fly west today.

At noon it was looking better. By complete coincidence, Gold and I launched within minutes of each other, but lift still wasn't that good. I top landed again higher to wait for a few minutes. My first crossing was very near and I needed altitude. Gold had been able to cruise low along the valley, and by the time I got in the air again, he was nearby. In fact, we were almost in the same thermal as conditions finally turned on for the day. I had spent quite a bit of time scratching and trying to get up along the edge of a large glacier, and then finally, we both climbed up to 3000 meters, and then 4000 meters.

The view from this valley, from 4000 meters, was amazing. I know I have said that about all of my flights, but this place in particular was spectacular. Behind me was the Aletsch glacier, the largest glacier in Europe, a stunning river of ice flowing down out of the high peaks. All around me were mountainous peaks that made 4000 meters seem like I wasn't very high at all. In the distance, I could finally see the Matterhorn (while it's iconic, it really isn't all that large compared to its neighbors), and even Mont Blanc in the distance.

So as Gold and I both climbed up sky high, I made the tough decision to let him go ahead. He had flown this area before and had a night pass. I couldn't see any way I was going to beat that. It was actually a relief to think that way, because it let me enjoy the flight and the scenery below me. Instead of pushing along the race, I went deeper over the glacier and took some photos, enjoyed the moments of my last flight in the Red Bull X-Alps.

Then I continued along the course, as I had my own goals regardless of whether I was now last in the race or not. I could see Gold ahead of me, and used some of his lines to show me where I needed to be going.   The wind was picking up now, and flying deep in the jagged peaks of the glaciers was beginning to make me nervous. By then it was time to cross the valley above the town of Visp. It was a big crossing, with the wind howling down in the valley. I let Gold go first, and saw him get quite low, but climb out again. By then I was crossing myself, and found that I was climbing in ridge lift, as the wind wrapped around from the main valley onto the ridge.

We were no longer getting as high as before, but I was tired and sore and wanted to keep pushing on. With a few meters over the ridge, I made the move into the Zermatt valley. It was just enough to turn the corner, but I didn't find much now that I was on the east side. Unbeknownst to me, Gold had crossed to the west side, which was now in shadow, and neither one of us was having much luck. I eventually found that I could Frisbee along using the ridge lift from the strong valley winds. Luckily no landing in the narrow valley was required!

The next time I saw Gold, I was passing him! Actually I thought he had been to the Matterhorn already, but that couldn't be. I continued to fly with my eyes on the prize, which was Zermatt.   The Turnpoint of the Matterhorn was a 5.5 km circle so I just needed to get close to it.   I had actually thought that the circle was somewhere in the town of Zermatt. When I got there, my Flymaster said 3.5km, which I thought was within the circle already and it just hadn't alarmed to tell me. Unfortunately, it really meant that I was still 3.5 km from the circle, which I didn't find out until I had already landed!

Bummer.   It would mean more walking to complete this turnpoint.

Chuck had been busy texting me updates about my race position and strategy, but unfortunately I didn't get them until hours after I landed. Guess my phone had chosen that time to act up for a while.

I had seen a few tandems flying down to the tiny little LZ in Zermatt, and I was mentally done in by that point anyway. I was like a horse coming home to the barn and all I could think about was getting on the ground finding my friends and supporters and enjoying a nice celebration dinner.   I found my tandem friend Phil after landing, and he broke the news that Turnpoint 7 was still a few km away at least, up the aptly named "Matterhorn Trail".   I took this in stride, and we agreed to meet for dinner after I had officially touched the Turnpoint circle.   Extra time would also allow my supporters to arrive on the train into town, as private vehicles weren't allowed in Zermatt, much less huge motorhomes.

Gold had flown over the turnpoint (like I could have if tunnel vision hadn't gotten in my way) and was now flying back down to the Rhone valley.   Ironically, the way the rules worked, the furthest person from Monaco gets eliminated. When Gold landed later, he was still further from the finish by a few kilometers than I was! He would have to walk a few hours of his night pass to get "ahead" of me officially, even though he was realistically further along the course than I was.

I was really happy to have landed safely for the last time in the race, and not at all sad that I chose to land early before it was necessary.   Temperatures in the Rhone valley were approaching 100 F that afternoon, and really the last thing I wanted to do was land in some random town to finish this race. The Red Bull X-Alps is a flagship race for the sport of paragliding, and I wanted to make my finish memorable for myself and for the race.   Finishing with Turnpoint 7 and celebrating in Zermatt was the perfect place.

But 5 km of trail was still standing between myself the moment where I could throw down my pack and finish in style. I know I didn't really NEED to tag the Turnpoint, but pride kept me walking along to this imaginary circle around the Matterhorn. The true hardship was that I was really hungry by then (I had napped through lunch) and didn't have any food or Swiss Francs. I should have bummed some off the tandem pilots, but didn't think to ask.

Anyway, those were the slowest few kilometers of the whole race, in my mind at least. Luckily the trail wasn't too steep, but I could still tell I was walking UP to the mountain. I called my mom for one last race update, then held my Flymaster in my hand until it ticked down to 0.00 and played the happy alarm to show I had made Turnpoint 7.

Jim had been walking up the trail behind me, and met me as I was heading back down to town. I was happy to see him and we were both excited to have made it through the race with no injuries or other problems! Chuck was waiting in town, and our first stop was for ice cream. Then we moved on to an Italian restaurant for my favorite meal, Pasta Carbonara. Finally Chris and Phil and their friends showed up, and we went to one of their favorite bars in Zermatt for a relaxing evening. I did my best to be lively and interesting, but I'm not sure if I was successful. More realistically, I was more tired than I had ever been and could only think of sleeping as soon as possible. At least I didn't fall asleep with my face in my Pina colada.

Their pictures of me that night looked pretty tough. I was sunburned, asleep on my feet, and walking very slowly. After a round of drinks, I had to go outside to give a phone interview, which ended up being a short video for the local station where my family lived in Iowa. Perhaps a drink loosened me up a little and I actually sounded ok? Either way, somehow we still made it back on the train to our motorhome, where we could sleep in just a little bit before driving down to Monaco for the awards ceremony coming up in just 48 hours.

Looking down at Aletsch Glacier

The Awards Ceremony

The race officially finished on Day 13 at noon. By then, 19 athletes had made it to the float in Monaco, 5 had quit or been injured, 5 had been eliminated, and 3 were left out on the course. By that evening, most of the athletes had congregated in Monaco for the final awards ceremony. It was a celebration that of all of us were safe and alive, and a chance to revel in our experiences and that of our supporters. It was also a great time to reconnect with other teams, many of which we hadn't seen since the gun went off in Salzburg.

So the 2015 Red Bull X-Alps was now in the record books. After dedicating so much time to training, preparing, and completing the race, tomorrow it would be time to return to normal life, even if many of the athletes were still limping! Fans all over the world would suddenly wonder what to do with their free time when not glued to live tracking. Athletes will think over their mistakes, and vow to come back better, stronger, and faster in the next edition.

After the awards dinner, (where athletes ate like we hadn't been fed in weeks), the announcements got underway. As each athlete was introduced (in reverse order of their finishing rank), the athletes and their supporters came forward to get their race flag and take a bow. Big cheers went up for Toma Coconea and Tom de Dorlodot, both of whom had been injured in the race. I'm sure they will be back stronger than ever in the next edition.

Perhaps this is an appropriate place to share a bit about my post-race recovery. In the days immediately following the race, I felt really good. Surprisingly good.

Post-Race Recovery

It wasn't until I finally got home to Utah a week after the race when I finally started feeling sore. This surprised me immensely, as such a delayed reaction wasn't really a typical recovery for me. Perhaps it was delayed because I had been traveling that whole week, driving to return the motorhome from Monaco to Germany, and enduring the overseas flights back to the States. Whatever the reason, I suddenly felt shooting pains down my hips and legs, which lasted almost a week. Massage helped a little bit, but time heals everything and eventually the pain receded. Within a few weeks of the race, I was back to running and mountain biking, and felt like I had recovered full strength within about a month.

Another recovery effect I often experience after an endurance event are crazy dreams about the event itself. A long adventure race is often said to be a whole lifetime lived within a few days. It's no wonder the mind doesn't have time to process all of it properly until later, given the physical exertion and lack of rest. During a race, I try hard not to think about what might go wrong. Perhaps you could call this repression, but I tend to believe that focusing on good outcomes is the way to avoid accidents. Whatever the reason, in my dreams I re-live the event, and each night the finish line gets closer and closer. But I also dream about all the things that could have gone wrong, too. I don't stop dreaming about it until finally my mind has worked through everything that happened and I reach the finish line.   I've come to accept these series of dreams as another interesting aspect of pushing myself to my physical and mental limits. The Red Bull X-Alps was no exception, and for a few weeks following the event, each night I dreamed of hiking and flying my way to Monaco, getting closer each time. Although this time, I only reached the finish line in my dreams, after only coming close in reality.

Possibilities...Could I have reached Monaco?

To be honest, I never thought I could arrive in Monaco. And it's hard to get somewhere you don't believe you can reach! So perhaps if I had believed in it more, I might have made it there. Perhaps not. But I do know that there are quite a few choices I could have made to help me further along the course.

My theory from the beginning was to learn the first half of the course really well. After all, it would be very hard to fly the second half of the course if I get eliminated in the first half! Aside from the fact that this turned out to be a very good weather year, in most cases, most of the athletes are happy to make it to France, much less the finish. Indeed, my training along the first sections of the course came in very handy. I knew where the launches were, where the best flying lines were, and the hiking trails between them. Specifically, I was able to make it to a main road for my night pass Day 3 because of the research and hiking I had done in that area. If I had needed to stop and study the maps, I might not have made the 9pm flight cutoff on my 3rd flight of the day. And in the Oetztal valley on Day 5, a previous flight helped me understand the valley winds, and prevented me from sinking out.

These are choices that helped me along the course. But what could have gotten me further in the race? Mostly, it was patience. Yes, it's a race, but it's a long race. Making a choice to go back and get a thermal behind me is worth it in the long run. Sticking with light lift rather than hoping to bumble into something is another.

What became difficult in the race during a long flight was maintaining my concentration. Even in the air, my hips and legs were aching, my feet were painful, and I found it hard to focus on flying. Perhaps I needed to eat and drink more in the air to retain my focus, but what I should have fought harder was complacency. My race goal was to not get eliminated, which is a lot different than wanting to finish in Monaco. If someone had told me that I HAD to reach Monaco before I could stop walking, then each kilometer would have counted a lot more! So I confess that after a good flight and a few hours in the air, mentally I would start thinking that I had done pretty well, and really, how far did I need to go today? Even the threat of walking after landing didn't bother me that much. Of course, such thinking is a good way to end up on the ground.

I also made choices to fly safely, which sometimes meant landing early. Especially in Merano, Italy, I was worried about high valley winds, and landed on Day 5 because I was worried about the North Foehn. Risking my life might have gotten me further, but it might have gotten me hurt too.

But there are other ways to fly further. Many teams, including Turner (USA4) and Villa (COL) had supporters who hiked up to launch with them to be wind dummies and fly with them along the course. Team flying is an easy way to go further and faster, yet my supporters were able to fly with me only twice.

Better supporter briefings en-route: Too many times in the air, I was wishing I had known where the other athletes had flown, to be able to take better lines. More than a few instances, it might have kept me in the air longer, and perhaps gotten me past some dangerous areas too. I was hampered in this with incomplete briefings by my supporter, and lack of internet access to check for myself. My supporter was certain to ask me after I landed why I hadn't flown a better line, but neglected to tell me before I launched what that line should be. It's hard to focus on the details when I'm tired after days of racing, but I should have been more proactive, to look at the route ahead of my big flying days.

One thing I don't think made any difference at all is gender. My average hiking speed was the same or only slightly lower than some of the men, yet the kilometers I covered on the ground were actually some of the highest by the middle of the race. But...the race is won or lost in the air. If I was a local pilot, and been flying longer, that raft in Monaco might have my footprints on it. Really, this is what I wanted to show the world, that **gender really isn't a factor** in a race like this. It's more about fitness, and knowledge, and the ability to make great decisions in dangerous conditions while flying tired.

My bottom line is that these thoughts on Monaco aren't regrets, only self-reflection. I am perfectly content with my race, and happy that I had a safe, enjoyable time along the route, without taking too many risks.

Over 11 days, I hiked 467 kilometers (290 miles). While hiking I gained 42,000 meters of vertical, which is the equivalent of climbing from sea level to the top of Mt. Everest almost 5 times. I flew 878 km (545 miles), which gave me lasting memories of some great flights over alpine scenery. I finished in 23rd place, successfully showing that I could stay ahead of many other competitors. I outlasted four eliminations, and only got caught by the fifth because of some unsportsmanlike race choices by another competitor.

My goals before the race were to:
Beat the other woman. I know it's silly but...CHECK
Beat one guy (or maybe eight!). CHECK
Not get eliminated first. CHECK
Not get eliminated at all. (Almost) CHECK
Make it to Switzerland. CHECK
Enjoy the experience. CHECK
Eat a lot of chocolate. CHECK
Stay safe. CHECK
Have fun. CHECK

Regardless of whether I compete again in later editions of the Red Bull X-Alps, I will remember this as a real highlight of my sporting career. Red Bull and Zooom put on an amazing race, and it was pretty cool to be interviewed, recorded, tracked live all over the world, and talked about. Beyond that, I just really appreciated the chance to compete in such a race. Thanks, Red Bull!

But wait...there's more! Following the main book is now a section written by my supporter Chuck Savall, who bent over backwards to make sure I always had what I needed during the race. His perspective is an interesting read. I also have a few more sections about the behind the scenes preparation and training for the race, if you are interested in doing anything like this yourself (or supporting someone else).

SPOTLIGHT: A Supporter's Perspective

"The Red Bull X-Alps from the Ground"
By Chuck Savall

I met Dawn in 2009 while paragliding in Iquique, Chile. She was the new kid on the block, and my first memory was of her doing some mild acrobatics above the Dragon Dune near Iquique. I asked someone who she was, and they told me Dawn was a brand new pilot who had only been flying several months, so I was impressed by her aggressiveness and bravery. Over the next several years, our paths would cross multiple times, as we both favored the same paragliding tour guides for Chile and Europe. We have now flown together in Chile, Slovenia, Utah, Italy, Austria, and Switzerland. We became pretty good friends by sharing some of these adventures, and I remained impressed by her tenaciousness in running, adventure racing and her approach to life.

As the Red Bull X-Alps 2015 was announced, I immediately thought about how qualified Dawn was to apply and compete. In the last few years she had become a stronger pilot as well as an accomplished adventure racer. I let her know I thought she should jump into the fray, and she told me that quite a few others felt the same way. Of course, Dawn went for it, but like many applicants, she probably soon regretted that decision! Once one realizes what they have gotten themselves into, the preparation and reality of this race can become quite daunting.

I had booked a paragliding tour through the South Tyrol for the spring of 2015, then realized that my trip would end about the time the Red Bull X-Alps 2015 was kicking off, so I thought I might stay longer to perhaps follow along as a spectator. But then I thought, why not offer Dawn any help that she might need, in whatever capacity I could? I hadn't flown the Alps enough to be of much technical help, but I figured an extra chase vehicle just might come in handy. With my airline pilot background, I also thought I could help out with the weather forecasts. As Dawn had never competed in the Red Bull X-Alps before, she wasn't sure what kind of help she would need, so we loosely agreed that I could tag along. I traveled up to Utah in March to sit down with Dawn and chat things through a bit, and also met her husband Jim, who I quickly found to be a kindred spirit. Dawn shared quite a bit of the logistical data she had already acquired, and we agreed to meet in Salzburg several days before the race start.

Before I left for Europe, Dawn and Jim asked me to help solve the problem they were having with Internet access challenges they were already facing during training in the Alps. They were pretty much restricted to Wi-Fi when they could find it, so their travels revolved around finding Internet access, which usually involved dragging their camper-van into a town, a hassle they were trying to avoid whenever possible. This Internet issue would become one of our biggest challenges during the race. I shipped some T-Mobile SIM cards for their phones to intercept them in Zermatt. These helped quite a bit, but still were not as fast as we are used to here in the States. Without a local European mobile account, high-speed cellular data usage was prohibitively expensive.

We also acquired some wireless hotspots shipped in from England, which added to the data flow. Interestingly for me, it also proved advantageous to have both Windows and IOS devices, as some apps ran better on one than the other. During the race, the Live Tracking was creepy-crawly slow and driving me nuts on my iPad, but when I switched it to my Windows laptop, voila, it worked a champ. More on this later, but I figure our Internet data and phone costs came to well over $3000 for the race, and that was for lousy service.

Our paths crossed once again in Italy prior to the race, where we shared some flying near Sand-in-Taufers, Italy from the Speikboden launch. We made a few more plans, then I traveled through Lake Garda, Slovenia and Czech Republic before meeting them near the Dachstein in Austria. We spent a day scouting the top of the Dachstein area, and also found a Via Ferrata to play around on. Dawn enjoyed the many Via Ferratas as a diversion from flying, as well as a way to stay in shape for the race!

About a week before the Red Bull X-Alps, I arrived at the Red Bull Athletes Camp outside Salzburg, just across the street from Red Bull's world headquarters. Things were still pretty quiet, but the camp soon began filling up with not only the Athletes and their supporters, but many fans that became squatters in the camp. I was surprised that race organizers didn't have a better handle on things here, and the place soon became overrun with people, vehicles, and garbage. We quickly exceeded the capacity of the facilities.

The town of Fuschl on Lake Fuschlsee is lovely, this was our home leading up to the race. It was interesting to see the human / team dynamics coming together for the varying athletes' teams. There were some obviously well-prepared groups, but there were also some that seemed cobbled together at the last minute. There was a surprising amount of dissent and tension amongst several teams. The tight living quarters didn't help, and I looked forward to seeing which of the teams would do well in the race, just based on how I saw them interacting during this lead-in week.

Not knowing what my actual daily role would be in the race, as we had left some of this open until we were at the camp and could better determine what our priorities would be, I had over-equipped myself as much as possible. I rented a van large enough to sleep in, and brought every laptop, iPad, cell-phone, data source and tech device I could fit in my luggage. This would turn out to serve me well, but the challenge was keeping everything charged up and online. During the race, we were constantly striving to keep all the devices running and the info flowing. We would soon learn that information is one of the keys to doing well. You need to be able to monitor the race progress through Red Bull's Live Tracking website, (a HUGE data hog), check multiple weather sources, monitor forbidden airspace, follow the race route as well as navigate the roads that access it, communicate with the rest of the team, monitor their locations as well as the athletes, not to mention get your daily Facebook / email / race website fix. Red Bull did supply each team with a mobile hotspot, but it did not have nearly enough data capacity for all of our needs. Our team ended up with multiple mobile phones with separate data plans, about 3 laptops, a half dozen iPads, 4 mobile hotspots, several DC to AC inverters, a large portable backup power source, and it still wasn't enough information or power. We all had to learn how long we could drain our vehicle's batteries before we had to run the engine to recharge everything. The last thing any of us wanted during the race was to wake up to a dead battery!

This year Red Bull added a "Prologue" race 2 days before the start of the actual race. I have to take a moment to give my opinion on this. First of all, the last thing any athlete wants two days before the start of a two week long balls-to-the-wall endurance event is a "warm-up" race. It does not fit into their training regimen at all. Next, it made the actual race completely unfair. The top three finishers in the Prologue were rewarded both a five minute head start in the actual race, as well as an additional night-pass. This means those three racers were allowed an extra six hours or more of racing time during the race. To me, it makes no sense to give the three athletes that are already the fastest and most skilled (which they demonstrated in the Prologue), both a head-start and extra racing time. It assured them a huge advantage. If you're going to give anyone a head-start, shouldn't it be the less strong competitors? If you must, give the Prologue winners a cash prize or some other reward, but not an unfair advantage against the other athletes. For many racers, the Red Bull X-Alps is the event of their lives, and I know they all expected a level playing field, which they didn't get.   Anyway, the Prologue did give us a chance to test equipment and strategies, although it was a brutally hot day and certainly took its toll on some racers. It did make the race sponsors happy, as well as attracting a crowd of spectators, giving fans a chance to get closer to the actual racing.

Red Bull loaded up the athletes with about 5 lbs. each of technical gear that allowed everyone to track and video the race. The athletes had to go through days of training and practicing with this gear, just to get it all sorted before the race. A couple days before the Prologue, the racers realized all of the communication equipment was based on mobile coverage, and there was no device that would allow a racer to communicate their location if they were outside of cell coverage. So on top of all the weight the athletes were required to carry, they each had to also supply their own personal GPS rescue device (SPOT or Delorme). There was a LOT of protesting going on in race camp about this. Dawn chose to not fly with VHF comm radios, as was common with most teams to save weight. I know this might seem odd to most paraglider pilots who usually fly with radios, but in reality, there would have been very few times radios would have worked during the race. Cell phones it is, or nothing at all, unless you drag your own satellite device along too.

By the time the race started, we had our support team duties pretty much sorted out. We planned to leap-frog our chase vehicles so that someone would always be near Dawn when she landed to re-fuel and re-equip her. Support team members are allowed to carry pretty much anything the athlete needs, except the equipment required by the race rules. So, extra food, water, clothing, climbing equipment, batteries, spare shoes, can all be shuttled by vehicle or on foot by the supporters. When athletes land after a flight, it becomes a race-car like pit-stop. Extra clothes stripped off, food and water replenished, shoes swapped out, a quick look at the maps or live flight tracking, grab the hiking poles and off they go. If you can rendezvous with them again before their next flight, then you can help keep their walking weight down, otherwise they have to carry enough extra gear for whatever hiking / climbing they have ahead of them, then also warm clothing for the next flight.

So obviously, the closer the support team can stay to their athlete, the easier their lives are and the more competitive they can be.   Jim was driving a large camper-van (large by European standards anyway, and something I was glad to not have to maneuver on twisty roads), so most days he was bringing up the rear. I ended up being point man because my vehicle was faster up the hills. Jim would get Dawn up early, feed and water her, jokingly tell her to get her lazy butt in gear, then kick her out into the cold morning. I could sleep-in a bit, then blast off to catch up with wherever Dawn had told us would be her next pit-stop. By the time I had rendezvoused with Dawn, Jim had broken camp and caught up with us, then we began the leap-frog.

Someone always had to stop to re-supply groceries, etc., which brought up one of our other challenges – finding ice. We Americans are used to being able to get ice pretty much at any gas station or grocery. Not so in Europe. We all had coolers in our vehicles, planning on stocking up and keeping stuff cold, but that never happened.   Therefore, we had to shop pretty much every day, which became a horribly inconvenient and time-wasting chore. If I were to do this again, I would find a small 12-volt portable fridge, but then that adds to the electrical charging supply challenge.

My personal goal was to always be within a 5 minutes or so of where Dawn landed, often I would pull up as she was still packing her gear. Between the Live Tracking and a free iPhone app that we used, "Friend Finder," we could keep pretty close tabs on real-time location. The Friend Finder app would also give turn-by-turn directions right to Dawn's location, and we could all keep track of each other as well. I spent a lot of time racing screen icons across Europe. This of course only worked when we had adequate mobile data coverage.   Problem in

Europe is when you get close to country borders, the cell coverage becomes spotty or non-existent as they don't overlap coverage, and much of the first half of the race was right along the borders between Austria, Germany, Switzerland, Italy and France. The high mountains block a lot of coverage as well. I got extremely frustrated at the times when I had no way to figure where Dawn was, often having to result to dead-reckoning and guessing which valley system she had chosen to fly. Luckily, there weren't too many times we couldn't give her good ground support, but I know the times we misconnected were pretty tough on her physically as well as for morale. Damned race is hard enough without all the glitches that pop up. I can't imagine how hard this race was before the technology we have today!

Dawn had what I consider amazing map-reading skills. She was able to see things on her relatively small cell-phone screen that I couldn't begin to see on a full-sized laptop or paper map. Pre-flying the route had to help considerably with this. She was working, planning and communicating constantly on her phone, whether she was walking, climbing, resting or even flying. I would get texts from her while she was in the air, frozen fingers and all, but she would only ask for help when there just wasn't information available to her on her own.

A supporter also has to be good at multi-tasking. These European twisty mountain roads are no place for distracted drivers, so when the workload started to get high, I just had to pull off the road and plan my next move while wasting as little time as possible. For me, much of the race was a high-speed drive through gorgeous scenery that I barely had time to look at. Most of the photos I took were out the side window of my quickly moving van. It's actually pretty rare that you will have your athlete in sight, so you rely heavily on all the tech and tracking. The times you can see the wings in the air can be quite exciting, especially when there is close racing going on. At least then you can stop looking at data screens and actually enjoy the pure thrill of the race right in front of your eyes.

Fortunately for me, I absolutely love driving, the more challenging the better.

Choosing and organizing a support team is a huge part of this race. From what I saw, just one supporter is probably not enough for most teams. If both the athlete and supporter live in the Alps, and fly them often enough to know them extremely well, then maybe one supporter is enough. Those teams don't have to think as much about where to fly, because they are already flying in their backyards. They already know the local weather and wind patterns, they are flying their home sites, and that knowledge is invaluable. Even so, just one supporter will be pushing his physical limits almost as much as the Athlete; with sleep deprivation, driving tired, mental anguish, and just plain exhaustion, all of which can affect decision making and performance. I heard several stories of sole supporters bonking while they were driving, and that is part of the reason the race only allows one all-nighter during the race for most teams now.

If your team isn't intimately familiar with the Alps, including which valley is favored on any given day, where the next camp spot will be, how the valley winds flow (and when), what is the Foehn up to today, where the next launch is and the easiest way to get there, how to strategize each and every move; then one supporter just isn't enough to be competitive. It also helps considerably to have two vehicles, one vehicle with a driver and another non-driver dedicated to weather, logistics and race tracking, the second vehicle to leap-frog with the athlete, one vehicle out front of the athlete awaiting their landing, the other behind if they need to backtrack or change route. With more than one support person, two vehicles can also make sleeping arrangements less confining, so everyone gets better rest. A second supporter also allows the ability to use wind-dummies more efficiently, if at all.

We had Jim helping take care of Dawn physically and mentally, shopping, cooking, finding camp locations, foot

massages, running checklists, tucking her in and waking her
up. For part of the race we had Jarek working mostly on
strategic planning and weather, pretty much glued to a laptop
day and night. For a while we also had Boga helping Jim out
with shopping and cooking. My job was to keep Dawn moving
at every transition between ground and air, and keep her
supplied with chocolate cake and pineapple juice. Even
splitting all the work, we put in long days, basically pre-dawn
to midnight. I never felt exhausted, but I'm accustomed to
only a few hours of sleep a night anyway. I do know that the
teams with small support groups all looked to be in pretty
rough shape as the race wore on.

Our team had its own personal challenges. Mostly, Jarek
thought he would basically be in charge of all the decision
making when it came to route planning and decisions, on
when and where Dawn should fly. Well, it just doesn't work
that way. The athlete is the ultimate decision maker, like the
quarterback of the team or the captain of the ship. The
supporters are there to supply the athlete with as much
information and advice as possible to help them make good
decisions, but ultimately, the final decisions are made by the
athlete. This doesn't mean they will always make the best
decision, as fatigue can often overwhelm their thinking
process, but it is their race to call. When your supporter tells
you that you will walk up a certain mountain at a certain time
in a certain way, and you tell him that you're too tired and
need to call it a day, or that your legs can't handle a steep
climb and that you would rather make a longer flat walk
knowing you will be faster that way, and he stomps off and
pitches a fit – well, that is a problem. As the race neared
completion, roles had to change to keep things civil, our main
supporter departed company and I had to take over his role as
the tech / weather guy. By now I had the weather sites dialed
in, but not much would change our race philosophy at this
point. This is why it seemed important for a race team to
spend enough time together, in adverse conditions if possible,
and well before a race of this sort, so they see if they can

endure and work together when the going gets tough.

We witnessed several teams fall apart, some that started as friends finished the race in discord. This type of event is as much mental as physical. These athletes push themselves harder than almost anyone can imagine. They get enormously frustrated by mistakes, both their own and those of others. Individual goals of supporters need to take a back seat to those of the athlete, as it is the athlete that ultimately has to cross the finish line. However, without the supporter, no athlete would finish. It's a fine balance of teamwork we must all strive for and achieve, to be successful in such a grueling race.

In fact, there were several teams in which the supporter was actually a better and more experienced pilot than the athlete. As much as those supporters would have loved to be competing, they chose not to, perhaps because they knew the physical demands would overwhelm their personal abilities, usually due to age or past injuries, or they didn't have the time to devote to the necessary training. Those teams faced their own challenges, when the athlete and the supporter disagreed on the plan, or the athlete just wasn't able to execute what the supporter knew to be possible under the conditions of the day. All of these human dynamics provided entertainment during the race, as on several occasions we would share overnight camp areas, allowing us to get a look at what was going on with other teams.

Dawn achieved considerably more than she set out to in this race. I was actually a bit surprised when before the race she shared that all she expected and hoped for was to not get eliminated in the first few days. But as she soldiered on, the expectations rose, first becoming to finish in front of some of the men, then to not get eliminated at all, then to make it to Zermatt or possibly beyond. We actually got so far beyond what we expected, that we had to go out scrounging for more maps. If not for another athlete deciding to drop out when he was only hours from being eliminated, she would have accomplished all those things. Almost all of her flights were personal bests, each day exceeding the last. She flew in an environment that was mostly foreign to her. She got spanked soundly on several occasions, but kept flying, smiling and enduring.

Some things I learned about Dawn were surprising to me during the race. As an endurance and adventure runner, she was very in tune with her physiological needs, and how to prepare for such an event. However, both Jim and I were surprised at how little she ate, compared to our perceived caloric demands of the race. She ended up getting cravings for things that helped her keep going. Finding chocolate cake was part of my daily routine, if it had cherries in it, even better, as well as pineapple juice, she went through several liters a day of the stuff, just quick and natural sugar-based energy. Her body seemed to be telling her exactly what it needed.

It was also interesting for me to read, after the race, in her rough draft of this book, where she revealed that she had some strong emotional ups and downs during the race as well as considerable physical pain. Of course, I imagined that anyone pushing themselves that hard would go through this, but even as she was, I never saw it. All I ever saw was her smiling like she was having the time of her life. Of course, there are those people that seem to laugh their way through pain and suffering. I'm not one of them.

Dawn got amazing support from her husband Jim. They both thrive on playful and sarcastic banter, but neither of them cuts the other much slack. He was also justifiably concerned about keeping her safe during the race, and I think this helped her avoid making some otherwise risky decisions. Jim was generously supportive of our entire crew, managing a big crew as well as keeping Dawn on the road.

Here are some of my personal observations from an American travelling in the Alps. This was not my first visit, but these are some of the reasons I love going back again and again. Europeans actually LIVE in their mountains, high up in places that we Americans would consider just too harsh and inaccessible. There are ski hills EVERYWHERE, most of them friendly year-round to paragliders as well. The mountains are accessible, in so many ways, there aren't many places you can't get to via a cable-car or lift, or a short hike from a road. Europeans know how to drive courteously and their roads are sporty and fun. They are actually helpful to tourists. Their ski hills double as pastures, cows are everywhere. Their hay pastures we would call black-diamond ski runs, many so steep the only way to harvest them is by hand. They have lovely lakes. The rivers run clean and pure. They plant flowers everywhere, even their cow pastures are fields of flowers. They all seem to drive BMWs, Porsches, Audis and Mercedes, cars we Americans consider exotic. Ice cream is EVERYWHERE, and it's amazing.

What I didn't like about travelling in the Alps was that ice was pretty much impossible to find, Internet data was prohibitively expensive for foreigners, they spray recycled liquid cow-shit in the air over their fields (on a windy day you can expect to get your car doused in the stuff), and the early morning church bells (apparently no one in the countryside is allowed to sleep in, ever). As they say, to travel – one must suffer ;-)

We finished the race officially in Zermatt on Day 11, but then drove down to Monaco for the awards ceremony. Of course, my vehicle's air-conditioning decided to give out, just as the temperatures decided to peak at 104°F, so I was not a happy camper anymore. Red Bull threw a nice party for the athletes, and it was fun to hear some of the crazy stories from the other teams. Many of the athletes were quite affected physically, barely able to walk, weak looking, beyond exhausted, and extremely happy to be finished with all the suffering, and to have achieved so much personally. Again, I was a bit miffed that Red Bull didn't spring for a nice well-deserved hotel room for the teams for the night of the awards, instead bussing us all to another hot and crowded campground. Oh well.

Personally, I thoroughly enjoyed almost every minute and aspect of the race. It was exciting, adventurous, gorgeous, challenging, educational and entertaining. We ended up in some absolutely amazing places, camped in deserted high mountains, saw stunning scenery, friendly people, great camaraderie, and felt part of something bigger. I discovered so many places that I need to get back to fly, without the pressure of having to keep moving. I would happily do the race again, but only with the right team under the right circumstance. It truly is one of the world's toughest and most adventurous competitions. I have to sincerely thank Dawn and Jim for allowing me to be part of their experience.

Below are some thoughts I have after participating in the Red Bull X-Alps.

Athletes:
- If you think the race will be hard, the race will be harder than you think.
- Train downhill – several athletes were doing fairly well until the first time they couldn't launch and had to hike downhill with all their gear. It rendered their legs and feet useless afterwards. I also heard this advice from some previous competitors. Most do a lot of hike-ups and fly during their training, but they never realize how important developing the muscles for down-hiking can be.
- Choose your team carefully, I would not recommend spouses, girl/boy-friends, relatives, or friends you aren't willing to risk losing.
- Give supporters well-defined roles as far in advance as possible.
- Pre-fly – pre-fly – pre-fly. If you haven't pre-flown the entire route 2 or 3 times and in several different manners and weather conditions, you will probably not be competitive.

- You don't have to win for this race to be a complete personal success, just entering and getting as far down the course as possible is amazing in its own right.

Supporters
- Make it fun for both yourself and your athlete.
- Plan WAY ahead.
- Sort out the technical and communication challenges before you leave your home country.
- Europe isn't America – don't expect to find many things you are used to finding easily in the US or your home country. Large shopping malls are few and far between, mostly only found in major cities. Once on the race route, you will not find much of anything outside of the larger grocery stores.
- Scout possible camping spots, places to shower, places to re-supply, roadside pull-outs, launches, landings, routes, valleys, ridges. More is better.
- Be adaptable and flexible.
- Pre-fly – pre-fly – pre-fly. Accompany your Athlete if possible during their route pre-fly.
- Enjoy the adventure.

Section 2: TRAINING AND PREPARATION

Applying to Enter the Red Bull X-Alps

Some people might say the most difficult part of the Red Bull X-Alps is making it through the selection process. Online applications are accepted about a year before the actual race, and selections are made nine months ahead of the starting gun. So it's a nail-biting process without a whole lot of guidance about what race officials are looking for. While only thirty-three applications are ultimately selected, as many as several hundred paraglider pilots and endurance athletes apply for each edition.

On the advice of former athletes and other pilots, along with my application, I requested several letters of recommendation from well-known paraglider pilots. I don't know if these were necessary, but I did get in, so perhaps they didn't hurt! I guess on some level, it may come down to who you know. After all, this race is elite both for the paragliding experience and the physical challenge, and it is possible to be perfectly qualified in both, but without a lot of hard facts to put on paper.

In October 2014 the athlete selections were revealed to the world, and to us. I had yo-yoed back and forth after I had applied from "They will never choose me" to "How could they turn me down, a qualified woman when they obviously haven't had any for years!". I have to admit I was on pins and needles waiting for that email. It came one morning as I was waking up for another day of driving the tractor on my family farm, during harvest season in Iowa. Talk about a world away from paragliding in Europe! The email said, "Congratulations, you have been selected for the 2015 Red Bull X-Alps!" My first words to Jim were, "Oh, S%#!"

Getting selected was really a mixed blessing. On one hand, I had wanted to do this race for a very long time. For me it was an ultimate challenge. On the flip side, I knew how much work and expense it was going to take to prepare properly for a race of this caliber.

Dawn Westrum 2015 Red Bull X-Alps Race Application

Red Bull: When and why did you begin paragliding?
Dawn Westrum: I first saw paragliders in Switzerland when I was in the US Army stationed in Germany. I knew I wanted to fly someday, and soon took a tandem flight in Norway where I was hooked! It wasn't until I got out of the Army that I had a chance to learn to paraglide in Colombia. This was in 2009 and since then I have been flying every chance I can get.

RB: Do you paraglide competitively? List rankings and events.
DW: I have flown in two competitions. I've wanted to do more but there aren't many chances in the States. I enjoy competing and want to test myself against other pilots. So far I have mostly concentrated on XC flying, in Chile, Colombia, the Alps, and in the Wasatch Range of Utah. I have had two articles published in the US Hang Gliding and Paragliding (USHPA) magazine. One is in the February 2014 issue about a long flight in Iquique, Chile. The second one is in the August 2014 issue, about XC valley flying in Roldanillo, Colombia. I spent 6 weeks in Colombia this spring focusing on solo XC flying. Rat Race Sprint 2013, I finished 3rd woman USA Open Distance Nationals 2013 in Salt Lake City, Utah. I am ranked the 18th woman on XContest (as of 8 Aug 2014). I am planning to do more competitions this winter in South America, and next year in Europe. If I am accepted into the Red Bull X-Alps, I will move to Europe early in the year and make it a priority to enter some competitions there as well as learn the course.

RB: What is your mountaineering experience? (Please give details of any claims and state clearly if an attempt or summit).
DW: I have climbed to 6,000 meters on Huayna Potosi

summit in Bolivia. Details are here http://hikerdawn.blogspot.co.at/2009/05/huayna-potosi-summit-bolivia-19975-feet.html
I have completed Via Ferrata (Klettersteig) routes 8 countries, including France, Spain, Slovenia, Austria, Switzerland, UK, Scotland, and Italy. More info is here: http://hikerdawn.blogspot.co.at/search/label/Via Ferrata
My highest elevation on a backpacking trip was in Peru, where I crossed a 4,870 meter pass on the Santa Cruz Trek. http://hikerdawn.blogspot.co.at/search/label/Peru
I have also spent 3 weeks on a NOLS (National Outdoor Leadership School) backpacking class in Montana, USA. There we crossed over high passes and lots of snow, and learned how to self-arrest on a glacier and safely cross snowfields. http://hikerdawn.blogspot.co.at/2013/08/nols-backpacking-expedition-beartooth.html
I have been climbing both indoors and outdoors for 20 years. I am qualified in both sport and lead climbing. I am certified as a Wilderness Emergency Medical Technician (WEMT) in 2013 by the National Outdoor Leadership School (NOLS) I learned orienteering and map reading in the US Army and have been navigating my way around the world ever since. I love maps, and by using them, I always know where I am and where I am going.

RB: What is your paragliding experience?
DW: I have been paragliding for 6 years in 10 different countries, including USA, Colombia, Chile, UK, Spain, Italy, Slovenia, Austria, Switzerland, and Turkey I have about 340 hours of airtime and 1100 flights. I have extensive experience with side hill and top landings, and I am confident that I can land anywhere I need to. I estimate I have top or side hill landed at least 700 times. I have done both hike and fly and vol biv paragliding, and I have the lightweight gear and the location (Utah Wasatch mountains) to make it easy to practice. I have completed SIV courses in Utah and in Turkey. I have my T-1 rating and I am working on getting my tandem

certification. I have trained under some of the pioneers in the sport of paragliding, including Ken Hudonjorgensen and Rob Sporrer.

RB: What is your adventure racing / endurance sport experience?
DW: My biggest adventure race so far has been the 2012 Adidas Terrex Expedition Adventure Race in Scotland. It was 5 days and 500 kilometers and included running, trekking, canoeing, canyoneering, via ferrata, and mountain biking. My teammates and I were able to work well together, stay uninjured, and we finished 10th overall! http://hikerdawn.blogspot.com/2012/09/adidas-terrex-sting-adventure-race-part.html
My biggest stage race was across England, where we spent 4 days racing over mountains including running, kayaking, swimming and mountain biking. I finished 3rd in the women's division. http://hikerdawn.blogspot.co.at/2011/08/adidas-terrex-coast-to-coast-adventure.html
The longest non-stop race I completed was 100 miles across Wales and England. http://hikerdawn.blogspot.co.at/2011/05/housman-hundred-101-mi-28-29-may-2011.html
I have completed 2 Ironman Triathlons, and over 60 marathons and Ultramarathons. I estimate that I have competed in 500 races and events, which include Adventure Racing, Ironman, Triathlon, Ultra Running, Mountain Marathons, Orienteering, Stage Races, and Volksmarches.

RB: What does your typical training week consist of?
DW: I don't think that training for ultra-running is anything typical, but I try to keep a good mix of activities in my weekly routine. Depending on what I am training for, I include running, trekking, swimming, rock climbing, strength workouts, and bicycling. I am working with a personal trainer to help me train specifically for the uphill hiking, strength and endurance I will need for this length of race. I have kept track of all my workouts since 2004, and I average about 600 hours

of training time and several thousand miles a year. It is hard to break it down further than that because some weeks are really intensive and some are for recovery. On a hard week, I typically do a hike and fly up to my local takeoff, go skiing or bike riding depending on the time of year, climb at the indoor climbing wall near my house, and run a marathon or ultra-marathon on the weekend. This can be between 15-20 hours of exercise. I live just a few miles from the Point of the Mountain paragliding site in Utah, so I am able to hike up to launch, and then either fly home or hike back depending on conditions. I will plan doing this several times a week for X-Alps training. I am also able to hike up to an XC launch in the Wasatch mountains from my house so I have the terrain available that will help me for this race.

RB: What are your best and worst adventure/flying moments?

DW: My worst moment in racing was at mile 76 of my 100-mile run. I kept telling myself that I had gone 3 marathons already.... but my mind kept reminding me that I still had one left! My legs hurt and it was cold and windy on a hilltop in Wales, and I must admit that I might have bawled my eyes out! Luckily another competitor came along to cheer me up, we had some food at a rest stop, and we spent the next 24 miles walking and talking and the time and the miles passed by quickly, believe it or not. It's a reminder to me that mood can get better just by eating, drinking, and talking to someone. To qualify for the 100-mile race, I had to run a long qualifying race and there were only a few near me that were available in England. The race I chose used a very interesting style of map, but at the start I was not looking at it and only following other racers. In fact I was distracted by talking to another runner! After a while we realized that there were less racers around us and we were lost, really lost. By the time we got back on the course, we had gone TEN miles out of our way extra, on a 50-mile race. This was very early in the race and the first checkpoint had almost closed before I arrived. I knew I had to finish this race to qualify for the 100 mile I wanted to enter, so

I kept going even though I had already run an extra 10 miles. I was the very last person for a while and then started catching up to a few people, then more. I was determined to finish and by the end I was famous at all the checkpoints because I was still running when everyone around me was walking. I did learn how to read the special maps but realized that following other people was never a good idea! So I guess my worst moment turned into a really good day after I determined to finish no matter what!

http://hikerdawn.blogspot.com/2010/10/rowbothham-round-rotherham-50-mi-60-mi.html

My best moment was my long flight in Chile I wrote about for the USHPA magazine. We had a really rough flight on the high cliffs above the Pacific Ocean, wondering if we could battle the winds far enough to make it all the way. The final turn is sometimes the roughest, but when we came around and we could see the city of Iquique, the winds were calm and we had an amazing high glide over the ocean to land on the beach in front of our hotel. I really value the idea of either leaving from my house or returning to it, on foot or bike or paraglider or whatever I am doing at the time. Human power rather than vehicle power, I guess you could say. So to be able to get all the way back to the hotel that day was really satisfying, and is a reminder of how cool it is to be able to fly like a bird, over land and even water!

http://hikerdawn.blogspot.com/2013/11/iquique-chile-paragliding-tour.html

RB: What are the sporting moments you are most proud of?
DW: When I was in the US Army in 2004, I was in good shape but hadn't really gotten into racing or long distances yet. In fact I hadn't ever run longer than 6 miles! My coworker asked me if I wanted to run a marathon. I blinked and said sure, when? He said this weekend (4 days from that day)! I still agreed, and finished my first marathon with absolutely no training! It was at that moment, I realized that I could do anything I wanted if I worked at it hard enough. Since then I

have just kept trying longer and longer races, and still haven't found my true limits. I am most proud of the fact that I have finished every race that I have started. I have never been injured and have been able to keep myself injury free through rain, wind, snow, and other extreme conditions. I lived in England for 3 years, and raced most weekends through lots of wet and mud and wind. Through it all I rarely had a blister and my feet stayed in great shape. I have been featured in a video about women pilots, which won the 2014 award for best Paragliding video at the NorCal Free Flight Film Festival http://we-are-pilots.com/two-part1/

RB: When and how did you first hear about the Red Bull X-Alps?
DW: Since the first moments I started paragliding, people started telling me that the Red Bull X-Alps would be the perfect race for me. I set my sights on it early as the perfect challenge for me to combine my two favorite sports!

RB: Have you competed in the Red Bull X-Alps before and if so, when?
DW: No

RB: What appeals to you about the Red Bull X-Alps?
DW: I have always been the type of person to aspire to do the hardest challenge I can find. This race is the ultimate challenge I can think of which plays to all of my strengths. I love maps and choosing new hiking trails and XC routes. I dance to the beat of a different drummer, as they say, and rarely can anyone I meet keep up with me either on the ground or in the air. Competing on this level would be a true test of my skills. I also want to prove that women can be competitive on a race of this length. I think that paragliding and long distance trekking are two of the few sports where men and women can compete almost equally. I believe that women can have as good or better endurance than men over long distances. Women have been breaking records in almost everything in the last 20 years, and I think this is a chance for me to show that

paragliding is a sport where they have an equal chance at being great. I want to show women everywhere that they are capable of doing more than they could ever believe, and that nothing will stop them except their own mind's limitations!

RB: What will be your strategy during the race?
DW: My strategy for the race will be to rely on my own judgment and decision-making. I have learned many times in the past that relying on other racers to make the decisions for me can lead to getting lost and not taking the best route. I will do a lot of pre-planning on the route and will try to hike and fly as much of the distance as I can before the race so I can make better decisions during the competition. I believe that my decision making skills are usually very good, and to help with that, obviously I will try to stay healthy, hydrated, well-fed and rested during the race, so that my brain functions on a high level and I can get as far as possible. This will help me make safe choices about when and where to fly, and when to stay on the ground.

RB: On average, over a third of the Red Bull X-Alps participants fail to finish the event. Why do you think you will make it?
DW: I have never failed to finish a race. Part of the appeal of racing to me is pushing my boundaries. I have continued to compete in longer and longer races and have never found one that I couldn't complete. I'm always looking for a new challenge and the Red Bull X-Alps race includes all my favorite activities, including planning, strategy, navigation, paragliding, and trekking. I feel like all of my outdoor experiences in my whole life have been leading up to this race.

RB: What scares you the most about the event?
DW: Obviously the whole race is scary! We will be out racing in conditions where pilots normally would be sitting in at home glad they are out of the elements. It will be hard to safely practice this, as no conditions are the same especially because the course is so long. However, what I like most about this race

is that I have my own choices about when to fly, so I will be able to make safe decisions for myself about the conditions.

RB: Have you ever done anything of this magnitude before?
DW: Yes. I believe the 2012 Adidas Terrex Expedition Race was comparable in terms of the training and preparation required before the race. We spent almost a year accumulating the gear we would need for 4 team members, including bikes, canoes, dry suits, harnesses, multiple sets of dry clothes, packs, food, etc. During that 5 day race, I got only 1 hour of sleep the first three nights, and still continued to race the entire 4th day while trekking 40 miles across the Scottish mountains. We did get some sleep on the 4th night! Of course the Red Bull X-Alps would be about twice as long as my expedition in Scotland. But I believe that preparation would be the same process. Step by step, getting gear and maps, breaking the race down into sections, conferring with my supporters. That is what I am best at and I look forward to the challenge. I'm dreaming about it already, actually!

Could I be healthy enough to race?

I was diagnosed early in life with Von Willebrand's disease. This is a hereditary disease with abnormal blood coagulation, resulting in prolonged bleeding after an injury. With a family history of this disease, my parents knew to check for it early on, and I got the short straw among my siblings. Having Von Willebrand's disease means that my blood doesn't clot very well, I bruise easily, I get a lot of nosebleeds, and surgical procedures can be very problematic. The disease was first described in 1926, but not understood until much later. I'm sure if I had been born a couple hundred years ago, I would have been a sickly pale child who never seemed to have any energy.

With increased blood loss because of Von Willebrand's Disease, especially after puberty, came a higher chance of developing iron-deficiency anemia. Statistics show that as many as 40% of all women are anemic in the USA, many of them undiagnosed. Someone with anemia might feel uncharacteristically tired, may look pale, and could have an abnormally high heart rate during exercise. I struggled with anemia throughout my teenage years, and even needed a blood transfusion as a soldier in the US Army, when my hemoglobin (G/DL) levels dropped as low as 4! (Normal is 12 to 15.5 G/DL). The difficulty in diagnosing anemia is that it comes on very slowly, after weeks or even months of slow decline in the quality and quantity of red blood cells. It's slow enough that at times during my life, I've just thought that I was getting older, and no longer able to run as quickly. That's rather an absurd thing to think in my 20s! So it's really not the Von Willibrands that limits my physical abilities, but the side effect of anemia, which at times has kept me from performing at my best.

I have tried virtually every natural diet possible, those full of iron-rich foods and healthy vegetables, but nothing has worked consistently. The unfortunate combination of Von

Willebrands and long distance running is a one-two punch. Surprisingly, the motion of running itself is tough on the blood! Pounding on hard surfaces such as blacktop or concrete can burst blood vessels in the feet from the force of impact. Not to mention that going for hours or days on end uses up a lot of vitamins and minerals in the body. After a lot of research, I've concluded that taking daily iron supplements is the only way for me to stay healthy. You can bet that for the last month before the Red Bull X-Alps I was very careful to take my iron, to avoid running on hard surfaces, and to do everything I could to be as healthy as possible!

I also think that my body's inability to produce healthy red blood cells has an effect on my VO_2 max. VO_2 Max is defined as the maximum amount of oxygen the body can use during a specified period of intense exercise. It is dependent on body weight and the strength of the lungs. Endurance in any sport is due to the lungs ability to deliver oxygen to the blood, and the heart's ability to pump it to the muscles. Less red blood cells mean less total oxygen to the muscles, which inhibits speed.

Ironically, it was anemia that got me interested in long distance sports. After getting a blood transfusion in the Army, I was suddenly raring to go! I had spent almost a year feeling weaker than normal and very pale, and couldn't understand why. So it was a relief to finally understand the disease and the side effects, and learn what I could do to mitigate the issues. Plus, I wanted to make use of all the energy I suddenly felt! So I did my research, began exercising more diligently, and signed up for an Olympic Triathlon. This eventually progressed to marathons, ultra-marathons, Ironman triathlons, and paragliding. The rest is history.

The other danger of Von Willebrand's Disease is that my blood doesn't clot as quickly as normal, and sometimes not at all. While I do pursue high-risk sports such as mountain biking and paragliding, I realize that if I were to have a serious accident out in the mountains, such as breaking my pelvis or femur, I probably wouldn't make it alive to the operating table.

Knowing this extra risk has made me take fewer chances in my activities. I knew that during the Red Bull X-Alps I might have to make a conscious decision to land sooner than I needed to, in order to save myself from a possible accident further on. This race was a great adventure, but no race is worth having an accident. I made a promise to my husband Jim that I would finish the race uninjured, and that was my biggest goal.

Photo Credit Vitek Ludvik

2015 Red Bull X-Alps Preparation

You could say that I've been preparing for this race since I started ultra-running back in 2005. I don't believe it is possible to train for a race of this magnitude in weeks or even months. I think it takes years of building up muscles, joint, tendons and bones to be able to withstand the pounding from the miles of walking that are needed, day after day for up to two weeks.

Once I was selected in October, about 9 months before the race, I approached training fairly scientifically, in an effort to do everything I could to get my body ready for this challenge. I hired a strength training coach, who based my weight-lifting workouts around getting all of my muscles toned up and ready for an endurance challenge.   We did this by using lower weights with lots of repetitions, and used a wide variety of exercises to keep me fit overall.

Twice over the winter I performed an Active Metabolic Assessment (more widely known as a VO2 Max test). This was done on a treadmill at the gym. After a warm-up, I started at a slow running pace, speeding up every 2 minutes until I couldn't run anymore. (At that point I was just trying not to fly off the back of the treadmill!) For the test, I wore a facemask, which measured my oxygen intake and carbon dioxide output, and a heart rate monitor. From the first test to the second, I was able to improve my VO2 Max score from 31.4 to 50.9!   My trainer said this was the biggest improvement she had ever seen within a few months, because of a combination of specialized training and getting my anemia under control.

I realize that a VO2 Max of 50.9 still isn't very high. All the training in the world wouldn't make up for my genetics, which evidently gave me a lot of slow-twitch fibers but not much pure speed. This meant I could go forever, but not get anywhere very quickly. I've always believed that I had gotten stuck with a small heart and lungs, but I'm just guessing there. Since this event, because X-Rays taken of my upper spine, I now learned that I have a very small airway (trachea), which also limits my oxygen uptake. For whatever reason, I was never going to win the 100 meter dash...but I go 100 miles without injury.

My pre-race training also included working with an endurance coach to set my weekly training workouts, so I could push myself without getting overtrained. My weekly training regimen included strength training, interval runs on the treadmill, and varying lengths of hikes with my pack. I was able to use the heart rate data from the VO2 Max Test to help me set my pace during my interval runs. By monitoring my heart rate, I could make sure I was training hard enough but not going too hard.

A Sample "Hard" Week of Training Looked Like This:

Monday - 30 minutes	Light Hiking or rest
Tuesday - 1 hour	Stair Climbing (sometimes with a pack)
Wednesday – 1 hour	Weight Training
Thursday – 90 minutes	Zone 3 Treadmill Run, 5 x 10 minute intervals at 7.9 mph, with 4 min rest.
Friday – 1 hour	Weight Training
Saturday – 8	Hike with pack, flat
Sunday - 4 hou	Hike with pack, hills

I kept a careful watch on my anemia by getting blood work done several times over the winter and spring before the race. I also incorporated massages after tough workouts to keep my muscles limber. During my strength workouts, I used an altitude mask to help expand my lungs and increase my red blood cells. Somewhat embarrassingly, this altitude mask made my breathing sound like Darth Vader, and I looked like an alien. I couldn't speak through it, and it was really hot. That being said, I think it really helped with my lung power, and I would use it again.

Of course, most people might argue that paragliding is the more important of the two disciplines of the Red Bull X-Alps, since the race isn't won on the ground, but in the air.   I've been paragliding since 2009, and while that might not seem like a long time (it really isn't), I have managed to get a lot of hours, flights and experience crammed into just six years.

Near our house in Utah is a wildly popular training hill known as the South Side of the Point of the Mountain.   Here I was able to really dial in my gear by doing repetitions on the 200-meter hill.   My goal was to get unpacked and set up to fly (and vice-versa) as quickly as possible.   By committing these movements to muscle memory, I could not only be fast at packing up and getting back on the trail, but I would know exactly what I needed to bring, how much, and what I could leave behind.   And it worked!   In the race, I always had water available to me in the air, I never left anything behind on launch, or forgot any piece of mandatory equipment.

During the spring, Jim and I were also able to spend six weeks down in Colombia, South America.   In this paragliding Mecca, I could hike the 15 km up to launch from my hotel 3-5 times a week, and then have long flights for days on end.   This really helped dial in my equipment and prepared me for the long, hot days experienced during the race.   We competed in a paragliding competition there, too, which always helps dial in flying skills.

Once we arrived in Europe, about two months before the race, my training became much more race specific.   Without dedicated locations for strength training, massage, and treadmill workouts, I used what I did have available; my paragliding pack, and the trails through the Alps.   So I hiked up to launch when I could, but made flying the priority. We also did quite a few Via Ferrata routes (climbs throughout the Alps which do not need specialized equipment but do require a good head for heights).   I believe it was this mix of Via Ferrata climbing which made up for any lack of strength training, since most Via Ferrata routes require good upper body strength.

Of course, physical training and long flights only go so far. Maps, routes, plans, and a working knowledge of the course were just as important. The official turnpoints for the 2015 race were released in March. So in April, the four 2015 USA Red Bull X-Alps athletes got together in the USA for a long weekend of strategizing. Honza Rejmanek, Gavin McClurg, Dave Turner, and myself, along with some of our supporters, pooled our knowledge in the hopes that it would help all of us to get further along the course.   Together we had previously flown, driven, and hiked a lot of the course already, which was helpful.   We also zoomed in on the terrain with Google Maps. We walked away from the weekend feeling much more confident about what could be accomplished during the race. Then, during our two months of training in the Alps, Jim and I tried to both see the race terrain from the ground, as well as fly it as much as possible.

With three weeks to go to the X-Alps, I started my taper. Each week I dialed back both the duration and number of workouts, finishing my longest training hike (52 km over 10 hours) on Jun 14. By the last week before the race, I wasn't doing much at all, following the old adage "You can't improve your race during the week before, but you can HURT it." Three weeks is a really long taper, I admit. It's probably not necessary to go that long, unless you are seriously overtrained and need complete rest. But I figured it would be a tough race of rather slow walking, and the length seemed to work out ok for me.

Race Clothing

For three months of training and racing in the Alps, I brought a wide assortment of clothing for all climates. Running tights, buffs, multiple warm layers, wicking t-shirts, gloves, rain jackets, and of course arm warmers. I used a little of everything for training as we had lots of cool, wet weather. I continually find it surprising how little clothing is usually required during intense training, even in cooler weather. I might start out in a fleece and long tights, but usually within a few minutes of walking, I would be sweaty and wishing for shorts and a lighter layer.

During the race, the temperature was very consistent over the 11 days. HOT. High temperatures were mostly in the 90s F (35 C). That made it pretty easy to get dressed for each day, in shorts and a t-shirt. Even on the days where it rained, I usually just threw my poncho over my pack and didn't need to add warm clothing underneath. The poncho itself was priceless. It kept my pack dry in situations where a raincoat and pack cover would allow dribbles of water to soak under the edges. I didn't want to carry a wet, heavy pack around if I could avoid it. The poncho did make it hard to use my trekking poles, as one of my hands was usually holding the poncho down during wind gusts. So I usually left my trekking poles in the vehicle when wearing my poncho, as that was just too many things to keep track of, and trip over.

Salewa sponsored the clothing for this year's Red Bull X-Alps, and I think they did a great job. Each athlete and supporter were provided with a rain jacket, fleece jacket, wind pants, shoes, wicking shirts, running shorts, headwarmer, and of course baseball caps.

I did find it slightly ironic that the women's race kit included two sleeveless shirts but no regular t-shirts. What, did they think this was some sort of fashion contest? I don't usually wear sleeveless shirts when walking outside all day carrying a pack. I find it very hard to regulate my temperature with my shoulders uncovered, and I would also get a nasty sunburn after just one day. I went back to race headquarters to beg for a normal t-shirt instead! This I absolutely loved, and actually bought another one of the same material. They were super lightweight, and I spent most of the race alternating between the two shirts, with Jim rinsing them out periodically as they did tend to stink like crazy. They kept me cool in the heat, so I didn't complain about the smell.

The most useful piece of kit I found was a thin pair of arm warmers. The thinner the better, and I kept a pair of these with me at almost all times when I was out training and racing. They might weigh an ounce, yet they can slide on and off in an instant--great for days when the sun and rain aren't sure what they want to do. I carried arm warmers almost all the time on the side of my pack, and could pull them on without removing my pack. This was much easier than putting on a long sleeved shirt, which would add another layer between my back and the pack. Saving that layer on my back saved a lot of extra sweating.

My go-to bottom layer was a pair of spandex shorts, usually the thinner the better and not too tight so they didn't chafe. If it was a little chilly I switched to a little longer pair of capris, or even full running tights. For this edition of the Red Bull X-Alps, shorts were almost always warm enough. After a few full days of sweating in the heat, I did get a little chafing and rash across my lower back and on my shoulders where the pack rubbed. I guess it's hard to avoid this, as I was sweaty most of the time. The rash was never too uncomfortable, and I really didn't give it a second thought. But since Salewa gave me a pair of running shorts, which were looser, I gave them a try about Day 4. The male athletes had gotten orange shorts while the women's were black and grey...I like bright colors so I may have been a little jealous. Plus the brighter colors make photos "pop". But I digress. Anyhow, I loved the loose fit of these shorts so much, that they became my go-to pair each morning. You can guess that after wearing them 8 days straight, sitting on pine sap, rocks, and in the dirt, I was happy to have gotten the black version!

The Salewa wind pants were also perfect for my flying gear. While they were light and thin, they seemed to keep me warm enough in my pod harness, so that my legs were never too cold. The warm temperatures on the ground during the race extended into the atmosphere as well, and our flying conditions were never very extreme. Of course, it's not easy to switch from record-breaking heat on the ground to near freezing temperatures in the air. Several times I had to launch still damp from my hike, and continue to fly while feeling chilled and wet. For my upper body, I had a thick down jacket to put over a fleece, and a rain jacket on top of everything, covered with my race jersey. On very high flights to 4000 meters, all these layers still weren't quite warm enough, but while in the air at low elevations, I got pretty warm. I never seemed to get the formula right. If I brought my light down jacket I would climb high and get cold, and vice versa. It was hard to predict how each flight would go, despite good weather forecasts.

As a note for the ladies, I never wore a bra the entire race. For sure, I usually do in running races and practically every other athletic event. However, this type of walking where my pack is always irritating my back, an extra layer of fabric would just add chafing and wet clothing. I had enough of that already, and a wet bra would have made it worse.

I used two kinds of socks, Smartwool light hiking socks and Drymax two-layer socks. Drymax socks have been my favorite foot covering since getting into adventure racing. They have an outer moisture-loving layer, which pulls wetness away from the inner side. Somehow my feet in these socks feel dry, even when soaking in sweat. These socks work particularly well in really wet conditions like England. For dryer conditions at home in the desert, I've switched to Smartwool socks, which seem to last forever and stay comfortable all day long.

When the rain really starts to fall, I add a pair of SealSkinz waterproof socks over my regular socks. With a mid-calf rise and elastic at the top, my feet stayed pretty dry even when splashing through puddles or a small creek. Of course it does start to feel like wearing a plastic bag over my feet, which is why a thin pair of liner socks was a must. Plus I had a pair of shoes a full size larger so the double socks fit without pinching my feet.

Speaking of shoes, I brought eight pairs of them with me to the race! That might have been overkill but I overheard rumors of a certain other competitor who brought 24 pairs along with him...perhaps eight wasn't that many after all? Half of my shoes were Salomon Sense Pro, my favorite type for long days out on the trail. They are light, while still providing protection from sharp rocks. I had two brand-new pairs for the race in blue and yellow, so I dared myself to wear one of each color in the race. I kind of liked the look, and continued it throughout, but I could never remember which ones I had worn that day already, and could only hope that Jim was switching me out with the correct fresh set of blue and yellow shoes!

Photo Credit: Markus Berger

The rest of my shoes were an assortment of brands, as I had read it was nice to change when the feet are sore. This might provide a different feeling to the soles of the feet, and perhaps help with foot problems. I even had a pair of ankle boots, which I thought might be required for mountaineering sections. Thankfully I never had to go on any snow, so never wore them. What I did wear a lot were my Hoka OneOnes. These shoes look a bit silly, as they are very padded and add an inch to my height! They are the anti-minimalist shoe and have a lot of sole, although still surprisingly lightweight. I bought these specifically for the race, thinking they might be good for long stretches of pavement. Indeed they were, and I wore them more than any other pair, for the days when I only had blacktop in front of me. These were also my big pair of shoes, sized up in case my feet swelled during the race. So they were handy to wear in the rain with the Sealskinz socks. My feet did swell a little, and I never could wear the smallest sized shoes I brought; they felt too tight every time I tried them on.

I was using Black Diamond trekking poles during much of the race, and always on the uphills. I've read that using poles can take as much as 16% of the weight off the legs. I expected my arms to get tired, but somehow the poles always helped push up the hills. On the flat roads I would often stow them back in the vehicle, as I liked to have my hands free to use my phone. What I did wear almost all day long was a very light pair of fingerless bike gloves. These helped protect my hands from the poles and from the terrain if I ever took a spill. They went right under my flying gloves and I'd almost forget they were on my hands at all times. I'm sure Jim had to remind me to take them off before going to bed at least once!

On my head was a perfectly graceless floppy hat; its only redeeming factor was that it kept the sun off of my neck and my ears. After forgetting to put sunscreen on during the first flight, I faced a losing battle in keeping sunburn at bay the rest of the race. I think many of the athletes found this difficult, after seeing many red noses at the awards ceremony! Most of the burn came in the air, as the sun always seemed to be on my face no matter which way I was flying. I only wear sunglasses when I'm flying, and the sunburn lines on my face after the race had a distinctive nose line from my glasses. On the ground, the hardest time of day for sun protection was walking west into the setting sun. While the rays might not have been as powerful as midday, I couldn't keep them off my face anymore. It always seemed to be the hottest part of the day too, and wearing a hat was often too sweaty to be comfortable.

Photo Credit: Markus Berger

Race Navigation

Of course all the flying ability in the world, or speed on the ground doesn't mean anything if you are walking in circles. It was important to have the right maps and the right technology, to allow my supporters and I to find our way down the race course each day. More importantly, we needed to find each other on the ground!

First of all, we needed maps. We started with paper maps, Kompass brand which covered most of Austria, Germany, Italy and some of Switzerland. With 1:50000 maps of the course for the first half of the race, I took a permanent marker and drew the approximate course lines on each map, and labeled each one on the front (Turnpoint 1, Turnpoint 2, etc). This allowed us to organize them, and find one quickly as we trained and raced. It also gave us an overview of the big route, which can be difficult to see on a computer screen.

Having road maps of the course wasn't the whole picture, though. At home, I had divided the course into smaller sections. Then I had printed four maps of each section, including a Google Earth overview, a road map, a terrain map, and finally a Skyways map from XCPlanner.(See examples below). XCPlanner is an online logging database where paraglider pilots can log their flights. Skyways then shows an overlay of these flights, and when they are all combined, it's a very enlightening view of where others pilots have flown. Of course, it's not a perfect system, as the sky around Kossen, Germany is almost black with flights, just because it's a very popular paragliding location. That doesn't mean it's easy to fly away from the Kossen valley! In other locations along the course, there were no flights logged at all, but perhaps only because the retrieves in that area were more difficult, causing fewer pilots to fly there. However, these four maps in conjunction with each other were an invaluable tool to see a glance; the flyable route, the drivable route, the hikeable route, and the terrain overview.

Out on the race, I never carried paper maps with me. Unless I hauled up several at once, I never knew if I would land with the right map, or find that I had flown right over the whole area and needed the next one. The perfect solution for this was the Kompass Map App on my iPhone. For $3 a map or $30 for everything, I could download the sections I needed, and have them waiting in my phone. Even in areas with no phone coverage, I could still zoom in on my trail. Even better, the GPS in my phone showed me where I was on the map. It took all the guesswork out of map reading. This worked all the way into Switzerland, where I fell off the area covered by Kompass, and had to switch to a Swiss Map. They also have an app, but since I hadn't downloaded it beforehand, it was almost impossible to get the maps to load during the race, with my slow data connection. Oops.

Finding my supporters (and vice versa) was also tricky at times. We used a combination of SPOT tracking, the live race tracking on the Flymaster, and an App on the iPhone called Friend Finder. None of these worked perfectly, but in the end we were always able to meet up again down the road.

Contrast this to Kari Castle's experience as the first woman to compete in the 2005 edition of the Red Bull X-Alps. This was before GPS and cell phones were commonplace, and she wasn't very familiar with the Alps either. "I would land in a valley, look up, and realize I had no idea which way the course went or where I could find another launch", Kari says. See Kari's SPOTLIGHT in Section 1 for more of her experience.

Below are sample maps that I used to plan my flights and routes before the race. These are all the same geographical area from Salzburg to Turnpoint 2, but they give very different views of the area, and together they paint a picture of what is possible in the air and on the ground.

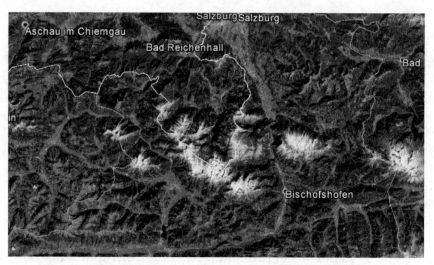

Day 1-2 Google Earth (Shows mountains and ranges)

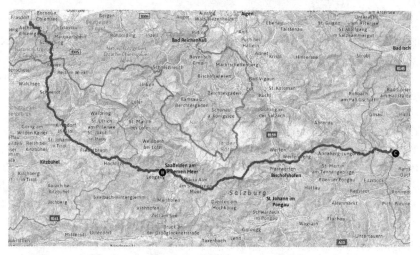

Day 1-2 Basic road map (Gives me an idea where my
supporters might drive)

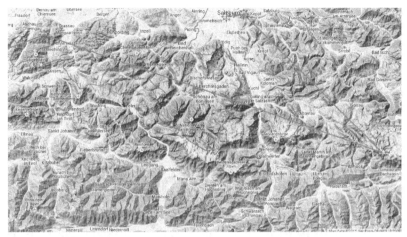

Day 1-2 XCPlanner (With Terrain and Turnpoints inputted)

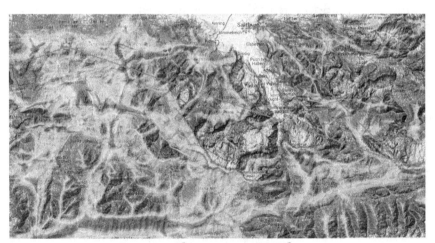

Day 1-2 Skyways on XCPlanner
(Dark Red shows where others have flown a lot)

Race Nutrition

I find that eating healthy while traveling is fairly difficult. When Jim and I are at home in Utah, we do eat quite well. Our normal fare includes fresh vegetable juices, fruit and veggie smoothies, salads, and other simple foods. We are blessed to have some really healthy restaurants near us including Jamba Juice (smoothies) and Sweet Tomatoes (salad bar). At home we don't each too much bread, pasta or meat.

Of course, that's really hard to do in Europe, when pastries are the simplest thing to find for breakfast and vegetarian options in restaurants are sometimes nonexistent. Since we were traveling in a motorhome, we decided to buy a blender in Europe (we couldn't bring ours over because of the voltage difference). This allowed us to get our daily servings of fruits and vegetables without trying too hard. My selection of veggies in smoothies included avocado, kale, broccoli, zucchini, and cucumber. These types of vegetables seem to blend up and disappear, whereas root veggies like carrots or beets give a distinctly gritty texture to the mix. Fruits for the smoothies included bananas, grapes, strawberries, apples; and whatever frozen fruit I could find in the grocery stores. In addition, I added a little nut milk for flavor, and a couple of scoops of a powder brought from home, which included chia seeds, creatine, dried wheatgrass, fiber, and chlorella. This overtly green powder provided lots of vitamins and minerals, but didn't necessarily add a great taste. For flavor, I sometimes used peanuts, peanut butter, cocoa powder and/or peppermint essential oil drops.

Race nutrition was considerably less healthy than I had hoped, but with a good training base I knew a few days of anything wouldn't hurt me. Actually I wasn't that stressed about it. Jim and I talked about race food a lot but never really came to any conclusions. I knew that being adaptable would be key, since every day would bring a new adventure. We stocked the motorhome with a mix of pasta, sauce, fruits, veggies, drinks, chocolate, snacks and water...and never turned down a fresh bakery pastry either!

Unlike a normal, structured race, the Red Bull X-Alps is all about adapting. While athletes in an Ironman triathlon can plan their race-day nutrition down to that last mouthful of Gu on the bike, this race would require me to take what each day gave me. On a hot day of walking down the road, I would need to eat and drink much more than on a day where I had a long, cool flight. Plus, I never knew how long I would be away from my support team and their supply of snacks.

My supporters were pretty worried about me the first few days of the race. They kept trying to shove more food in me, more calories, and more often. I was so hot and dehydrated that I could barely stand the thought of eating. It's hard to chew dry foods when you are walking down a road roasting in the sun. So I drank a lot of my calories, and it worked out great. On the first day I found I loved the taste of pineapple juice, and so I drank lots of it the rest of the race. Somehow it was just the perfect solution to calories and hydration. I didn't plan that all but it worked out that way.

Eating during the race was more like a tortoise than a hare. I was going really slowly on the ground, and even when I was walking quickly, it is metabolically still pretty slow. Nothing like the 100-meter dash or even running a marathon. Most of my calories were coming from fat, because my body had time to access those energy stores while I was walking. All I had to do was keep eating small amounts of calories often enough to keep my blood sugar up to feed my brain. Honestly, it took my supporters a few days to understand, but I kept saying "I haven't bonked yet and I walked 70 km today". I think by the middle of the race they finally believed I knew what I was doing!

I'm also sure my supporters will tell you I was a picky eater. I subsisted on juice, smoothies, chocolate, Nutella, cheese, potato chips and apples while hiking, with the occasional piece of chocolate cake thrown in. (I'm sure I turned up my nose at perfectly good (but dry) pastries just because I knew I couldn't begin to chew them). One takes breathing through the nose for granted, but during exertion that's not enough airflow, so my mouth was open a lot and really dried out. Try eating a few saltine crackers without any liquid to wash them down, and that's about how my mouth felt all day long during the race.

What I really craved was a cold drink in the heat, anything cold, but ice was almost impossible to come by and the inside of Chuck's cooler felt more like a sauna. Bubbly drinks were my next best happy place, and Chuck could be counted on to always have something fizzy for my resupply.

Dinners were also a little haphazard, based on where and when I would land. On Day 1 we happened to pass by a familiar town in the evening with a great pizza joint. That made dinner easy. Otherwise, if I would be hiking for a while, they could drive ahead of me and prepare a meal of pasta and pesto. I was also happy when I could take snacks with me to last a while, so my supporters could go find a meal in town and have a little down time. I think they were taking better care of me than they were of themselves, which got them all a little run down. (Then the tables were turned and I got to lecture THEM about getting enough to eat!)

Liquids were the most important thing. Often, as I started my climb up to launch for the day, I was loaded down with up to four bottles of water, Coke and/or juice. I always planned to use two on the way up the hill, and keep two in reserve for the flight and my next climb, if it happened I landed out away from support vehicles. I know several times I ended up carrying water up the hill unnecessarily, but also at times it was so hot I drank every bit of what I had. Carrying extra water saved me from waiting around for the vehicles after landing. So if the extra weight slowed me up a little overall, I made up for at other times, like on Day 1, when I didn't see my support team over 7 hours and two big flights.

I almost never drink caffeine in training. Since it's a blood thinner and I have thin blood already, I figure there's no need to tempt fate. I do make an exception for racing, but wasn't sure how this would work in the Red Bull X-Alps. It's not a short race; it would turn out to be an *eleven day* race (for me anyway). Plus, drinking caffeine makes the body release adrenaline stores. Drink too much of it, and there might not be enough adrenaline left when it's really needed. After days of racing, this could actually be a problem. So I had planned on drinking caffeine (in the form of Coke) only when I thought I would really need it, but always before noon, so that it wouldn't keep me awake at night. I guess I'm sensitive like that. I made an exception for my night pass, as a shot of Coke at midnight really kept me going!

So I was very happy to find that after the first few days of drinking caffeine each morning, I found I really didn't need it anymore. My energy levels had normalized during the race, and although I was tired I could keep going steadily. The exception was the last day of my race, when fatigue really caught up to me, along with the mental tiredness of knowing it was my last day.

USA Athletes Honja Rejmanek, Dawn Westrum,
Gavin McClurg and Dave Turner;

Meeting to discuss the 2015 course.

Dealing with Fear

Fear is a very subjective, unpredictable emotion.   On some nights when I'm home alone, you couldn't pay me enough to walk downstairs into the dark basement. It's an unnatural fear of the boogieman (which of course doesn't exist) but at 11 pm occasionally my brain no longer accepts that. On other nights, I put on a headlamp and walk through the mountains all by myself, and the darkness doesn't bother me at all.

Much of this difference is just how I control the thoughts about my fears. If I sit on launch and think about all the things that could go wrong during launch or the flight or the landing, then I am focusing on the negative.

Controlling fear is as important on a macro scale on the micro. When my application into the race was accepted, I experienced angst on a large scale. I was suddenly saddled with 1038 km of terrain which I hadn't seen before, and would need to fly and hike without much time to prepare. I didn't really know where to start in my preparation. Yet, as soon as I arrived in Europe, began buying maps and looking at the route, the fear dissipated to a large extent.   It's amazing how much education conquers fear of the unknown.

Fear also lessens with comfort level. I recently gave a talk about the Red Bull X-Alps to my local paragliding club.   I'm not terribly comfortable with standing in front of a crowd and certainly don't seek out such things. I confess I was a little nervous ahead of time.   However when I arrived at the meeting, and saw that I knew most of the people and felt they were excited to hear what I had to say, suddenly it felt it a lot easier.

So knowledge and preparation and comfort level can really help mitigate fear.   However things can go wrong quickly in the air (or on the ground!) and it's also important to keep a level head in emergencies. I think all pilots have had a day where they felt on top of the world on a great flight, and then soon afterwards flew into bad air where suddenly it became a fight to stay alive.   It's important to be able to switch gears and find new priorities very quickly.   While a few minutes before, it was OK to think about taking photos and having a snack, now every brain cell needs to refocus on staying alive and making good, safe decisions. The ability to focus on the important things (like the steps to staying safe) also helps mitigate fear, by knowing you are doing everything you can to keep yourself alive.   Freaking out will just cause harm. So the first small step of conquering fear is not letting yourself feel paralyzed.

Will Gadd wrote a very interesting article about leaving yourself a safety margin in dangerous conditions. http://www.explore-mag.com/Gadds_Truth_Have_a_Margin . Cross-country paragliding surely falls in this category almost all the time! I agree with his ideas, and I think that leaving a margin also helps with the fear factor.   By thinking through the dangers ahead of time and giving yourself more time and space to react, it's possible to tamp down the fear and make better decisions with a cool head. Potentially saving the day.

What about the call of nature?

Women in paragliding and other aerial sports don't have many choices when it comes to relieving themselves inflight. Unlike men, we can't simply use a condom catheter or even just hang it all out in the air. For long flights I've always went with the cheap, easy solution of a bulky, ignominious adult diaper. This allows me to urinate multiple times in the air, and so far I haven't had any leaks. The hardest part is usually finding a quiet place to take off the diaper after landing, especially if I'm being mobbed by people or kids in the LZ! I've also experimented with a women's version of a tubing system, meaning a vaginal insert which runs in a tube out to my foot, so I don't have a soaked diaper to carry around after a long flight. This "works" but I haven't used it enough to say that it's a failsafe option, and I also use a light diaper just in case of leaks.

My choice for the Red Bull X-Alps was to use...nothing. I figured that I would be naturally dehydrated during the race, as I would almost always have a big hike up to launch before getting in the air. Plus, unlike a regular paragliding competition, it's certainly allowable to top land anywhere, if that necessity should come up.

Indeed, while I did have some longer flights during the 11 days of the race, I never felt that I was landing because I needed to pee. The heat and the dehydration did their job and I was never suffering with a full bladder. I realize that flying tired and dehydrated makes it difficult to think clearly, so I did bring water and snacks during each flight. However, while I would take a sip or bite here or there, I never found that my thought clarity suffered from not eating or drinking. Or perhaps it had and I didn't know it?

Comparing Training Strategies

Three radically different (but successful) ways of training for the Red Bull X-Alps

Gavin McClurg (USA2)

Gavin approached physical training about as scientifically as it is possible to be. With his trainer Ben Abruzzo giving him specific workouts, he incorporated strength training, specific race training, and lots of hard endurance workouts. Strength training came in the form of power workouts like CrossFit. Long endurance events consisted of marathons while carrying his race kit.   Gavin did one marathon in February, two marathons in a row in March, three marathons in a row in April, and four in March. His training culminated in five straight marathon walks in June while carrying full race kit. Although Gavin was 43 years old and had bad knees, he was able to overcome these obstacles by strengthening his body, and using his physical resources wisely. He was so muscular at the race that his nickname during the race quickly became "Big Guns" McClurg. Even a few days before the race start, he could still be seen pumping out multiple repetitions of lunges and pushups.

This scientific focus extended to Gavin's flying preparation as well. His supporter, Bruce Marks, was very familiar with the Alps and was able to give great insight on flying routes as well as hiking routes. Together they used all the resources they had, including the flyways on XCPlanner, and athlete track logs from previous editions of the X-Alps.   While the route changes every year, it does tend to use some of the same big turnpoints, and these places can be key locations for race-time decision making and making big moves. However, it wasn't enough for Gavin to study the route, he also arrived early enough to fly the whole 1000 kilometers of the race course. Some sections he even did several times over some sections to see what might work better.   Talk about knowing the route forward and backwards...Gavin once flew over my head in the Oetztal heading against the race route! At the time I wondered why that would be a good idea. But I concluded later that time spent in the air, even going the wrong way, was better than not seeing the route from the air at all, or having a short flight while fighting the wind.

Gavin's method definitely paid off, getting him into Monaco in 8th place, the first American to ever reach the finish in the history of the Red Bull X-Alps. Gavin avoided any knee problems, continuing to hike strongly until the end, even with blisters. His daring flight on Day 8 across Switzerland bumped him up 10 places on the leaderboard, and couldn't have happened without him studying the route, and knowing when to take a risky line in great weather conditions.

Dave Turner (USA4)

Dave's preparation for the race consisted of completing the whole 1038 Km of the route on foot (or in the air) in training, without cheating by taking vehicle rides along the course. This helped him live up to his nickname of the "Lone Wolf". He was able to make it to Monaco in training, with just a week to spare before the race preparation started in Fuschl. Of course Dave wasn't moving for 18 hours a day in training like he would be during the race! Rather, he would walk up to a launch, have a flight for the day, then maybe walk down the road a little further that evening. His mileage was probably between 20 and 40 km a day (on average) during the month or so it took him to get to Monaco. I don't think he ever took a day off.

The bonus of this method was that Dave was mentally getting into the race strategy ahead of time. It's hard to recreate that mental stress in training, but Dave's insistence on walking or flying every step of the route (even in practice) meant that his choices had big consequences. The need to keep flying, knowing that it would save him lots of walking down the road, would be a big motivator to stay in the air. It also made his choices very simple. Walk, or fly. I would envy this focus each time I checked the flying conditions, trying to decide if wanted to drive to Switzerland to fly the next day, or back to Italy, or start over in Austria, or just take a day of rest.

The downside of a one-way trip to Monaco for Dave meant no backtracking. When it was raining, foggy or un-flyable, Dave saw a lot of pavement pass under his feet, but didn't have much time flying in the mountains. During one particularly long stretch of bad weather, he barely flew between Turnpoints 1 and 3 at all. I was with Dave and his supporters during some of this time, and I didn't find this time useful for when I would cover this ground in the race, but I was able to return to the area later and fly it in good weather.

It was also possible that Dave didn't take enough time off to rest during this training time and taper before the race. He certainly broke all of the conventional rules about tapering! Not many people could have kept up that kind of mileage day after day, without feeling run down eventually. Would this lack of rest cause him to bonk during the race?

Happily, Dave showed himself to be strong during the race by walking 660 kilometers, more than any other competitor by a long shot. So race-specific fitness, without strength workouts or tailored training plans can be just fine, too. I think Dave proved that achieving the race mentality of the Red Bull X-Alps was just as successful as a regimented training program.

Dawn Westrum (USA3)

My own training was a tale of two halves. I had done my base training for more than ten years of ultra running, triathlon, and adventure racing events. With 9 months to go to the starting gun, I then hired two personal trainers, one to create my endurance-training schedule, and one to coach me through my strength workouts. I began doing weight workouts about twice a week, mostly upper body and core as I was getting quite a lot of leg workouts outside of the gym. My endurance coach had me doing one long hike with my pack every ten days to two weeks, plus a weekly Zone 3 or 4 heart-rate interval run on the treadmill, along with other runs and walks designed to get me going long.   I also incorporated massage to loosen muscles tight from hard efforts.

While in Colombia during the winter, I hiked nine miles on a steep trail up to launch every other day for 5 weeks in a row. These hikes, combined with long flights almost daily, was probably the best race specific training I could do ahead of arriving in Europe to see the route.

So this strength and endurance training continued until we arrived in Europe.   There, almost everything structured went right out the window!   We arrived about two months before the race, which is either way too long or not long enough, depending on how you look at it.   It's not nearly enough time to adequately cover the whole course; only living locally could help with that.   At the same time, it's a long time to be away from home.

So my workouts in Europe were balanced around the weather. When it rained and I couldn't fly, I would do long road walks, knowing that a big part of the Red Bull X-Alps could be walking down the valleys.   When we wanted a break from thinking about the race, we incorporated a few Via Ferrata climbing routes, which I know were really good for my upper body, and kept me strong.   Plus they were fun and I wanted Jim to enjoy his time here this summer as well.   Driving me around in the motorhome all the time did get boring.

I'd like to say I walked up oodles of hills to launch, but I really didn't.   To get good flights where I was alert and not tired from walking up to launch, I made use of roads and cable cars where I could.   If that meant I could spend more time in the air flying the route, then it was worth it.

Of course training for the race also included flying as much as I could.   With changing weather conditions and a lot of rain during May and June, we were forced to chase flyable conditions across Austria, Germany, Italy and Switzerland, and it wasn't always easy to know what decision to make. I had decided early on that statistically I wasn't very likely to make it to Monaco. But there was a very good chance I would see the first half of the course. You might think, "Duh, of course". Since I knew I couldn't reach the second half of the course unless I had already successfully flown and hiked the first half, I decided to focus on the first half. I figured if I got past halfway in the actual race, I would just wing it! But if I could drive, hike and fly the first half, perhaps even multiple times, then I would be likely to cover this section more quickly. So when I reached Switzerland and about halfway in training, I turned around and went back to Austria. Of course this started causing me anxiety on Day 8 of the race when I got to Switzerland and ran out of beta (why didn't I keep going?!?).

I thought a lot about my taper, which is the rest period before my last big workout and the start of the race. With limited reserves of speed compared to the guys, I figured the best thing I could do, would be to arrive at race day well rested and raring to start. With this in mind, I started cutting back my workouts with three weeks to go. My last long workout was a 50 km hike carrying my pack with a few hills about the middle of June. Of course I still stayed active but not to the extent I had before. The last week before the race, I rested as much as I could, ate healthy when possible, and did only very short, intense workouts. This would keep my muscles firing quickly but not fatigue them.

But honestly, I wondered if I had done enough. In the week before the race, I was worried that I hadn't trained nearly enough at all, as self-doubt began to creep in. I think that's a fairly normal thing to worry about before a race of this length! But by then it was too late to get any stronger, and an attempt to do so would only cause injury and impede muscle recovery.

After the race, I was really pleased with my endurance, walking further and longer than I had thought possible. I also flew a lot longer and further than I had hoped, proving that my study of the course and my training efforts had paid off.   I concluded that lots of time on my feet was ideal preparation for such a long race, as I spent approximately 100 hours walking during the 11 days of the race!

Photo Credit: Vitek Ludvik

Section 3: Results and Athlete SPOTLIGHTS

Results Chart, 2015 Red Bull X-Alps

Rank	Team	Athlete	Supporter	Finish Time	Distance to Goal (as the crow flies)	Km Walked	Km Flew	Km Total
33	FRA1	Clément Latour	Barnier Philippe	Did Not Start	DNS	0	0	0
32	GER2	Yvonne Dathe	Thomas Ide		840 km, eliminated	135	210	345
31	SUI2	Samuel Vurpillot	Martin Müller		755 km, eliminated	266	192	458
30	COL	Alex Villa	Stefan Hodeck		635 km, eliminated	349	542	891
29	ESP	Ivan Colás	Ainhoa Garcia		611 km, withdrew due to injury	309	567	876
28	GER1	Michael Gebert	Tobias Böck		575 km, withdrew	347	604	951
27	RSA	Stephan Kruger	Konstantin Filipov		575 km, eliminated	353	666	1019
26	ROM	Toma Coconea	Daniel Pisica		555 km, withdrew due to injury	417	613	1030
25	AUT4	Pascal Purin	Florian Ebenbichler		531 km, withdrew due to injury	350	752	1102
24	BEL	Thomas de Dorlodot	Sebastien Granville		499 km, withdrew due to injury	276	718	994
23	USA3	Dawn Westrum	Jaroslaw Wieczorek		375 km, eliminated	467	878	1345
22	AUT2	Gerald Gold	Othmar Heinisch		302 km, did not finish	496	1234	1730
21	GBR	Steve Nash	Richard Bungay		178 km, did not finish	557	1454	2011
20	USA4	Dave Turner	Krischa Berlinger		140 km, did not finish	660	1140	1800
19	AUT3	Stephan Gruber	Claus Eberharter	11 Days and 6 hours +48-hour penalty		431	1687	2118
18	SUI3	Michael Witschi	Yael Margelisch	11 Days and 22 hours		499	1638	2137
17	SWE	Erik Rehnfeldt	Peter Back	11 Days and 21 hours		582	1792	2374
16	POL	Pawel Faron	Piotr Goc	11 Days and 20 hours		584	1617	2201
15	USA1	Honza Rejmanek	Jesse Williams	11 Days and 17 hours		570	1910	2480
14	KOR	Chi-Kyong Ha	Yun Jae Rju	11 Days and 15 hours		439	1914	2353
13	SUI4	Peter von Bergen	Philippe Arn	11 Days and 12 hours		451	1720	2171
12	CZE	Stanislav Mayer	Petr Kostrhun	11 Days and 8 hours		499	1804	2303
11	FRA3	Nelson de Freyman	Thomas Punty	11 Days and 2 hours		546	1836	2382
10	NZL	Nick Neynens	Louis Tapper	10 Days and 18 hours		485	2023	2508
9	GER4	Manuel Nübel	Christian Scheineis	10 Days and 17 hours		430	1733	2163
8	USA2	Gavin McClurg	Bruce Marks	10 Days and 4 hours		498	1560	2058
7	NED	Ferdinand van Schelven	Anton Brous	9 Days and 22 hours		497	1550	2047

6	ITA	Aaron Durogati	Ondrej Prochazka	9 Days and 6 hours		367	1808	2165
5	FRA4	Gaspard Petiot	Laurent Pezet	9 Days and 5 hours		275	2090	2365
4	FRA2	Antoine Girard	Demelin Mathieu	9 Days and 5 hours		359	2085	2444
3	AUT1	Paul Guschlbauer	Werner Strittl	9 Days and 4 hours		446	1620	2066
2	GER3	Sebastian Huber	Martin Walleitner	8 Days and 22 hours		480	1583	2063
1	SUI1	Chrigel Maurer	Thomas Theurillat	8 Days and 4 hours		405	1654	2059

Athlete Spotlights

Yvonne Dathe (GER2)

Supporter: Thomas Ide

Nationality: Germany

Age: 38

X-Alps Rookie

Rank: 32nd, Eliminated in 1st Round

Total Distance: 345 km

Hiking: 135 km

Flying: 210 km

Yvonne Dathe was one of two women chosen for the 2015 Red Bull X-Alps. Dathe has been a paraglider pilot for 20 years, learning to fly with her dad, who was also one of her supporters. She competed in the 2014 X-Pyr, a similar race in the Pyrenees, but held in opposite years from the X-Alps. Dathe is also a tandem pilot, flying on every good weather day for the last eight years. She has been the German ladies paragliding champion for three years.

After a good flight on Day 1 of the X-Alps, Yvonne landed near the back, but close to other pilots, and like them spent the second day mostly walking because of poor weather. Caught in a long valley with poor launching options, she did high up to a launch SE of Kossen, but her flight from there wasn't able to get her to Turnpoint 3 that night.

Still struggling at the back by Day 3, Dathe made several flights but the winds were against her, which limited airtime and caused long hikes. She passed the Kampenwand early that morning, and then made it across the Inn Valley to Germany near her home town. But it wasn't enough to get ahead in the race.

Inexplicably, according to race strategists, she did not pull her night pass on Day 3, even though she was just barely ahead of last place athlete Nick Neynens (NZL).   According to race rules, the last athlete is eliminated at 6 am on Day 4, and another athlete every 48 hours thereafter.   Not using her night pass allowed Neynens to pass Dathe in the middle of the night.

Yvonne's goal was to have fun and do her best.   She said after elimination that her race was too short, but that she still enjoyed the experience.

Samuel Vurpillot (SUI2)

Supporter: Martin Muller

Nationality: Switzerland

Age: 46

X-Alps Rookie

Rank: 31st, Eliminated in 2nd Round

Total Distance: 458 km

Hiking: 266 km

Flying: 192 km

Samuel Vurpillot has been flying since he was 19. Considering he is one of the older competitors in the race, that's a long time, almost since the birth of paragliding itself! He has competed in many shorter hike and fly competitions, and is an experienced mountaineer. His supporter Martin Muller was a former Red Bull X-Alps competitor, finishing 3rd in 2007. They did plenty of research on the route, and knew what they were doing and where they were going.

However, success in the Red Bull X-Alps requires a little bit of luck as well as experience. Vurpillot might have gotten the worst weather luck of the entire Red Bull X-Alps in 2015. Landing near the back on Day 1, his race turned into a walk-a-thon for the next four days. With rain, then wind, and more rain, and some more wind, he was unable to fly much at all, for four days straight. In each of those days he walked up to 75 km, suffering the blisters and pain you might expect from that much time pounding the pavement.

In some cases, he arrived at a good launch, just hours too late, to see that the weather had changed and flying wasn't possible. Facing elimination on Day 5, he walked to a launch overlooking the Inn Valley, but found it too windy to make a last flight to escape his fate. Vurpillot make it just past Turnpoint 4. At least the hut where he stopped his race had good goulash soup and a warm fire!

Alex Villa (COL)

Supporter: Mayer Zapata

Nationality: Colombia

Age: 38

X-Alps Rookie

Rank: 30th, Eliminated in 3rd Round

Total Distance: 891 km

Hiking: 349 km

Flying: 542 km

Arriving only 10 days ahead of the race and never having been in the Alps before, Alex Villa gave the race his best effort. Villa had previously participated in the 2014 X-Pyr, where his native language of Spanish came in handy. In the Red Bull X-Alps, he had his best flight on Day 1, staying up with the main pack and making it almost to Turnpoint 3 by that evening.

Villa then saw volatile Bavarian winds and rain get in the way of progress for the next few days. On Day 5 he was able to fly again, but high winds make for tricky airtime and he had a very dangerous landing in the Oetztal Valley. Inexplicably, he then chose to hike up and over a 3000-meter pass rather than stick to the lower, easier route over the Timmelsjoch Pass. Even worse, the winds were not right at the top, so he had to walk down the other side!

On Day 6, Villa ascended another difficult hike only to sink out again. The conditions for flying weren't very good for anyone in that area at the time, and Villa choose to make another high climb on the direct route to the next turnpoint, rather than taking a longer, easier route. This allowed Ivan Colas (ESP) to pass him in the air and get ahead of the elimination by a small margin. Alex never gave up, walking quickly into the night during his night pass in a last effort to get ahead of Colas. The distance was too great to make up, and Alex was eliminated after Day 7, just short of Turnpoint 5.

Author's Note: Researching Alex's route choices for this book were heartbreaking for me. Alex is a great pilot and friend of mine from my travels down to Colombia, and I had high hopes for him in the Red Bull X-Alps. This shows it is truly difficult to come into such a complicated place like the Alps without any experience, and make good route choices under pressure of such a race. Neither Alex nor his three supporters had much experience with flying or hiking in the Alps, and this was certainly a detriment for them in this race.

Ivan Colas (ESP)

Supporter: Iñigo Arizaga

Nationality: Spain

Age: 36

X-Alps Rookie

Rank: 29th, Withdrew due to Injury

Total Distance: 876 km

Hiking: 309 km

Flying: 567 km

Ivan Colas struggled physically during the 2015 X-Alps. He had been very successful in the 2012 X-Pyr, battling it out on foot during the final day, and finished second to Inigo Gabiria (by only 1 minute) after 7 days and 11 Hours of racing! However, a pulled muscle in his calf early in the 2015 Red Bull X-Alps slowed his walking pace and caused him considerable pain. On Day 4, he was only walking a few kilometers per hour and it didn't look good.

Colas continued on against all odds, putting in a lot of painful kilometers on the ground, and finally got a key flight from the Timmelsjoch Pass into Italy. This allowed him to pass Alex Villa (COL) and arrive at Turnpoint 5 at Cima Tosa, earning him another two days of racing.

In a controversial move that some fans called unsportsmanlike (but not against the rules), Colas quit the race only 15 hours ahead of what would have been his elimination. The elimination then fell on Stephan Kruger (RSA) instead, shortening his race by 48 hours. This also had a domino effect on author Dawn Westrum, causing her elimination on Day 12 rather than being able to continue until the official finish of the race.

Toma Coconea (ROU)

Supporter: Daniel Pisica

Rank: 26th, Withdrew due to injury

Nationality: Romania

Total Distance: 1030 km

Age: 40

Hiking: 417 km

Has competed all seven editions of the X-Alps!

Flying: 613 km

Toma Coconea is a legend in the X-Alps. He is the only athlete to compete in every edition of the race, and he has reached the float in Monaco three times. He has finished second twice, one of them in 2007, when he walked 1000 km, (over 75% of the course!) on foot. He has an incredible amount of fans following him during the race, and covers ground quickly on foot.

Toma came close to breaking airspace on Day 1 (which comes with a 48 hour penalty) but his flight track logs proved him clear of any violation, so he continued on. On Day 2, Coconea wanted to get ahead of some bad weather, and pulled a night pass, where he headed out into the Bavarian flatlands for a 117 km march through the night. To keep his spirits high, a loyal fan even ran with him through some of the darkness!

In the Oetztal valley on Day 5, Coconea chose to hike up to the glacier at 3000 meters to launch into Italy. That didn't pay off, but on Day 6 the winds were just right for him to fly into Turnpoint 5 in Brenta Dolomites. His three flights for the day brought him close to Tonale pass.

Unfortunately, his 2015 race was cut short on Day 7, near Bernina Pass in Switzerland. On a day with high winds, he found rotor at a very high altitude (3800 meters) and couldn't fly fast enough to escape it. He got trapped in a valley, landed while flying backwards, and was dragged over some rocks. He fractured his arm, cut his face, and broke some teeth.   After surgery and three months of recovery, he is now back at 80%, and says he plans on toeing the starting line in 2017.

Michael Gebert (GER1)

Supporter: Tobias Beck

Nationality: Germany

Age: 35

Previous X-Alps: 2005, 2007, 2009, 2011

Rank: 28th, Withdrew

Total Distance: 951 km

Hiking: 347 km

Flying: 604 km

Michael Gebert was no rookie in this race. With four past X-Alps under his belt, he has the distinction of having finished in 6th place three times! Although he skipped the 2013 edition, he looked to be in great shape for 2015. Gebert runs comfortably with his pack and his average hiking pace is higher than many athletes.

Gebert had a great start to the 2015 edition of the X-Alps, and along with the top half of the pack managed to make it to Kossen on Day 1, just short of Turnpoint 3. His place on the leaderboard remained in the top half through Day 5. In strong winds, he climbed up the glacier at the end of the Oetztal valley, which enabled him to fly all the way to Turnpoint 5 in the Brenta Dolomites and beyond that evening.

On Day 6 his status took a turn for the worse, finding headwinds and being forced to walk over the Bernina Pass of Switzerland. He flew and walked back into Italy before stopping in Chiavenna. Gebert retired from the race at the end of Day 7, stating that conditions were too difficult for him to proceed.

Stephan Kruger (RSA)

Supporter: Konstantin Filipov

Nationality: South Africa

Age: 33

X-Alps Rookie

Rank: 27th, Eliminated in 4rd round

Total Distance: 1019 km

Hiking: 353 km

Flying: 666 km

It's a long way from South Africa to the Alps, so Stephan Kruger arrived early to get some time in the Alps before the race start.   Unfortunately, bad weather plagued his Alps training, along with flying restrictions due to a G7 summit!

With his two Bulgarian supporters Konstantin and Sunshine, Stephan had a few misadventures during the Red Bull X-Alps. During a rain and windstorm the night of Day 3, several large tree branches fell on their vehicle during dinner, narrowly missing Konstantin's head.

Without pre-downloaded electronic maps (the supplied race phone did not have a data connection), Stephan was forced to rely on his supporters to tell him which way to go at most trail junctions.   When phone signals got spotty in the deep mountains, he was sometimes lost, in his own words "for hours at a time".

That didn't stop him from getting some key flights along the way.   On Day 1 he stayed near the front half of the pack, almost reaching Turnpoint 3.   On Day 5, he was almost near the back of the pack (due to a few of those "lost in the woods" episodes), yet managed to fly ahead of several competitors and work his way back up the leaderboard.

His luck ended on Day 8, when a headwind prevented a valley crossing into Switzerland.   Thinking he was safe from the 4th elimination after reaching Switzerland, Kruger was surprised by Ivan Colas's (ESP) decision to quit the race early.   This forced the elimination onto the South African athlete, who took it with good grace.

Pascal Purin (AUT4)

Supporter: Florian Ebenbichler

Nationality: Austria

Age: 26

X-Alps Rookie

Rank: 25th, Withdrew due to Injury

Total Distance: 1102 km

Hiking: 350 km

Flying: 752 km

Pascal Purin might only be 26, but he's been flying since he was nine years old, and has over 12,000 flights! He is now a test pilot for Nova, and has been known to skip school to go flying.

Purin landed near the back of the pack on Day 1, but with what seemed like premeditation, he pulled his night pass on the first night. This allowed him to move up from 27th place to 10th place on Day 2, after having a great flight across the Bavarian Alps from Turnpoint 3 in Aschau.

After a long rainy walk up the Oetztal Valley on Day 4, Purin climbed up near the border to launch on a side hill on Day 5. However, strong north foehn conditions meant a difficult flight and he landed deep in the main spine of the Alps. He was able to hike up and launch again, but it cost him time, arriving near Turnpoint 5 in the Brenta Dolomites back down in 22nd place.

Day 7 was a difficult one for Purin. After traversing a mountainside in Switzerland, conditions weren't right and he sunk out back down to the valley. The next morning, he relaunched further up the valley, this time having a wonderful early flight around Turnpoint 6 at Piz Corvatsch.

Landing at Maloja Pass near St. Moritz, it was again very windy and turbulent. Purin attempted to hike up to fly again, but spent several hours walking around the mountain without finding a place to launch, due to switching winds and strong gusts. He eventually had to hike back down to the valley floor. With injured legs, he then withdrew from the race. Pascal confided at the time that he had promised his mother he would give her grandkids, and he didn't like the conditions he was flying in.

Tom de Dorlodot (BEL)

Supporter: John Stepels

Nationality: Belgium

Age: 30

Previous X-Alps: 2007, 2009, 2011, 2013

Rank: 24th, Withdrew due to Injury

Total Distance: 994 km

Hiking: 276 km

Flying: 718 km

Tom de Dorlodot is passionate about bivouac flying. He has crossed many major mountain ranges alone with just his paraglider for company, racking up 7000 km of solo flying. He also loves the Red Bull X-Alps, making 2015 his fifth attempt at the race. He's never finished higher than 10th place, and he would like to change that this year.

Dorlodot had a good first day of flying, but then again so did everyone else, leaving him in 15th place. He stayed solidly in the middle of the pack through Day 4, as flying conditions were poor for several days. He admitted it was hard to get ahead on foot, as 15 km (which is what separated him from athletes in the Top 10) is hours on the ground but only a couple of thermals in the air.

Tom continued to chase the leaders as the weather improved, catching a break on Day 5. From the Italian side of Timmelsjoch Pass, he had an epic flight all the way to Turnpoint 5 in the Brenta Dolomites, finally reaching Tonale Pass that night. Good flying conditions continued the next day, seeing Dorlodot pass Turnpoint 6 in the air above St. Moritz, still maintaining his place in the middle of the pack.

On Day 7 the weather still cooperated, but with stronger northwest winds than before. Tom was flying together with Ferdy van Schelven (NED) and Manuel Nubel (GER4); they found they could soar the windy NW faces, rather than thermal up on the sunnier south sides.   They were passing north of Chiavenna, Italy and hoping to make it back into Switzerland soon.

While trying to cross the main spine of the Alps in a remote spot along the Italy/Switzerland border, Nubel just made it over the ridge onto the west side and surged ahead. Dorlodot and van Schelven sunk just below the level of the saddle and into the lee of the wind, forcing them to land, luckily near a trail leading over the pass.

They were quickly at the pass, but the mountains were steep and filled with rocks, looking like a dinosaur spine along the highest ridge. Together they found a small spot where it looked safe to launch, even though it was close to small cliffs below them. Ferdy was able to get away safely, but a few minutes later, Tom launched into a bad cycle. His glider didn't inflate and as his feet left the ground, the wing collapsed. Dorlodot fell, then slid down about 15 meters of rocks, spraining his foot and ripping his glider to shreds.

Without phone coverage in the area, Tom used his emergency SPOT Locater Beacon to call for help. He was disappointed that his race was over, but optimistic about his foot. With no broken bones, he was expected to make a full recovery within a month.

Dawn Westrum (USA3)

Supporter: Jim Sorensen

Nationality: USA

Age:37

X-Alps Rookie

Rank: 23th, Eliminated in 5th Round

Total Distance: 1346 km

Hiking: 468 km

Flying: 878 km

Enough about me, already!

Gerald Gold (AUT2)

Supporter: Othmar Heinisch	Rank: 22nd, 302 km from Goal
Nationality: Austria	Total Distance: 1730 km
Age: 38	Hiking: 496 km
X-Alps Rookie	Flying: 1234 km

An Austrian native, Gerald Gold had a great first day of flying, and managed to stay up near the middle of the pack through Day 2. He was perhaps the only athlete to tie a container to the front of his harness, allowing him to both walk down the road and eat pasta at the same time! Gold continued racing despite car trouble with his support vehicle, which eventually spent some time in a repair shop before getting back on the race route. He did have great fan support from being a local pilot, and mentioned that fans in Nassereith, Germany even welcomed him with a handmade sign!

After walking through a couple of days of rain, on Day 5 Gerald flew into Italy through strong north Foehn winds. He had a rough top landing on the hills west of Merano, getting dragged and bruised. The winds escalated into the evening, and eventually he had to walk down the hill rather than relaunching.

At Turnpoint 6 in Switzerland, Gold faced strong west winds and decided to make progress going north rather than west. While this route had been flown earlier by Rehnfeldt (SWE), conditions weren't ideal anymore, and Gold wasn't able to make his choice pay off. He was forced to walk much of the extra distance, especially as he eventually turned west to find the winds still not favorable.

This slowdown in his race, and choices by other athletes meant that on Day 11 he was facing an elimination. Gold managed to avoid this by having a great flight past Turnpoint 7 at the Matterhorn, and pulled his night pass to get ahead of the author that evening. Gerald's goal for the race was to make it to Mont Blanc, which he did with style, pulling into Chamonix just as the clock was counting down to stop the race!

Steve Nash (GBR)

Supporter: Richard Bungay

Rank: 21st, 178 km from Goal

Nationality: Great Britain

Total Distance: 2011 km

Age: 52

Hiking: 557 km

Previous X-Alps: 2011

Flying: 1454 km

The oldest competitor in the race, Steve Nash had his best flight on Day 1. He laughed as he flew over the Dachstein, and made it 130 km in the air, very happy with his flight. Along with other athletes, Nash was plagued by bad weather and storms for the next couple of days, as well as battery charger problems on his van. To get the van charged back up it needed to stay in a campsite, forcing Nash to spend a wet night in a sponsor's new car in a raging thunderstorm!

The western winds, which had kept Steve from reaching Monaco in 2011, reared an ugly head on Day 6, just when he needed to fly directly west. During one exciting landing in Italy, Nash managed to smash his face into his instruments, and bled from a cut lip. Just past Checkpoint 5, Steve became the only competitor to hike up and over the Passo de Laco Scuro at 3000 meters! Luckily he was able to launch from this pass, and reached Switzerland that evening.

Nash didn't believe the spirit of the race allowed for wind-dummies, so if his supporter flew with him, it was only with him or behind him, not out in front. On Day 7, Nash had a great flight, tagging Turnpoint 6 and making it to Italy despite strong headwinds. Hiking back up into Switzerland on Day 8, this became his most exciting day in the air. On his second flight, he narrowly missed colliding with a rusty cable arcing across a valley, and landed after completely losing his concentration. Another hike-fly-hike brought him to the top of the Nuefenen Pass with barely enough time to lay out his wing and fly down to the valley before the 9 pm flying deadline. Nash called this late evening flight "terrifying" like flying down through a waterfall. He landed safely in a very windy valley, and fell asleep on his wing before his supporters could drive down to meet him!

Weather conditions in the Goms valley leading to Zermatt weren't terribly favorable for the next couple of days. Despite short flights into headwinds, Steve was forced to walk to the turnpoint in Zermatt, after getting his first shower in 8 days! An inversion in Zermatt made it hard to fly, even after hiking up to 2500 meters. He was able to barely tag the turnpoint in the air, but after flying back down the valley, high west winds kept him from turning west to Mont Blanc.

Nash made up for lost time during the last couple days in the race, tagging Turnpoints 8 & 9 and making the big turn south to Monaco. He even had time to meet up with his flying mentor in France! Alas, the race ended with Steve still 178 km from Goal.

Author's Note: It is with great regret that I mention Steve Nash passed away on August 31, 2016. Steve was halfway through a paragliding and hiking journey through Mongolia. Originally he was traveling with his friend Gareth as part of their "Spiralling the Steppes 2" paragliding adventure. Gareth was forced to leave the trip after some heavy landings hurt his back. Nash took his remaining food and was continuing on alone, when his tracker stopped moving in the middle of a valley. He was found murdered with his passport and money stolen, but his expensive paragliding gear left untouched. It was a senseless death, and friends all over the world were shocked and saddened. Steve will be remembered by his local flying club as "a true inspiration, happy to share his knowledge, skills & adventures in the most enthusiastic ways. Nicest guy you would ever want to meet."

Dave Turner (USA4)

Supporter: Krischa Berlinger

Nationality: USA

Age: 33

X-Alps Rookie

Rank: 20th, 140 km from Goal

Total Distance: 1800 km

Hiking: 660 km

Flying: 1140 km

For Dave Turner, the Red Bull X-Alps would be his second attempt to reach Monaco. After all, he had walked or flown every step of the way in training just a month before the race!

Turner had a nice first day, but so did everyone in this edition of the Red Bull X-Alps, and so he landed near the back of the pack that evening. His legs took over from there, walking at least 70 km on Day 2 and pulling his night pass to get him to a launch for the third day. But the weather wouldn't cooperate and it was back to walking for a while. He finally got a break with a late evening flight into the Oetztal valley but stayed low in the standings.

Turner had a couple great flights on Day 6, hopping from Turnpoints 5 to 6 in about 24 hours. This helped him climb back up the standings, reaching the middle of the pack and propelling him through Switzerland. With competitors all around him, and in good flying conditions, Dave joined a flurry of white wings flying to the Matterhorn, and reached Turnpoint 7 in the air on Day 8.

High winds and heat meant a day full of walking the next day past Mont Blanc, but Day 10 brought good conditions and another day in the air for Dave. A couple of flights took him through Annecy and the final turnpoint before Monaco.

If his race blog is any indicator, Dave might have eaten the most of all the competitors! His supporter was able to find him pizza, doner kebabs, and everything else needed to fuel a hungry athlete. But Dave was working it off quickly, as he walked the most of all competitors in the race by almost a hundred kilometers! 660 km in 12 days is enough to make anyone hungry.

Turner was the closest competitor to Monaco who didn't finish the course, with a heartbreaking 140 km left to walk and fly. In true "Lone Wolf" style, Dave didn't quit the race when the clock reached zero. Instead, he skipped the awards ceremony, waved goodbye to his supporter, and finished the course under his own steam.

Stephan Gruber (AUT3)

Supporter: Florian Eder

Rank: 19th, Finished in 11 Days, 6 Hours + 48-Hour Airspace Penalty

Nationality: Austria

Age: 29

X-Alps Rookie

Total Distance: 2118 km

Hiking: 431 km

Flying: 1687 km

Stephan Gruber had a cracking start to the 2015 Red Bull X-Alps, flying in the lead pack on what would be an exceptionally great flying day for the start of the race. By the end of the flight he was in the lead, and in Germany, having flown all the way from Turnpoint 1 past Turnpoint 2 and very near to Turnpoint 3! Whether it was confidence or advance planning, Stephan pulled his night pass on the first night (having declared it at noon, before his flight had really even got off the ground). The night pass allowed Gruber to walk south in the Inn Valley, launching further south than anyone in the lead pack. Flying solo down the Inn and then across the German Alps, he was able to reach Turnpoint 4 in Aaschau still in third place.

Now back, the lead pack motored its way down to Italy, where Gruber reached Turnpoint 5 on Day 5. He continued to progress into Switzerland; however, with strong North Foehn winds, conditions were dangerous. He was alarmed to see Michael Witschi, whom he had been flying with for hours, lose control of his wing, pull his reserve, and land in a lake. Witschi was ok, and had swum to shore by the time Gruber arrived.

By Day 6, flying conditions had improved. A pack of three had pulled ahead of the rest, but Stephan was near the front of about 18 pilots fighting it out above Turnpoint 6. He then spent night 7 high in the mountains on the Swiss/Italy border, allowing him to fly down the next morning. Gruber's favorite part of the race was flying at 4,500 meters over the Matterhorn. When his feet were back on the ground after that flight, he suffered from the record breaking heat, but was buoyed by fans that would drive by him and cheer him on. Day 9 put him back on the ground walking through France waiting out the high winds. But the final two days of Gruber's race brought good weather, great flying, and a speedy journey to the finish in Monaco.

His most exciting moment of the race might have been landing near an elephant. While approaching the final Turnpoint in Peille, too late he realized there were clouds which would force him to land, unknowingly in the backyard of Princess Stephanie of Monaco! The police took him away, but he was released when the race organizers explained the situation. Unfortunately, Stephan got a 48 hour airspace penalty for this mistake, costing him seven places in the standings, but still allowing him to finish on the float in Monaco.

Michael Witschi (SUI3)

Supporter: Yael Margelisch

Nationality: Switzerland

Age: 37

X-Alps Rookie

Rank: 18th, Finished in 11 Days, 22 Hours

Total Distance: 2137 km

Hiking: 499 km

Flying: 1638 km

Michael Witschi's first day of flying landed him near Turnpoint 3, but too late in the day to reach the mountaintop. Unfortunately, although he was at the Turnpoint early the next morning, thunderstorms came through and forced him and a couple of other athletes to walk down from the turnpoint instead of flying.

Flying skills and more walking kept him in the top five for the competition on Day 3, when he reached Italy. Michael then joined a string of athletes on the road up to the Brenta in the rain. Reaching Turnpoint 5 early the next morning, he was able to fly down in improving weather. This would turn out to be an exciting day for Witschi, however. Day 5 had been forecast to have very strong North Foehn winds and dangerous flying conditions. After crossing the border of Switzerland in the air at 3,600 meters, Witschi flew out of a calm lee of a mountain and into strong head winds. His glider took a collapse, and he pulled his reserve for the first time in 17 years of flying.

The wind blew Michael (under reserve) over Lago di Poschiavo, and he quickly undid his harness buckles to escape as soon as he smashed into the water. He only needed to swim 150 meters to shore, but it was cold and against the wind and he was dressed in layers of cold weather flying clothes. Help arrived quickly and salvaged his wing and gear. Witschi was determined to continue the race, and since his water landing occurred near the end of the day, managed to dry out his gear overnight. He didn't even lose his 5th place in the standings!

Michael dropped a few places in the leaderboard during the middle of his race, but managed to stay in the top half of the field. On Day 8, he was in good company with other athletes around Turnpoint 7. Flying above 4000 meters near the Matterhorn, he flew the direct line toward Mont Blanc. Even landing out deep in the mountains couldn't slow him down, as the next day he was able to get in the air despite strong tailwinds and progress toward Mont Blanc. Rounding the last Turnpoint in Annecy on Day 10, Witschi had some problems with a broken line on his glider. After messing with it for a while, his support team finally fixed it with a knot. The result? His glider flew, but always pulled to the left side. The flying wasn't that great anyway, as the air was very stable.

The delay cost him places in the standings, but what was important now for Witschi was getting to Monaco before the race ended. Having saved his night pass, he now used it on the last night, walking the last 85 km to make it to Monaco, and finished within 2 hours of the time cutoff!

Erik Rehnfeldt, (SWE)

Supporter: Xavier Potier

Rank: 17th, Finished in 11 Days, 21 Hours

Nationality: Sweden

Total Distance: 2374 km

Age: 48

Hiking: 582 km

X-Alps Rookie

Flying: 1792 km

Quickly dubbed "Erik the Viking", Erik Rehnfeldt stayed comfortably in the top half of the field for most of the 2015 Red Bull X-Alps. Eric reported that his race had a lot of ups and downs, so much that it was hard for him to keep track of all the days! He said his supporters were great, and really helped keep him fueled and moving down the course. He also realized that small mistakes can have big consequences. Here is a section from his blog telling about the last days of this challenging race, in his own words:

"I am a little disappointed with my final placement (17th) in the comp. I felt like I deserved to be around 12th place, next to Team CZE (Stanislav Mayer) and Team FRA3 (Nelson De Freyman) with whom I had caught up with in Annecy and also been close to many times during the race. But the difference is so small sometimes.

Let me explain to give you an idea (not to make excuses ;) The same day as we passed Annecy, I tried to take off in the evening with Stanislav above the Maurienne valley to make a glide down the valley. I missed my first takeoff attempt and when I finally got in the air there were no more thermals at all. So I had to fly straight down in the valley, but Stanislav had manage to follow the ridge and gain maybe 10-15 km over me, just in one glide! Because of this, I reached the takeoff maybe 1h after Stanislav the following morning, and this turned out to be critical since the weak thermals were already blown apart by the NW wind that got stronger and stronger by the minute.

I then spend hours on this take off trying to fly the east side, then the west side, only to bomb out and hike up again. Finally after 5 hours without making any progress, I flew down in the valley to hike up to the Galibier Pass from where I would launch the following day for my flight close to Peille, the last TP above Monaco. All this to describe how little can make a huge difference in the end. Of course there have been many situations like this for everybody during the race, but still it was quite frustrating for us.

I am of course very happy to have reached Monaco. We have had many flyable days this year, and I imagine for those of you following the live tracking, it all seemed like quite "easy" conditions. But the reality was far from that. Many days we had strong headwinds and VERY turbulent conditions in lee side thermals. I heard many of the pilots placing in the top ten saying that they were honestly really happy to have arrived in Monaco in one piece and alive! I felt the same way. My previous experience from paragliding is mostly from competition flying and XC flying. And I can tell you that if there would have been a PWC, the tasks would have been cancelled most of the days due to strong winds and / or to strong lee sides causing dangerous conditions. I do not say this to try to impress but rather to make it more clear that the conditions were not easy this year even if we had many flyable days. After all it took Maurer one day more to reach Monaco this year than 2013.

But all this made me even more happy for my last flight from Galibier. I know when we took off that it could be done. But during the flight I did not dare to think that I might make it all the way to Monaco. In the end (after about 170 km flight) I landed only about 40 km hike (24 km in straight line I believe) from the last TP, and we realized that we could make it!!! I landed quite high because down in the valley there were almost nothing for landing. It took me 45 minutes only to get down from the mountain. After that Mathieu and I started to run towards Peille. We had 2 hours in the evening and then another 6 1/2 in the morning, so we gave it all we had in the evening to make as much progress as possible. In the morning we continued at almost the same speed, until we realized that we had enough time to reach Peille before the deadline at 11h30, and also that we would not have time to catch up with any of the pilots in front of us who had used their night passes to advance during the night.

What a nice feeling to arrive. Incredible!!! I have never in my life felt anything like it. I have never before made an adventure so demanding both physically and mentally. What a victory to arrive. It will take some time to really sink in. I am so happy to have achieved this goal. So much preparation, time, thoughts and money has gone into this project. It is something like a crown on my paragliding achievements. I am more proud of reaching Monaco in 17th place than finish 4th in the Paragliding World Cup (Annecy 2009)! The Red Bull X-Alps is much more my style. I love the adventure part of it. But next time I think I prefer to do it without the competition aspect. It gives more freedom to enjoy the fantastic mountains and scenery that I pass through, because the mountains I have flown in are really spectacular!!! An unforgettable and incredible human and physical experience ! Thank you all again for cheering me on !!!!" / Erik

http://www.eriksadventureblog.com/red-bull-x-alps-2015-team-swe-reaching-the-goal-in-monaco/

Pawel Faron (POL)

Supporter: Piotr Goc

Nationality: Poland

Age: 41

Previous X-Alps: 2011, 2013

Rank: 16th, Finished in 11 Days, 20 Hours

Total Distance: 2201 km

Hiking: 584 km

Flying: 1617 km

With his signature white sunglasses and ready smile, Pawel Faron was ready to reach Monaco. The year 2015 would be his third attempt at the Red Bull X-Alps. When talking about the previous editions before the race, he said his two experiences were very different from each other. In the rainy year, he walked a lot, really trashing his legs, and it took him months to recover physically. In the race with better weather, he got to fly a lot more, and physically he was fine very quickly after the race. But he hadn't reached the finish and was anxious to get to the float in Monaco. The year 2015 would be his year to do that!

Faron had a good start to his race, but a tough second day which saw him fall down the standings. He rallied to fly with a gaggle of competitors on Day 3, allowing him to make up some distance across the German Alps. After landing, he found himself (along with 5 other pilots) walking in record heat along a valley with no launches at all. Pawel put his head down and kept covering ground.

After turning the corner of the Zugspitz on Day 4, heat gave way to cool winds and rain, and a long walk up the Oetztal valley toward Italy. The middle pack of athletes came together at the border above Timmelsjoch pass, launching into strong tailwinds the next morning. The North Foehn winds were dangerous, but still propelled them into the Brenta and Turnpoint 5. They were able to land, sign the board, and continue flying further that day. Faron made it over another big pass that day and near the border of Switzerland.

Three days of fine flying conditions were then enough for Pawel to cross Switzerland and set his sights on Mont Blanc. On Day 9, high winds made flying difficult, but by then he had reached France and focusing on Monaco. The weather again improved on Day 10, allowing for good flights past the turnpoint in Annecy and heading south.

Pawel would end up walking 110km on the last night to finish the race before the time cutoff, and those painful kilometers were evident in his limping stride at the award ceremony the next day. He narrowly beat out Rehnfelt (SWE) who (having used his night pass earlier in the race) was forced to stop for the night just a few kilometers from the finish. Regardless of finish placement, Pawel and his large contingent of supporters were pleased and proud that he had finally reached Monaco.

Honza Rejmanek (USA1)

Supporter: Jesse Williams

Nationality: USA

Age: 40

Previous X-Alps: 2007, 2009, 2011, 2013

Rank: 15th, Finished in 11 Days 17 Hours

Total Distance: 2480 km

Hiking: 570 km

Flying: 1910 km

Honza Rejmanek has competed in more Red Bull X-Alps than just about anyone except Toma Coconea (ROM). He's been successful, too, with a 3rd place finish in 2009 to put him on the podium. Traveling to and competing in this race takes most of his vacation time for the whole year, and each time he competes, Honza swears it will be his last. But Monaco had eluded him; even in 2009 for 3rd place, he was still 139 heartbreaking kilometers from the sea. 142, 139, 181, and 101 km; those are the distances he had left to Monaco each year he competed. The year 2015 would be his year to try and finally finish the race.

Day 1 would set the tone for a successful race, allowing him to fly over the Dachstein for the first time, rather than slowly and painfully walk up and over the massif. Landing within a few kilometers of Turnpoint 3, Honza knew the weather the next day wouldn't be as good.   He patiently waited out rain showers interspersed with extreme heat, and made it to Turnpoint 4 in Germany by Day 4. Just south of there, he gambled on a break in the rain showers and hiked up to a really steep launch near the Inn Valley. Taking to the air here saved him at least 30 km of walking, and moved him up on the leaderboard, not to mention being highly rewarding mentally!

On Day 5, Rejmanek joined much of the middle of the field in launching on the border of Italy on a very windy day. He had good company in the air, and arrived at Turnpoint 5 in Cima

Tosa at the same time as at least 5 other athletes. That's a lot of fives, high-fives I'm sure!

Another day would see him reach Switzerland and the top half of the field. A meteorologist by trade, Rejmanek was elated to get to fly the wave phenomena (for the first time) over Switzerland. He found smooth, steady lift which carried him up and over cloud base and up to 4,300 meters. His flight for the day lasted for 8 hours, and while he couldn't stay in the wave as long as he wanted, it helped carry him along his way to Monaco.

Then with three days to go to the time cutoff, Honza found himself in the same location as he had been in the 2013 edition. Then, he wasn't able to finish. This time, the forecast was looking better, and he said there was still hope left. Rejmanek calls this race the perfect game, because it's not possible to get through it with brute force. "You have to think", he says, "and this year the competitors have gotten really good at thinking".

On Day 10, Rejmanek was one of ten athletes to pass the turnpoint in Annecy and head south to Monaco on the final leg. The weather would be his friend here, as blue skies promised more chances to fly. At least, he flew well up until the last day of his race, which had hot and stable weather, forcing him to do lots of walking. A couple of other competitors managed to nip by Honza in the air that last day, but his goal was bigger than the leaderboard. His night pass, saved for the last night, allowed him to finish within a few hours of the time cutoff. And for the first time in five editions, Honza Rejmanek got to fly down to the float in Monaco.

Chi-Kyong Ha (KOR)

Supporter: Yun Jae Ryu

Nationality: South Korea

Age: 39

X-Alps Rookie

Rank: 14th, Finished in 11 Days 15 Hours

Total Distance: 2353 km

Hiking: 439 km

Flying: 1914 km

Sometimes called the Korean Dragon, Chi-Kyong Ha had never been higher than 2000 meters before arriving in the Alps. Luckily the altitude didn't turn out to be a factor for him, although the heat did. Hachi, as he was known to his friends, said his favorite day of the race was Day 1. He had been nervous about the airspace, but then just had an amazing flight almost to Turnpoint 3. However, Day 2 was just the opposite. Getting caught in a thunderstorm early in the morning on launch meant walking down instead of flying. He put in a lot of road miles that day, in record heat. This would take a toll on his feet, causing him foot pain and blisters for the remainder of the race.

Slipping a few places on the leaderboard, and now near the back of the pack, Hachi walked much of the route through Germany as bad weather and lack of launches kept him grounded. Improving weather albeit high winds helped him assault the leaderboard starting on Day 5, when he flew almost to Turnpoint 5 in Italy.

Day 6 gave Hachi a little setback, as he took a very "unique" line to get into Switzerland. Luckily he was able to take to the air to cross the high mountains which were blocking his progress west. He said "During the middle of the race I launched in very poor conditions that I didn't think I could fly in. But I took off and fought strong turbulence, went up to a high altitude and flew further than I believed possible. I hit the jackpot that day!"

The chance to climb to the middle of the leaderboard came on Day 8, when good flying conditions dominated the area. On a day when many competitors were having great flights, Hachi took a risky line in the high mountains, heading straight west to the Matterhorn rather than curving north. This paid off for him as he tagged Turnpoint 7, now in 15th place.

Hachi found the last section of the race to be the most difficult. Altitude restrictions forced him to land only 23 km from goal, but it was hard to find landing places. The curvy roads added kilometers to his route, and by the end he was really happy he could stop walking on his painful feet.

Upon reaching Monaco, Hachi said "It really is a great achievement. It was a miracle! Even I cannot believe that I made the goal in such poor conditions. The moment I reached the goal, Monaco, I cried. It was a reward for the pains of a hard race."

Peter Von Bergen (SUI4)

Supporter: Phillippe Arn

Nationality: Switzerland

Age: 29

X-Alps Rookie

Rank: 13th, Finished in 11 Days 12 Hours

Total Distance: 2171 km

Hiking: 451 km

Flying: 1720 km

Peter Von Bergen, known as "Peter of the Mountain", was one of two wildcards selected for the 2015 Red Bull X-Alps (The other was Dave Turner). He got off to a good start on Day 1, landing in Kossen near Turnpoint 3 in the top half of the field. He even had time to film a bit while flying, calling the thermals "beautiful, not too strong, not too rough".

Unfortunately on Day 2 Von Bergen ripped up his race glider, but was able to get another one very quickly, so that it didn't interfere with his flying. Peter didn't mind the penalty on Day 3, which allowed him to get an extra two hours of sleep, saying it was really helpful! But his equipment problems continued, as his race Flymaster was now broken. He would use his own vario until another one was provided by the organization. All this didn't slow him down as he moved up to 8th place in Germany.

On Day 5 Peter celebrated his birthday while racing...he was now a big 3-0. He was moving up in the standings, too, now in 5th place and part of a chase pack of several pilots.

Evidently Peter ate too much birthday cake (just kidding), because on Day 6 he wasn't feeling very well. His supporter Phillippe, who usually hiked up with him to launch, made him rest longer before flying, and Von Bergen fell to 17th in the standings.

Now very happy to be in his home country of Switzerland,

Peter took a line after Turnpoint 6 that was well to the north of any other athletes so far in the race. It worked for him, though, and allowed him to maintain his place in the middle of the field. On Day 8, Von Bergen found himself already thermalling at 9:30 in the morning. But he loved his country so much, that he said he just wanted to stop and enjoy the view!

Continued intestinal problems would plague Peter off and on during the race (if the repeated photos of toilet paper rolls on his race blog are any indication!). Nubel (GER4)'s supporter would help him out a little bit, but at times Von Bergen was only moving at about 30% of his physical capacity.

Despite his sickness, Peter powered through Switzerland and into France, flying with competitors all around him, and almost catching up to the top 10 near Annecy. Now in a group of about 6 pilots, it was race for 11th place with 200 km to go. Good flying weather ensued, allowing all of them to make fast progress. Peter fell behind the group for a while, but caught up to some again with good flights on his final push to Monaco.

Von Bergen might have suffered during the 2015 Red Bull X-Alps, but he and his supporter always seemed to be smiling and enjoying themselves, whether it was in the air or sleeping in their self-customized race van.

Author's Note: It is with great sadness that we note Peter Von Bergen passed away on March 19, 2016. He was doing paragliding acrobatics low over the ground in Fiesch, Switzerland when something went wrong. He didn't deploy his reserve, and was already dead when paramedics arrived. I will remember Peter for his big smile, and the paragliding world mourns his passing.

Stanislav Mayer (CZE)

Supporter: Petr Kostrhun

Nationality: Czech Republic

Age: 25

X-Alps Rookie

Rank: 12th, Finished in 11 Days 8 Hours

Total Distance: 2303 km

Hiking: 499 km

Flying: 1804 km

A true rookie in the paragliding world, having only been a pilot for five years, Stanislav Mayer got his race off to a great start by coming second in the Powertraveller Prologue. He would finish in 2h 22m, only a minute behind the winner Guschlbauer (AUT1)!

Mayer had a great start to his main race too, sleeping at the hut after making it to Turnpoint 3 on the first day. Flying near Merano, Italy, Mayer saw a very scary black cloud, and spiraled down to land to avoid rain and maybe a gust front. He was very angry a few minutes later, when the black cloud dissipated and other competitors flew overhead! Despite this, Mayer kept hard on the leader's heels through the first few days, using his night pass in Italy on the 3rd night to try and reach the front. This helped him get to Turnpoint 5, but unfortunately in the face of strong winds he couldn't capitalize on his efforts to catch the leaders.

Stanislav was familiar with the Red Bull X-Alps, having been a supporter in 2013 for Michal Krysta, who finished in France but short of Monaco. Mayer was able to fly while supporting Krysta, but appreciated how hard it was too. This time around, his two supporters didn't see eye to eye about their roles, and there were arguments in camp as the race started. "I had a friend who came to help with the hiking and also my official supporter too. They had a clash. My friend wanted to enjoy his time, spend moments with nature, while my official supporter is very performance-orientated. So one will want to keep the car running to charge instruments in the evening and the other will want to turn it off to listen to the birdsong!" said Mayer.

He wished he had prepared more for flying in bad weather. Since he lived relatively far away from the Alps, most of his trips to train here were in good weather, since that made it worth the drive. Mayer said the scariest moment of his race was in Germany. "I jumped over a col with only 20 meters spare into the leeside and was getting thrown down towards a big ridge of trees. I thought, 'help, I'm going to end up in the trees,' but then I hit this strong thermal in the middle of nowhere. It was such good luck. I was so happy, and I am so happy to be here now!"

Almost to Switzerland on the evening of Day 5, Mayer was hiking with Witchi (SUI3) and Gruber (AUT3). He was behind them perhaps 10 min after taking longer to finish his dinner. They launched and crossed the wide valley, and then the wind came up very strong and Mayer got stuck on the hill. He would spend the night up on the mountain, catch up on a lot of sleep, and wait to fly until the next day. He was disappointed, but then relieved when he heard that conditions were bad, and Witchi had thrown his reserve and landed in a lake! He lost a few places from waiting, but eventually made up some ground. Mayer was the only athlete in the race to visit Lake Como. Perhaps he just wanted to take a swim? Regardless of his navigation strategy, it worked out, bumping him back up to the top 10 for a little while.

Day 9 was tough for everyone, as high winds made flying difficult for everyone. Mayer attempted a flight north of Mont Blanc but was soon back to walking along with other competitors in the area. He made up for lost time on Day 10, by team flying into Annecy with Pawel Faron (POL), Nelson de Freyman (FRA3), and Stephan Gruber (AUT3). After all top landing to sign they board at Turnpoint 9, they flew together another 60 km south towards goal. Mayer may have been the pilot with the least years of flying experience, but he successfully arrived in Monaco, becoming one of nine athletes to finish within the last 24 hours of the race.

Nelson de Freyman (FRA3)

Supporter: Thomas Punty

Nationality: France

Age: 23

X-Alps Rookie

Rank: 11th, Finished in 11 Days 2 Hours

Total Distance: 2382 km

Hiking: 546 km

Flying: 1836 km

At 23 years of age, Nelson de Freyman might be the youngest athlete in the 2015 Red Bull X-Alps, but he's already been paragliding for 8 years and mountaineering for longer than that! In 2013 he was a Red Bull X-Alps supporter for Antoine Girard, who finished third in the race, so Nelson knows what it will take to get to Monaco for himself.

Nelson made the mistake of going too hard at the start of the race. Although he finished the first flight near the front of the pack, after a couple of days he was down in 21st place. "At first I didn't want to take a rest to stop and eat. I then realized I needed to slow down and spend more time resting and thinking, and then my race was better. I started to come back and catch up the lead group and play with them for two to three days. That was a very nice experience", said de Freyman.

He made his big move near Turnpoint 5 in Italy, moving up as high as 6th for a while, with the three French athletes together in the standings. This lasted across Switzerland, finally breaking apart near the Matterhorn, where competitors took wildly different paths to get across the 4000 meters peaks toward Mont Blanc. Nelson wanted to try something different, heading north instead of west. This admittedly didn't work very well, and forced him to try and make up ground on his feet. De Freyman said he experienced every emotion possible during the race, but he kept smiling. His youth and strong training regimen allowed him to keep running throughout the competition.

Luckily conditions in his home country of France were good, allowing Nelson to stay in the air and off his feet. He found himself in good company on Day 10 with other competitors, and together they made great progress from Mont Blanc, past Turnpoint 9 in Annecy, and then toward Monaco. That night, he used his night pass to pull ahead of these athletes, and the next day flew most of the rest of the way to Monaco.

De Freyman set his sights high. He didn't want to just finish the race, he wanted to be in the Top 10. At the finish, he says he found the race tougher than expected. "This year conditions were very strong. I really never flew in these kinds of conditions. So for me that was a very tough experience and scary. But every day got better and at the end they were manageable", says Nelson. Next time? He'll be trying to win.

Nick Neynens (NZL)

Supporter: Louis Tapper

Rank: 10th, Finished in 10 Days 18 Hours

Nationality: New Zealand

Total Distance: 2508 km

Age: 32

Hiking: 485 km

X-Alps Rookie

Flying: 2023 km

Nick Neynens did not have a good start to the 2015 Red Bull X-Alps. The first to take off from the Gaisberg, he had thermaled up and was ready head out, when he realized he had a big knot in his lines. He had to land to fix it, putting him down the field. Once past the Dachstein and Turnpoint 2, he flew the southern side of the hills, which was much lower than where most competitors had flown, which put him on the ground in the very back of the pack. Nick spent the next two days in poor weather, in last place, knowing he needed to get ahead of someone before the elimination at 6 am on Day 4. Along with many people at the back of the field, he pulled his night pass on Day 3, walking most of the night to finally move up a few places and avoid elimination.

The highlight of his race was in the Italian Dolomites. It was amazing scenery, and finally he was able to see other competitors around him. Not to mention, he completed a lot of the kilometers in this race wearing flip-flops. Yep, Nick thought "jandals" as they are known in New Zealand, kept him from getting blisters, especially in the rain, and he wore them often in the race.

Neynens continued to slowly move up the leaderboard, until he finally got a break on Day 8. In 19th place and still in Italy north of Lake Como, he had the best flight of his race, passing Turnpoint 7 in Zermatt. The crux of this flight was clearing a col near the Matterhorn by inches...he even had his legs out of the harness to run across the glacier, if necessary! Luckily it wasn't, and finally he was back in the game in 10th place after 170 km of flying!   This earned him the nickname "Comeback Kiwi".

By Turnpoint 9 in Annecy, Neynens top landed in style and even reached as high as 9th place for a while...not bad for someone who had come from 32nd place days before!   But his adventure wasn't over.   After a good flight that day, Nick landed too close to a tree and dropped his wing over it. He and his supporters would spend the next couple of hours (in the pitch black) picking his lines out of the thorns. Nick called it "all part of the adventure" and seemed pretty upbeat about it.   He said his good flights were helping to even out his mistakes.

Nick was able to get several good flights through the French Alps to Monaco, and collected the final coveted spot in the Top 10. On his final night, he was still several kilometers short of the finish, though, and with his night pass expended, had to wait until the next morning to cross the line. Finally, his flip-flops could be put to good use landing on the float in Monaco!

Manuel Nübel (GER4)

Supporter: Christian Schineis

Nationality: Germany

Age: 27

X-Alps Rookie

Rank: 9th, Finished in 10 Days 17 Hours

Total Distance: 2163 km

Hiking: 430 km

Flying: 1733 km

Although Manuel Nubel suffered a broken patella during training for the Red Bull X-Alps, that couldn't stop him from toeing the start line as a confident rookie. He enjoyed the prologue, but like most athletes couldn't wait for the main event to get started. On Day 1 Manu had a great flight, landing near the back of the Kampenwand. Unbeknownst to him, fans were worried about him being stuck in a tree way back near the start...his GPS tracker had broken while in the air. Luckily he was fine, although suffering from the effects of sunshine, headache, and dehydration during the long flight.

His headache had a chance to recover the next morning, though, as he waited out a rain shower on launch at Turnpoint 3. Manuel then suffered through the heat for the next couple of days, staying quietly in the top half of the field, and was the only one to climb up the side of the Zugspitz in order to fly down to Turnpoint 4 in Lermoos. On Day 4, crossing the Inn Valley in rainy weather meant zigzagging around big hills, but luckily he was able to fly down from the second one, making it into the Oetztal Valley. There he joined most of the middle of the field of competitors, all slogging up the valley through rain showers, and hoping to fly the next day into Italy.

While many competitors decided to walk up and over the Timmelsjoch Pass at 2500 meters, Nubel and a few others chose to head up the Similaun hut at 3019 meters, both on the border of Austria/Italy. Since both groups were able to launch into strong North Foehn winds, it's unclear if the extra effort was worth it, but "Manu" used the winds to his advantage, able to fly to Turnpoint 5 and to land there in difficult conditions. He continued his flight that day much further, almost arriving in Switzerland before stopping at the mandatory 10:30 cutoff.

Day 6 was another good flight past Turnpoint 6, with Nubel consistently flying in the top half of the field, with plenty of competitors around for company. Flyable weather brought him through Switzerland and into France, and then he had a long hot walk down the Sion valley to Mont Blanc. Despite high winds on Day 9, Manu managed to fly while other competitors were grounded, moving him into 10th place. His flights would allow him to land in Annecy and continue further that evening.

Despite landing in a tree in France, and being separated from his supporters for hours, Nubel couldn't be deterred. He spent two more days flying south to Monaco, head to head with Neynens (NZL), finally passing him by using his night pass on the last night. After going 25 hours straight to finish the race, he arrived in Peille in the wee hours, knowing he could rest before flying down to the raft the next morning. Nubel called getting to Monaco the most intense ten days of his life. He said that it was hard to realize that he was finished because he was so exhausted, but that he was really happy to be done.

Gavin McClurg (USA2)

Supporter: Bruce Marks

Rank: 8th, Finished in 10 Days 4 Hours

Nationality: USA

Total Distance: 2058 km

Age: 43

Hiking: 498 km

X-Alps Rookie

Flying: 1560 km

Gavin McClurg's first Red Bull X-Alps had more ups and downs than that average athlete, and that's saying something. His extensive training regime in the months leading up to the race earned him the nickname "Big Guns" McClurg. His glory came early, in the Powertraveller Prologue, finishing third in 2h 24m. This earned Gavin an extra night pass and a five minute head start in the main race.

Gavin's flying skills and extensive research earned him 4th place after Day 1, arriving in time to sleep in the hut for the night at Turnpoint 3. Unfortunately, an early morning rain shower forced him and 3 other athletes to walk down from the turnpoint rather than fly. Other competitors who waited, were able to fly down later, not exactly catching the walkers, but more importantly saving their bodies from a steep descent. Climbing up to launch later that afternoon in brutal heat would give McClurg really bad blisters. "I tried to take a shortcut" he said, "by bushwhacking up a steep slope". When Gavin found the road again, he saw other athletes who had obviously followed a trail and had an easier time of it. He fell to the middle of the pack through Germany in the midst of record heat and then cold rain. He would use the first of his two night passes here to regain some ground on his competitors.

A few days later his fortunes fell again. Between Turnpoint 4 in Germany, and 5 in Italy, he choose a solo line to the west of the other athletes, which didn't pay off. Gavin's competitors were able to take advantage of strong north winds to speed them south, and he fell to 22nd place.

From there, McClurg had nowhere to go but back up. On Day 8, he chose a risky line directly to the Matterhorn across high mountaintops where no roads led to where he wanted to go (had he landed). He stayed in the air, and his research paid off, so when he finished his flight that evening, after 160 km and nearly to Mont Blanc, he was in 7th!

McClurg said his supporters were a great help, and that they had fun even while suffering, with no arguments at all. After one particularly grueling day, they offered him a can of cat food for dinner, before sending him back out on the course!

Now in France, he was in home territory (if that can be said of an American) having visited and flown here several times over the years. That didn't mean it would be easy though. Unfavorable winds slowed his progress at times, and forced him to take risks that he usually wouldn't. At one point, which Gavin called "the worst flight of his life", he was descending in downdraft at -22m/s, which is almost free fall. He considered landing in a pond just for a softer surface, but managed to get to the ground safely while staying dry.

At nightfall on his final day, he pulled his night pass and just kept walking over 100 km in 16 hours to finish the race. He might have won the award for the worst blisters in the race, and said he wanted to quit with just a few kilometers left to walk, but he made Monaco. In doing so, he became the first American to finish the race by landing on the float in Monaco.

Ferdinand van Schelven (NED)

Supporter: Anton Brous

Rank: 7th, Finished in 9 Days 22 Hours

Nationality: Netherlands

Total Distance: 2047 km

Age: 31

Hiking: 497 km

Previous X-Alps: 2011, 2013

Flying: 1550 km

Ferdinand van Schelven was no stranger to this race. Neither was his supporter. Anton and Ferdy were friends for 10 years, and have now competed as a team in three editions of the Red Bull X-Alps. With so much experience together, Anton knows when to push Ferdy to keep going, and when to stop and get some rest. Anton gets a break from driving each morning by hiking up to the first launch of the day with Ferdy...and then hiking down again, saying "my wing is quite large. I tried hiking with it once, but at the top I was totally wasted."

In 2015, the team didn't get off to that great of a start. After landing near the back of the pack on Day 1, heat and then rain meant a struggle to continue down the course. Ferdy blamed the extreme heat in the 2015 edition of the race for his blisters. He'd never had blisters before in the Red Bull X-Alps, and this made his motivation to stay in the air stronger. But he actually loved walking in the rain, and during a stretch of bad weather, called himself the "Walking Dutchman" rather than his usual "Flying Dutchman". But when Ferdinand looks up while flying, he finds encouragement on his wing. When financing this race through a crowdfunding site, he asked his donors to write down motivational messages on stickers, which he placed on the fabric. He was also helped with motivation by a surprise visit during the race by his brother and girlfriend who hiked along with him for a while.

After Day 5 of van Schelven's race, he had barely arrived in Switzerland, and was still in the bottom half of the field with more than half the distance still to go. It was time to turn on the afterburners. From 20th place in the standings, during the next two days he passed other competitors like they were standing still, arriving via a direct flying line to Mont Blanc, now in 5th place!

In France for the rest of the race, Ferdy continued his solo assault on the terrain, lucking out with windy but otherwise good flying weather while heading south to Monaco.   With competitors closing in behind him, he used his night pass on the last night to cruise into Monaco the next morning. Neither of them got much sleep that night, but Ferdy took time to notice that it was exactly two years before that he had arrived in Monaco for the previous edition of the race!

Ferdy was nothing if not consistent. This was his second time arriving in Monaco, with three impressive showings in the Red Bull X-Alps; 7th in 2011, 6th in 2013, and 7th again in 2015. He's been telling his supporter that it's his last race for three editions now...but will 2017 be a 4th?

Aaron Durogati (ITA)

Supporter: Ondrej Prochazka

Nationality: Italy

Age: 29

Previous X-Alps: 2013

Rank: 6th, Finished in 9 Days 6 Hours

Total Distance: 2165 km

Hiking: 357 km

Flying: 1808 km

Aaron Durogati arrived in Monaco before, as a rookie in the 2013 edition of the Red Bull X-Alps. He hopes to better his 7th place finish this time. But aside from the entire field having good flights on the first day, Aaron didn't enjoy the first few days of the race. Bad weather, bad decisions, and bad luck seemed to plague him as he pushed through Germany. On Day 2, he arrived at the Kampenwand Turnpoint early in the morning, only to have a rain shower pour down. Aaron and a few others elected to walk down rather than wait for the rain to stop.

Still in the Top 10, but wanting more, Durogati got a few key flights to reach Lermoos at Turnpoint 4, but the winds always seemed to be against him. Only his girlfriend could coax a smile to his face after a tough flight near the Zugspitze, which didn't seem to earn him any distance. Lingering pain in his ankle made bad weather miles on his feet less enjoyable, but didn't seem to slow him down.

On the morning of Day 4, Aaron was very happy to arrive to arrive in his hometown of Merano, Italy. Even better, he had managed an early morning flight down from the Timmelsjoch pass, just before another rain shower came through. It wasn't a great day for flying through Italy, but Aaron knew the area well and made good progress toward the Cima Tosa. The next day he used his local knowledge to fly near and then away from Turnpoint 5, arriving in Switzerland that evening.

But it was on Day 6 that Durogati made his big move, flying across a few borders and major mountain passes, and into the Top 5.   Then, nearing the Matterhorn on Day 7, he was able to hook up with Antoine Girard (FRA3) and Gaspard Petiot (FRA4).   Their teamwork in the air allowed them to fly further, faster and longer than they would have alone. Realizing this, they stayed together for the better part of 3 days, which is how long it took them to get close to Monaco. Flying in 4th, 5th, and 6th places, their team flying put Durogati, Girard and Petiot within reach of Paul Guschlbauer (AUT1), who had taken a westerly line south of Annecy, costing him energy and time.

Now the four of them were within striking distance of Monaco, and within sight of each other.   The teamwork came to an end, and it was every man for himself.   Durogati made the first move, broke away to almost catch up to Guschlbauer, and gambled on a shortcut which could get him the podium. Unfortunately, Aaron would sink out about 10 km short of Peille, forced to walk to the finish while the others flew on.

Durogati arrived in Monaco to the rapturous cheering of his fans.   When he caught his breath, Aaron said that this edition of the Red Bull X-Alps was very dangerous, more than usual. He knew it would be hard, he expected it to be hard, but there were many windy days this time, which made it tough and dangerous.   He was happy to arrive at the finish without any injuries.

Gaspard Petiot (FRA4)

Supporter: Laurent Pezet

Nationality: France

Age: 34

X-Alps Rookie

Rank: 5th, Finished in 9 Days 5 hours

Total Distance: 2365 km

Hiking: 275 km

Flying: 2090 km

Gaspard Petiot didn't know if he would physically survive the X-Alps. Going into the event with knee problems, he didn't expect to last more than a couple of days. Petiot would end up doing more in the 2015 Red Bull X-Alps than just hanging in there, though...he was usually gunning it at the front. However, his strategy was different than the rest of the field. Necessity is the mother of invention, and because he couldn't walk very much, he knew he needed to fly more. He top landed in the afternoon when he could, to save him walking up the next morning to fly. Petiot found that after the first few days of the race, he was still fresh while everyone else was tired from walking. And because walking was so much slower than flying, he didn't lose much distance on the ground and could easily make it up in the air.

Petiot landed in the Top 10 after a good flight on Day 1. Choosing to wait at Turnpoint 3 until the rain had cleared the next morning, he lost a few places in the standings, but easily made it up once he got in the air. A good flight across the German hills brought him near to Lermoos and Turnpoint 4. Even then, he chose to hike up and fly down for short flights rather than pound out extra miles on the ground.

Day 3 got him across the Italian border and closer to Merano, where he would sleep high up in a valley and was ready to launch early the next morning. Even in bad weather, Petiot made good progress in the air, and by the fifth afternoon, he was in 4th place and in Switzerland. A lead pack of three had pulled away, but a chasing pack of 7 pilots had all come together, and a little bit of teamwork allowed them to pass Turnpoint 6 in the air and continue on. Durogati (ITA) and Petiot had been near each other almost the whole race so far, and leapfrogged positions as first one and then the other would get low while flying. They might have flown together more than anyone else in the competition, and together they managed to pull ahead of the next chasing pack. Pausing for an early night, Petiot again chose not to put in mindless miles on the tarmac, but to wait for the morning and launch right above where he had landed.

The stretch of good weather continued, allowing Gaspard to cover more distance in the air, and then top land above the town of Brig, close to the Matterhorn. Early the next morning, he would fly across the valley to side hill land, and then hike up a little to be ready for the midday flight. Joining him were Durogati and Girard (FRA2). They might not have known it at the time, but this trio would continue to work together for the next three days. Flying was good, and they passed Mont Blanc, then Annecy, and set off towards the final Turnpoint at Peille.

After working together with Durogati and his fellow countryman Girard for so long, the alliance broke apart with less than 50 km to reach Monaco. All three were chasing Guschlbauer (AUT1) and hoping to get a coveted 3rd place podium. Durogati made his move first, breaking away and then sinking out with 10km to go. The weather was changing and anything was possible. Girard was far back in the distance, and it was now Petiot who was chasing close to Guschlbauer. Guschlbauer pulled ahead to nab 3rd, and Petiot landed just a couple agonizing kilometers short of Peille. He pushed through his knee pain to run the last few kilometers to the finish, but it wasn't enough...Girard came from behind, flew over his head, and landed at Peille just minutes before Petiot arrived, out of breath and covered in sweat.

Petiot's race to Monaco was remarkable for how little he
walked. Only 275 km, when most athletes were covering 400
or 500 km on their feet. Several times, he choose to land up
high while the flying was still decent, rather than glide another
few kilometers down the course line. This of course would
save him a lot of climbing the next morning to get back up to
launch! Luckily, the weather cooperated with this style of
racing, and allowed Petiot to stay more rested, which created
better decision making in the air.

Antoine Girard (FRA2)

Supporter: Pascal Gautheret

Nationality: France

Age: 35

Previous X-Alps: 2013

Rank: 4th, Finished in 9 Day 5 Hours

Total Distance: 2444 km

Hiking: 359 km

Flying: 2085 km

Antoine Girard is a philosopher, interspersing his regular Red Bull X-Alps Facebook updates with his favorite quotes. After a great first day of flying, he evidently believed he must pay a price for it in blisters. When a monsoon hit him at Turnpoint 3, he opted out of hiking down with other competitors, and waited for the weather to clear. However he didn't wait long enough, and landed in turbulent conditions with a soaked, heavy glider. Day 2 continued to not be kind; Girard got his first blisters, and the flying didn't go so well. He now sat in the bottom half of the field, still with high spirits.

Girard called his two support vehicles Command-Car and Fan-Bus, and together with his multitude of fans, they seemed to take good care of him both on the ground and in the air. No stranger to success, he finished 3rd as a rookie in the 2013 Red Bull X-Alps, and expected to do well this time, too. But he reflected on the vagaries of the weather in a race like this. "If you are stuck in the rain or in the wind in the middle of a hostile range, while others get fine flying weather, the gap widens very fast. One can hope the followers may catch good flying weather while the leaders get stuck. Usually this does not happen... strangely. Weather is not fair play." said Girard.

Indeed, the leaders reached the Southern Alps on Day 3 and enjoyed improving weather, while Girard and the middle of the pack get stuck in two days of poor conditions with weak flights. He was forced to wait on launch for hours for the clouds to clear.

"Patience is the key to content" - Mahomet

Meanwhile, his supporters waited impatiently down on the road for the Girard to fly again.   They reported on their day: "Not a free minute from 4h30 to midnight : maps, computers, tablets, electronic failures, shopping, driving hundreds of km in a day from valley to valley, repairs, champion care, feeding, photos, videos, uploads, three to six friendly journalists following us with cameras, interviews, drones overflying us some times...The phone rings more than 100 times a day. We have an average of two arguments per day, followed, within an hour, by a good laugh."

Day 5 was Antoine's comeback day. Despite a broken brake line, he caught up to many competitors and moved past Turnpoint 5 at the Brenta on a very windy day.   He finished the day in 9th place, up from 19th place, but not without a cost. His final glide in waning daylight brought him over thick forests, forcing him to continue past the time cutoff, and spiral dive to finally get down to a clearing a few seconds after 9 pm. This would earn him a 3 hour penalty. He didn't get much sleep either, staying up late to fix his brake line.

"No need to rush, just start in time" - La Fontaine

Day 6 brought strong westerly winds which impeded progress, but Girard still made good flights, moving up to 6th place, but unable to land up high as was his plan. With the three-hour penalty enforced for landing after 9 pm, he would need to rush the next morning to get to a launch, as the good weather continued to smile on the race.   His fans would worry as his GPS tracker was broken, but Antoine was still out there chasing down the leaders.

"The man who has no imagination has no wings" - Muhammad Ali

Day 8 would see Durogati (ITA) and Petiot (FRA4) join forces with Girard to pull away from the rest of the field, still chasing Maurer (SUI1), Huber (GER3), and Guschlbauer (AUT1). The three worked together for the next couple of days, with Girard occasionally unable to keep up. He called Durogati and Petiot "madmen" for their moves across the Matterhorn. As a team they fly most of the rest of the way to Monaco, until the bonhomie ended and each one vied for the coveted 3rd place finish. Guschlbauer almost allowed himself to be caught, but sneaked ahead to finish just 10 minutes ahead of Girard. Then it was down to the three. Durogati made a move out front, but got caught in the sea breeze and landed with 10 km still to go. Petiot got very close to Peille, landing and just needing to run a couple of kilometers left to the final Turnpoint.

"Petty impatience confounds great projects" - Confucius

However, Antoine, who had been left far behind, was still in the air and determined not to walk any further on his blistered feet. One of his supporters, whom he titles "Cloud-Control" was familiar with the area and instructed him on how to avoid the sea-breezes. Indeed, Girard reached Peille from the air, just minutes before Petiot got there on foot.   On a damaged glider, Antoine had somewhat of a crash landing at Peille, and only later realized that he actually broken his foot. In the euphoria of the moment, he just labeled it a "little bruise".

"All means are good as long as they are efficient" - JP Sartre

Paul Guschlbauer (AUT1)

Supporter: Werner Strittl

Nationality: Austria

Age: 31

Previous X-Alps: 2011, 2013

Rank: 3rd, Finished in 9 Days 4 Hours

Total Distance: 2066 km

Hiking: 446 km

Flying: 1620 km

Paul Guschlbauer started off strong in his third Red Bull X-Alps, winning the Powertraveller Prologue in 2h 21m. This earned him an extra night pass during the race, and he would use both of them to help maintain his race position over the course. From the start, Guschlbauer was gunning for the top spot. Having finished third in his rookie year in 2011 (only a heartbreaking 9 km from Monaco!), he reached the sea in his second attempt, this time in 9th place. This time he set his sights on keeping up with Chrigel Maurer (SUI1).

In the main race, Guschlbauer was one of the top three pilots to make it to Turnpoint 3 the first day, allowing him to fly down and make some distance on the rest of the competitors. Day 2 was a race for the lead, as Chrigel and Guschlbauer flew parallel paths along the German Alps, finally meeting up again at Turnpoint 4 in Lermoos. Then it was Chrigel who pulled ahead in Italy, leaving a chase pack of 5 pilots just behind him.

The weather on day 4 wasn't great, and no one made much progress at the front. If anything, the chasing pilots made up a little ground. Guschlbauer used the first of his night passes here to walk a few kilometers and be ready to fly the next day. His girlfriend hiked with him during the night, and with her long legs, Paul could barely keep up! The following day in very windy conditions, Maurer, Guschlbauer and Huber (GER3) pulled away from the rest, now almost 80 km ahead of the chasing pack. However, launching on the glaciers for the first time in the race, Paul opened his pack to find 2 left gloves and no sunglasses at all! His supporters had to go find him eye drops that night, after he landed with mild snow blindness from flying at 4500 meters.

The lead at the front increased by day 6, when Chrigel rounded Turnpoint 7 at the Matterhorn and continued via the safe/traditional route heading back north to Mont Blanc. Guschlbauer arrived at the turnpoint later that evening, and hiked up to spend the night in a hut at 3000 meters. He would choose to fly south from there into Italy, hoping for good winds to bring him over very high ridges to Mont Blanc. This worked out ok, but he wasn't able to make up any time on Chrigel, and Huber was chasing from behind also on the southern route.

Day 8 saw all three of them round Turnpoint 9 in Annecy and head for Monaco. While Maurer had gone due south from there, Guschlbauer skirted west around the Ecrins mountains at 4,000 meters. There was no going back, yet the winds on his side were too strong to fly. Paul finally got a windy flight across Lac de Serre-Poncon late in the evening, but by then he had already lost a lot of ground.

Firmly in second place at the beginning of the day, Day 9 would see Huber overtake Guschlbauer and push him back to 3rd. Still struggling too far to the west, the end of the day would see the trio of Durogati (ITA), Girard (FRA2), and Petiot (FRA4) work together to push Guschlbauer back to an unbelievable 6th place.   Fans were devastated, but Guschlbauer deployed the second of his night passes, to cover 20 km and move back up into 3rd.

With about 100 km to go, exhausted from his night pass, he was in a four way race for 3rd place. Staying just ahead of the chasing pack, he fought off an attempt by Durogati to catch him.   Durogati landed just short, as well as Petiot, leaving Girard to come from behind and chase Guschlbauer to Peille in the air.

Finally Guschlbauer was able to fly in and land at the Peille launch to narrowly claim third. Or would he? His wing fell and landed in the bushes just behind Turnpoint 10. Luckily his supporters and some fans were close by, and with many helping hands, they had his wing out in just 10 minutes. Guschlbauer could then run to the finish, narrowly reaching it ahead of Girard to finally capture the third place podium. After racing for almost 10 days and 2000 km, the podium was decided by only a few minutes!

Sebastian Huber (GER3)

Supporter: Martin Walleitner

Nationality: Germany

Age: 29

X-Alps Rookie

Rank: 2nd, Finished in 8 Days 22 Hours

Total Distance: 2063 km

Hiking: 480 km

Flying: 1583 km

Sebastian Huber made a nice start to his rookie year, landing in the top 10 near Turnpoint 3 on the first day. Then he was in well-known territory, flying near his local training hill the next morning. He wouldn't have time to do much more than wave, though, as he was hot on the heels of the leaders, and indeed made up ground, finally stopping for the night just short of Lermoos at Turnpoint 4. Flying south into Italy on Day 3, Huber was now in second just behind Chrigel Maurer (SUI1) with a gap open behind him. Suddenly he was somebody to watch. Could rookie Huber finally give three-time winner Maurer a run for his money? The ceiling of Huber's support vehicle was covered with relief maps of the whole route, allowing him to visualize his moves along the race course. Perhaps he was also visualizing a win.

Huber would drop back to 3rd after passing the Brenta dolomites, as Guschlbauer (AUT1) used his night-pass to catch up and pass him overnight. Strong winds blew them along on Day 5, and Huber used them to his advantage, opening an 80 km gap back to 4th place. When good weather settled in (still with strong afternoon valley winds), Sebastian would make it to the valley leading to the Matterhorn. Grounded for the evening, he set off at a run to Turnpoint 7, even managing to give an interview on the go without sounding out of breath!

Hoping to fly over the big peaks directly to Mont Blanc, Huber launched near the Matterhorn, but found the winds taking him south to Italy, following second place Guschlbauer.

Meanwhile Maurer was well on his way to Annecy, while the two chasers still had to somehow get around the glaciers near Mont Blanc, the rules stating that athletes had to pass north of the massive peak. Huber would spend the next day, luckily still flyable, on a spectacular flight around the glaciers. Because of airspace limitations around Mont Blanc, this circular flight would take some time, but it was also beautiful. That afternoon, more flights took him to Annecy and Turnpoint 9, still solidly in third.

Day 9 saw Sebastian flying quickly south toward Monaco, and doing the unthinkable; catching up to Guschlbauer, who had taken a windy line to the west and been grounded while others were flying. When the thermals gave up that evening, Huber was within striking distance of Monaco, and by using his night pass, he did just that. He finished the next morning, to the elation of his family and friends, who had traveled down to cheer him at the end. With his second place finish, he also won the Mazda rookie trophy, a behemoth of a statute, which weighed much more than his paragliding pack, that's for sure!

Christian (Chrigel) Maurer (SUI1)

Supporter: Thomas Theurillat

Nationality: Switzerland

Age: 32

Previous X-Alps: 2009, 2011, 2013
(AND WON THEM ALL)

Rank: 1st, Finished in 8 Days 4 Hours

Total Distance: 2059 km

Hiking: 405 km

Flying: 1654 km

Christian Maurer might as well have had a target on his wing, as everyone was gunning for him in 2015. After winning three straight editions of the Red Bull X-Alps, all by wide margins (a full day ahead or more at the finish) his competitors had upped their game, and hoped to finally give Maurer a run for his money. But would it be enough to keep "Chrigel the Eagle" from splashing down first in Monaco?

Chrigel had streamlined his race this year, and was traveling light. Even his support vehicle would produce no CO_2, as his four-time supporter Thomas and Maurer's girlfriend had managed to fit everything into a Tesla electric car! They would be there to get him just what he needed on the ground, and back in the air again quickly. With no vehicle large enough for sleeping, Maurer planned to use huts whenever he could, or sleep on the ground when that wasn't possible. With years of experience, Thomas and Chrigel have learned that "less is more" when it comes to the gear they will need to finish the race, and obviously they have made their method work very well. His supporters often hike up to launch with him to make sure he gets in the air quickly...after all, he usually has great flights, so they will have plenty of time to chase him in the vehicle the rest of the day!

At the start of the race, Maurer pulled off an extraordinary flight on a day when everyone was having great flights.   He was one of three athletes to land near Turnpoint 3 in Kampenwand, hike up, and still fly down that evening, opening up a 10 km gap just that quickly.   Chrigel was then in a good position to hike through rain showers the next morning on the way to launch.   When the sun came out, he and Guschlbauer (AUT1) were able to fly 80 km and land at Turnpoint 4 in Lermoos.   At one point Chrigel got low over the trees, but managed to save his flight and continue on.   That evening he hiked up to a hut, had a good dinner and could look forward to good flying conditions the next day.

But his good mood that evening was punctured a bit by news of a penalty.   Along with most of the athletes, Maurer had taken a wrong turn in Salzburg heading up to the Gaisberg launch, and organizers were going to give everyone a six hour penalty for this mistake.   Maurer was furious and his supporter Thomas was soon on the phone talking to the organization, which ultimately reduced the penalty to two hours.

Chrigel continued in the lead, but for the first time, he had competitors hot on his heels.   On Day 3, now in Italy, he landed on the wrong side of a river, adding distance to his hike to Turnpoint 5 in Cima Tosa.   After accepting the Brenta trophy early in the morning for being the first competitor to this turnpoint, Maurer was lucky to get a gap in the rain showers to fly down, but he walked 70 km over the rest of the day in poor weather.

By Day 6, Chrigel was still out front in Switzerland, chased closely by Guschlbauer and Huber (GER3), but these three had opened up an 80 km lead on the rest of the field.   He was able to reach and pass the Matterhorn, but 50 km headwinds at times stopped Maurer in his tracks.   That night, he stayed up late at a friend's house, getting his torn harness sewn back up for the next day.   He would miss some sleep, but he was also still in the lead.

High winds then gave Chrigel an unusual day...he spent it mostly walking toward Mont Blanc rather than flying. But he still had the advantage, as his two chasers had dropped into Italy from the Matterhorn, and seemed to be stuck on the wrong side of Mont Blanc.   Day 8 would find Maurer hiking up to Annecy and ready to round the corner south to Monaco. He did see Guschlbauer that day, but it was in opposite directions as one headed into Turnpoint 9, and one out. Chrigel had 25 km of lead and there was still 300 km to go.

The weather cooperated and Maurer made fast progress to the finish, covering 200 km that day and now with just 98 km left to go.   Thanks to a few mistakes by the chasing group, he was all by himself in the lead. He would fly into Peille in style the next afternoon, landing at the golf course just behind the turnpoint. This flight was pretty special for him, as he was able to fly above and alongside the clouds near Peille.   He saved the final flight down to the float for the next morning, saying "Enough flying for today".

Afterward, Chrigel said that he was really happy to win, but that he had made some mistakes this year, unlike in 2013 where he almost had a perfect race.   But he was glad that his leg (broken last fall) hadn't given him any trouble. Winning for the fourth time puts Maurer in a class of his own. It also keeps the record perfect for the Swiss...together they have won all seven editions of the Red Bull X-Alps.

Appendix A – Via Ferrata Information

Many books are available (and more popping up every day) about Via Ferrata (allow known as Klettersteig). Since they are graded by length, difficult level, and exposure, there is something for everyone, but always a very fun day out in the hills.

http://www.klettersteig.com/rmaps01/root2_austriawest.htm

http://www.oetztal.com/climbing-via-ferrata-stuibenfall

http://www.montafon.at/en/holiday_worlds/summer-activities/rock_climbing/via-ferratas

http://www.viaferrata-fr.net/cartefrance.php

http://www.ramsau.com/en/summerholidays/climbing/#jfm ulticontent_c607-2

Appendix B – Travel Insurance and Health Care

Insurance

- **Www.Dolomitiemergency.It** All Europe Covered For Emergency Heli-Vac To Hospital, only 22 Euro Per Year. Web Site Is Mostly Italian.

- **Medjet Assist** – Emer Evac From Anywhere In World Via Jet / Helicopter

Travel Hospital / Health Care

- **Img Patriot International** Travel Accident Insurance W/ Adventure Sports Rider – Buy It Only For Length Of Trip, 6 Weeks Cost $200 For $500,000 Policy

- **Good Neighbor Insurance** – Global Underwriters – International Diplomat With Specific Additional Sports Riders

- **Spot And Delorme** Have A Good Rescue Policy They Sponsor If You Own One Of Their Devices

Appendix C – Map Information

- Paper Copies Of All Topos For "Big Picture" Planning
- Pre-Downloaded Digital Maps For Offline Areas And Athlete Hiking
- Kompass Wanderkarte Maps – Austria Only – Apple App Best, Laptop Hard To Figure Out As Only In German
- Rest Of Europe – Www.Maps.Me
- Download Before Leave Home As Very Slow And Expensive To Do Once In Europe
- Download Into As Many Devices As Possible For Backup
- Ipads / Tablets / Laptops Work Much Better For Maps Than Smaller Screens
- Skyways Maps Of Frequently Flown Areas – Have To Select XContest And Set Thermals To Skyways: Http://Xcplanner.Appspot.Com/
- Glide Planner: Http://Glideplanner.Appspot.Com/
- Off-Road Route Planning: Www.Outdooractive.Com Http://Www.Alpenvereinaktiv.Com/En/Tourplanner/
- Paragliding Map App And Website: Http://Www.Paraglidingmap.Com/
- Pre-Download And/Or Print Routes / Legs / Turnpoints / Skyways Maps / Topos / Elevation Profiles / Previous Year Routes / All Waypoints
- Book – "Best Flying Sites Of The Alps" In PDF
- French Paragliding Vol-Libre Site Map
- Road Maps Of All Countries – Draw Route Legs And Turnpoints Onto Road Maps
- Get X-Alps Supplied Airspace Maps At Athlete Camp
- Kml Files For Google Earth Display - .Igc Files For Playback And Scoring
- http://www.alpenvereinaktiv.com/en/tourplanner/
- http://www.hikeandfly.info/hikeandfly/home.aspx
- http://www.austrianmap.at/amap/index.php?SKN=1& XPX=637&YPX=492

- http://glideplanner.appspot.com
- http://xcplanner.appspot.com
- http://www.airwolves.net
- http://www.xcmag.com/2014/05/map-of-flying-sites-in-the-alps/
- http://xcplanner.appspot.com/?l=free&p=_vvbHyksnA uf@%7DpK%60%7B%60AglcBigw@dvtF%60l%60Axa mGzdvFjcU%7Djp@bfmEnisA%60ldL%7C%60[d~yC_ ~Bpk%7CBvrxKc~fF%7ChCeyB&s=20.0&a=0
- App- Butterfly Avionics Freeflight
- http://www.doarama.com/info

- Online maps for much of the route:
- AT: http://www.austrianmap.at/
- DE: http://geoportal.bayern.de/bayernatlas/ (Chose Amtl. Karte in the top right of the map)
- IT: http://www.pcn.minambiente.it/viewer/
- CH: http://map.geo.admin.ch/
- FR: http://www.geoportail.gouv.fr/accueil (Click Cartes (IGN) in the top left of the window)

Appendix D – Weather Information

- Weather.Com For Local Current Winds And Forecasts
- Almost Every Mountain Has A Live Wx Site: Ski Areas, Paragliding Sites, Gondolas, Etc. – Check All These Out And Bookmark While Pre-Flying Routes
- Valley Winds Critical And Usually Different Than Altitude Winds – Usually Flows Same Direction As Rivers, But Some Don't – Study And Learn Online
- Austro Control – Login= Guest/Guest Http://Www.Flug-Wetter.At/Segelflug/Index.Html
- Dhv Wetter - Http://Www.Dhv.De/Web/Wetter
- Www.Sat24.Com   Rain Patterns
- Radar: Http://Www.Weathercast.Co.Uk/Radar/Europe.Html
- Wind: Http://Www.Windguru.Cz In 2d Mode For Winds Aloft (Use Phone App Instead Of Website)
- Find A Website That Has Foehn Wind Forecasts – Very Important
- http://meteo-parapente.com/?lang=en
- https://www.windyty.com
- http://www.sat24.com/?culture=en
- http://www.wetteronline.de
- http://www2.wetter3.de
- http://www.flug-wetter.at/segelflug/fra_thmo.html#
- http://www.windguru.cz/int/
- http://www.wunderground.com/wundermap/

Appendix E – Internet/Phone Information

- For Laptop And Back-Up For Everything Else - Tep Wireless Wi-Fi Hotspot (Will Get Some High-Speed Per Day, Then Slow Speed) – Worked Well Enough To Allow Live Tracking To Work
- For Cell Phone Talk / Text / Data - T-Mobile Family Plan Sim Talk/Data Cards W/ Minimum High Speed-Data As All Will Be Slow Speed In Europe
- For Tablets – T-Mobile Data Only Sim Cards W/ Minimum Data
- Use Campground Wi-Fi When Possible (All McDonald's Also Have Fast Wi-Fi)
- Consider Buying A Cheap Multi-Sim Europe Phone Online Before Leaving Home, Then Can Use One Phone For Different Voice / Data Plans – However Consider The Fact That You Won't Have iPhone Or Android Apps In That Cheap Phone

Suggested Devices - Supporters
- **Laptop** Was Best For Live Tracking, Was Only Device That Would Allow Full Speed Live Tracking – Ipads / Iphones Would Not Do This Because It Is An App, While Laptop Website Worked Great. Handy To Have Both Windows And Apple IOS Capability
- **iPad** With Topo Maps Downloaded For Areas With No Internet
- **iPad Mini** For Navigation – Google Maps Worked Best – Also For "Find Friends" App, (Best For Tracking Everyone But Only Works On Apple Devices, We Also Used "Life360" App Because It Works On Apple And Android)
- **iPhones** For Calls / Texts
- European **GPS** for driving directions

2015 Red Bull Supplied Devices –Athletes

- Race Phone -Only Good For Communication With Race Control And Tracking Backup, No Internet
- Garmin Virb Camera (Take A Go-Pro Foot Or Knee Mount And A Selfie Stick To Allow For Nice Angles On Videos)
- Flymaster Vario – For Live-Tracking – Will Have Airspace Pre-Loaded In It
- Back-Up USB Charger
- Garmin GPS
- Personal Smartphone For Primary Communications And Nav/Maps
- Personal SPOT/Delorme For Areas w/o Cell Signal (Be Sure To Set Everyone Up On Notification Lists)
- Airspace Backup And Study Before Race – Flyskyhy App

DC Power

- Charging Athletes Devices Overnight Proved To Be The Biggest Challenge – Our Goal Zero Power Block Charged From 12v Or 110v In Campgrounds, It Could Keep Up With Everything Except A High-Draw Laptop Charger
- Make Sure Rental Vehicles Have At Least Two 12v Taps And/Or USB
- Two Or More Y-Cords W/ Double USB Adapters On Both Ends
- Increase Fuse Size To Avoid Blowouts – Take Extra Fuses
- Monitor Heat Where They Plug Into Lighters – I Melted One
- Do Not Run Laptop Through These (May Be Ok With Inverters That Run Cool , Have Cooling Fans)
- Small Single 110v Inverters Not Powerful Enough
- Use Fan-Cooled Dual 110v Outlet / Dual Usb Inverters, Will Run Fairly Cool
- I Found A Special One (Sine Wave) For Laptop, Others Can Ruin Laptop Chargers

- My Laptop Direct To 12v Charger Got Way Too Hot To Use, But Normal 110v (120 Watt) Wall Charger Worked Ok When Fed Off A Fan-Cooled Inverter
- Take A 12v Cable That Can Run From Battery Clips Into Vehicle (Maybe Have To Punch A Hole Through Firewall) To A Cigarette Plug For Additional Power Source And To Power An Inverter From Vehicle Battery

CPSIA information can be obtained
at www.ICGtesting.com
Printed in the USA
LVHW080046290622
722356LV00014B/726